Ownership Economics

This book presents the first full-length explanation in English of Heinsohn and Steiger's groundbreaking theory of money and interest, which emphasizes the role played by private property rights.

Ownership economics gives an alternative explanation of money and interest, proposing that operations enabled by property lead to interest and money, rather than exchange of goods. Like any other approach, it has to answer economic theory's core question: what is the loss that has to be compensated by interest? Ownership economics accepts neither a temporary loss of goods, as in neoclassical economics, nor Keynes's temporary loss of already existing, exogenous money as the cause of interest. Rather, money is created as a non-physical title to property in a credit contract secured by a debtor's collateral and the creditor's net worth.

This book is an edited English translation of a highly successful German text, and offers the first book-length treatment of a theory which has received much interest since its first appearance in articles in the late 1970s.

Gunnar Heinsohn is Professor Emeritus at the University of Bremen, Germany.

Otto Steiger, who passed away in 2008, was a Professor at the University of Bremen, Germany.

Frank Decker is an economist based in Sydney, Australia.

Routledge frontiers of political economy

1 **Equilibrium Versus Understanding**
Towards the rehumanization of economics within social theory
Mark Addleson

2 **Evolution, Order and Complexity**
Edited by Elias L. Khalil and Kenneth E. Boulding

3 **Interactions in Political Economy**
Malvern after ten years
Edited by Steven Pressman

4 **The End of Economics**
Michael Perelman

5 **Probability in Economics**
Omar F. Hamouda and Robin Rowley

6 **Capital Controversy, Post Keynesian Economics and the History of Economics**
Essays in honour of Geoff Harcourt, volume one
Edited by Philip Arestis, Gabriel Palma and Malcolm Sawyer

7 **Markets, Unemployment and Economic Policy**
Essays in honour of Geoff Harcourt, volume two
Edited by Philip Arestis, Gabriel Palma and Malcolm Sawyer

8 **Social Economy**
The logic of capitalist development
Clark Everling

9 **New Keynesian Economics/Post Keynesian Alternatives**
Edited by Roy J. Rotheim

10 **The Representative Agent in Macroeconomics**
James E. Hartley

11 **Borderlands of Economics**
Essays in honour of Daniel R. Fusfeld
Edited by Nahid Aslanbeigui and Young Back Choi

12 **Value, Distribution and Capital**
Essays in honour of Pierangelo Garegnani
Edited by Gary Mongiovi and Fabio Petri

13 **The Economics of Science**
Methodology and epistemology as if economics really mattered
James R. Wible

14 **Competitiveness, Localised Learning and Regional Development**
Specialisation and prosperity in small open economies
Peter Maskell, Heikki Eskelinen, Ingjaldur Hannibalsson, Anders Malmberg and Eirik Vatne

15 **Labour Market Theory**
A constructive reassessment
Ben J. Fine

16 **Women and European Employment**
Jill Rubery, Mark Smith, Colette Fagan and Damian Grimshaw

17 **Explorations in Economic Methodology**
From Lakatos to empirical philosophy of science
Roger Backhouse

18 **Subjectivity in Political Economy**
Essays on wanting and choosing
David P. Levine

19 **The Political Economy of Middle East Peace**
The impact of competing trade agendas
Edited by J.W. Wright, Jnr

20 **The Active Consumer**
Novelty and surprise in consumer choice
Edited by Marina Bianchi

21 **Subjectivism and Economic Analysis**
Essays in memory of Ludwig Lachmann
Edited by Roger Koppl and Gary Mongiovi

22 **Themes in Post-Keynesian Economics**
Essays in honour of Geoff Harcourt, volume three
Edited by Claudio Sardoni and Peter Kriesler

23 **The Dynamics of Technological Knowledge**
Cristiano Antonelli

24 **The Political Economy of Diet, Health and Food Policy**
Ben J. Fine

25 **The End of Finance**
Capital market inflation, financial derivatives and pension fund capitalism
Jan Toporowski

26 **Political Economy and the New Capitalism**
Edited by Jan Toporowski

27 **Growth Theory**
A philosophical perspective
Patricia Northover

28 **The Political Economy of the Small Firm**
Edited by Charlie Dannreuther

29 **Hahn and Economic Methodology**
Edited by Thomas Boylan and Paschal F. O'Gorman

30 **Gender, Growth and Trade**
The miracle economies of the postwar years
David Kucera

31 **Normative Political Economy**
Subjective freedom, the market and the state
David Levine

32 **Economist with a Public Purpose**
Essays in honour of John Kenneth Galbraith
Edited by Michael Keaney

33 **Involuntary Unemployment**
The elusive quest for a theory
Michel De Vroey

34 **The Fundamental Institutions of Capitalism**
Ernesto Screpanti

35 **Transcending Transaction**
The search for self-generating markets
Alan Shipman

36 **Power in Business and the State**
An historical analysis of its concentration
Frank Bealey

37 **Editing Economics**
Essays in honour of Mark Perlman
*Edited by Hank Lim,
Ungsuh K. Park and
Geoff Harcourt*

38 **Money, Macroeconomics and Keynes**
Essays in honour of Victoria Chick, volume one
*Edited by Philip Arestis,
Meghnad Desai and Sheila Dow*

39 **Methodology, Microeconomics and Keynes**
Essays in honour of Victoria Chick, volume two
*Edited by Philip Arestis,
Meghnad Desai and Sheila Dow*

40 **Market Drive and Governance**
Reexamining the rules for economic and commercial contest
Ralf Boscheck

41 **The Value of Marx**
Political economy for contemporary capitalism
Alfredo Saad-Filho

42 **Issues in Positive Political Economy**
S. Mansoob Murshed

43 **The Enigma of Globalisation**
A journey to a new stage of capitalism
Robert Went

44 **The Market**
Equilibrium, stability, mythology
S.N. Afriat

45 **The Political Economy of Rule Evasion and Policy Reform**
Jim Leitzel

46 **Unpaid Work and the Economy**
Edited by Antonella Picchio

47 **Distributional Justice**
Theory and measurement
Hilde Bojer

48 **Cognitive Developments in Economics**
Edited by Salvatore Rizzello

49 **Social Foundations of Markets, Money and Credit**
Costas Lapavitsas

50 **Rethinking Capitalist Development**
Essays on the economics of Josef Steindl
Edited by Tracy Mott and Nina Shapiro

51 **An Evolutionary Approach to Social Welfare**
Christian Sartorius

52 **Kalecki's Economics Today**
Edited by Zdzislaw L. Sadowski and Adam Szeworski

53 **Fiscal Policy from Reagan to Blair**
The left veers right
Ravi K. Roy and Arthur T. Denzau

54 **The Cognitive Mechanics of Economic Development and Institutional Change**
Bertin Martens

55 **Individualism and the Social Order**
The social element in liberal thought
Charles R. McCann Jnr

56 **Affirmative Action in the United States and India**
A comparative perspective
Thomas E. Weisskopf

57 **Global Political Economy and the Wealth of Nations**
Performance, institutions, problems and policies
Edited by Phillip Anthony O'Hara

58 **Structural Economics**
Thijs ten Raa

59 **Macroeconomic Theory and Economic Policy**
Essays in honour of Jean-Paul Fitoussi
Edited by K. Vela Velupillai

60 **The Struggle over Work**
The 'end of work' and employment alternatives in post-industrial societies
Shaun Wilson

61 **The Political Economy of Global Sporting Organisations**
John Forster and Nigel Pope

62 **The Flawed Foundations of General Equilibrium Theory**
Critical essays on economic theory
Frank Ackerman and Alejandro Nadal

63 **Uncertainty in Economic Theory**
Essays in honor of David Schmeidler's 65th birthday
Edited by Itzhak Gilboa

64 **The New Institutional Economics of Corruption**
Edited by Johann Graf Lambsdorff, Markus Taube and Matthias Schramm

65 **The Price Index and its Extension**
A chapter in economic measurement
S.N. Afriat

66 **Reduction, Rationality and Game Theory in Marxian Economics**
Bruce Philp

67 **Culture and Politics in Economic Development**
Volker Bornschier

68 **Modern Applications of Austrian Thought**
Edited by Jürgen G. Backhaus

69 **Ordinary Choices**
Individuals, incommensurability, and democracy
Robert Urquhart

70 **Labour Theory of Value**
Peter C. Dooley

71 **Capitalism**
Victor D. Lippit

72 **Macroeconomic Foundations of Macroeconomics**
Alvaro Cencini

73 **Marx for the 21st Century**
Edited by Hiroshi Uchida

74 **Growth and Development in the Global Political Economy**
Social structures of accumulation and modes of regulation
Phillip Anthony O'Hara

75 **The New Economy and Macroeconomic Stability**
A neo-modern perspective drawing on the complexity approach and Keynesian economics
Teodoro Dario Togati

76 **The Future of Social Security Policy**
Women, work and a citizens' basic income
Ailsa McKay

77 **Clinton and Blair**
The political economy of the third way
Flavio Romano

78 **Marxian Reproduction Schema**
Money and aggregate demand in a capitalist economy
A.B. Trigg

79 **The Core Theory in Economics**
Problems and solutions
Lester G. Telser

80 **Economics, Ethics and the Market**
Introduction and applications
Johan J. Graafland

81 **Social Costs and Public Action in Modern Capitalism**
Essays inspired by Karl William Kapp's theory of social costs
Edited by Wolfram Elsner, Pietro Frigato and Paolo Ramazzotti

82 **Globalization and the Myths of Free Trade**
History, theory and empirical evidence
Edited by Anwar Shaikh

83 **Equilibrium in Economics**
Scope and limits
Edited by Valeria Mosini

84 **Globalization**
State of the art and perspectives
Edited by Stefan A. Schirm

85 **Neoliberalism**
National and regional experiments with global ideas
Edited by Ravi K. Roy, Arthur T. Denzau and Thomas D. Willett

86 **Post-Keynesian Macroeconomics**
Essays in honour of Ingrid Rima
Edited by Mathew Forstater, Gary Mongiovi and Steven Pressman

87 **Consumer Capitalism**
Anastasios S. Korkotsides

88 **Remapping Gender in the New Global Order**
Edited by Marjorie Griffin Cohen and Janine Brodie

89 **Hayek and Natural Law**
Eric Angner

90 **Race and Economic Opportunity in the Twenty-First Century**
Edited by Marlene Kim

91 **Renaissance in Behavioural Economics**
Harvey Leibenstein's impact on contemporary economic analysis
Edited by Roger Frantz

92 **Human Ecology Economics**
A new framework for global sustainability
Edited by Roy E. Allen

93 **Imagining Economics Otherwise**
Encounters with identity/difference
Nitasha Kaul

94 **Reigniting the Labor Movement**
Restoring means to ends in a democratic labor movement
Gerald Friedman

95 **The Spatial Model of Politics**
Norman Schofield

96 **The Economics of American Judaism**
Carmel Ullman Chiswick

97 **Critical Political Economy**
Christian Arnsperger

98 **Culture and Economic Explanation**
Economics in the US and Japan
Donald W. Katzner

99 **Feminism, Economics and Utopia**
Time travelling through paradigms
Karin Schönpflug

100 **Risk in International Finance**
Vikash Yadav

101 **Economic Policy and Performance in Industrial Democracies**
Party governments, central banks and the fiscal–monetary policy mix
Takayuki Sakamoto

102 **Advances on Income Inequality and Concentration Measures**
Edited by Gianni Betti and Achille Lemmi

103 **Economic Representations**
Academic and everyday
Edited by David F. Ruccio

104 **Mathematical Economics and the Dynamics of Capitalism**
Goodwin's legacy continued
Edited by Peter Flaschel and Michael Landesmann

105 **The Keynesian Multiplier**
Edited by Claude Gnos and Louis-Philippe Rochon

106 **Money, Enterprise and Income Distribution**
Towards a macroeconomic theory of capitalism
John Smithin

107 **Fiscal Decentralization and Local Public Finance in Japan**
Nobuki Mochida

108 **The 'Uncertain' Foundations of Post-Keynesian Economics**
Essays in exploration
Stephen P. Dunn

109 **Karl Marx's *Grundrisse***
Foundations of the critique of political economy 150 years later
Edited by Marcello Musto

110 **Economics and the Price Index**
S.N. Afriat and Carlo Milana

111 **Sublime Economy**
On the intersection of art and economics
Edited by Jack Amariglio, Joseph W. Childers and Stephen E. Cullenberg

112 **Popper, Hayek and the Open Society**
Calvin Hayes

113 **The Political Economy of Work**
David Spencer

114 **Institutional Economics**
Bernard Chavance

115 **Religion, Economics and Demography**
The effects of religion on education, work, and the family
Evelyn L. Lehrer

116 **Economics, Rational Choice and Normative Philosophy**
Edited by Thomas A. Boylan and Ruvin Gekker

117 **Economics Versus Human Rights**
Manuel Couret Branco

118 **Hayek Versus Marx and Today's Challenges**
Eric Aarons

119 **Work Time Regulation as Sustainable Full Employment Policy**
Robert LaJeunesse

120 **Equilibrium, Welfare and Uncertainty**
Mukul Majumdar

121 **Capitalism, Institutions and Economic Development**
Michael Heller

122 **Economic Pluralism**
Robert Garnett, Erik Olsen and Martha Starr

123 **Dialectics of Class Struggle in the Global Economy**
Clark Everling

124 **Political Economy and Globalization**
Richard Westra

125 **Full-Spectrum Economics**
Toward an inclusive and emancipatory social science
Christian Arnsperger

126 **Computable, Constructive and Behavioural Economic Dynamics**
Essays in honour of Kumaraswamy (Vela) Velupillai
Stefano Zambelli

127 **Monetary Macrodynamics**
Toichiro Asada, Carl Chiarella, Peter Flaschel and Reiner Franke

128 **Rationality and Explanation in Economics**
Maurice Lagueux

129 **The Market, Happiness, and Solidarity**
A Christian perspective
Johan J. Graafland

130 **Economic Complexity and Equilibrium Illusion**
Essays on market instability and macro vitality
Ping Chen

131 **Economic Theory and Social Change**
Problems and revisions
Hasse Ekstedt and Angelo Fusari

132 **The Practices of Happiness**
Political economy, religion and wellbeing
Edited by John Atherton, Elaine Graham and Ian Steedman

133 **The Measurement of Individual Well-Being and Group Inequalities**
Essays in memory of Z. M. Berrebi
Edited by Joseph Deutsch and Jacques Silber

134 **Wage Policy, Income Distribution, and Democratic Theory**
Oren M. Levin-Waldman

135 **The Political Economy of Bureaucracy**
Steven O. Richardson

136 **The Moral Rhetoric of Political Economy**
Justice and modern economic thought
Paul Turpin

137 **Macroeconomic Regimes in Western Industrial Countries**
Hansjörg Herr and Milka Kazandziska

138 **The Political Economy of the Environment**
Edited by Simon Dietz, Jonathan Michie and Christine Oughton

139 **Business Ethics and the Austrian Tradition in Economics**
Hardy Bouillon

140 **Inequality and Power**
The economics of class
Eric A. Schutz

141 **Capital as a Social Kind**
Definitions and transformations in the critique of political economy
Howard Engelskirchen

142 **Happiness, Ethics and Economics**
Johannes Hirata

143 **Capital, Exploitation and Economic Crisis**
John Weeks

144 **The Global Economic Crisis**
New perspectives on the critique of economic theory and policy
Edited by Emiliano Brancaccio and Giuseppe Fontana

145 **Economics and Diversity**
Carlo D'Ippoliti

146 **Political Economy of Human Rights**
Rights, realities and realization
Bas de Gaay Fortman

147 **Robinson Crusoe's Economic Man**
A construction and deconstruction
Edited by Ulla Grapard and Gillian Hewitson

148 **Freedom and Happiness in Economic Thought and Philosophy**
From clash to reconciliation
Edited by Ragip Ege and Herrade Igersheim

149 **Political Economy After Economics**
David Laibman

150 **Reconstructing Keynesian Macroeconomics Volume 1**
Partial perspectives
Carl Chiarella, Peter Flaschel and Willi Semmler

151 **Institutional Economics and National Competitiveness**
Edited by Young Back Choi

152 **Capitalist Diversity and Diversity within Capitalism**
Edited by Geoffrey T. Wood and Christel Lane

153 **The Consumer, Credit and Neoliberalism**
Governing the modern economy
Christopher Payne

154 **Order and Control in American Socio-Economic Thought**
U.S. social scientists and progressive-era reform
Charles McCann

155 **The Irreconcilable Inconsistencies of Neoclassical Macroeconomics**
A false paradigm
John Weeks

156 **The Political Economy of Putin's Russia**
Pekka Sutela

157 **Facts, Values and Objectivity in Economics**
José Castro Caldas and Vítor Neves

158 **Economic Growth and the High Wage Economy**
Choices, constraints and opportunities in the market economy
Morris Altman

159 **Social Costs Today**
Institutional analyses of the present crises
Edited by Wolfram Elsner, Pietro Frigato and Paolo Ramazzotti

160 **Economics, Sustainability and Democracy**
Economics in the era of climate change
Christopher Nobbs

161 **Organizations, Individualism and Economic Theory**
Maria Brouwer

162 **Economic Models for Policy Making**
Principles and designs revisited
S. I. Cohen

163 **Reconstructing Keynesian Macroeconomics Volume 2**
Integrated approaches
Carl Chiarella, Peter Flaschel and Willi Semmler

164 **Architectures of Economic Subjectivity**
The philosophical foundations of the subject in the history of economic thought
Sonya Marie Scott

165 **Support-Bargaining, Economics and Society**
A social species
Patrick Spread

166 **Inherited Wealth, Justice and Equality**
Edited by Guido Erreygers and John Cunliffe

167 **The Charismatic Principle in Social Life**
Edited by Luigino Bruni and Barbara Sena

168 **Ownership Economics**
On the foundations of interest, money, markets, business cycles and economic development
Gunnar Heinsohn and Otto Steiger; translated and edited with comments and additions by Frank Decker

Ownership Economics

On the foundations of interest, money, markets, business cycles and economic development

Gunnar Heinsohn and Otto Steiger
Translated and edited with comments and additions by Frank Decker

LONDON AND NEW YORK

First published 2013
by Routledge
2 Park Square, Milton Park, Abingdon, Oxon OX14 4RN

Simultaneously published in the USA and Canada
by Routledge
711 Third Avenue, New York, NY 10017

Routledge is an imprint of the Taylor & Francis Group, an informa business

© 2013 Gunnar Heinsohn and Karin Steiger; selection and editorial material, Frank Decker

The right of Gunnar Heinsohn and Otto Steiger to be identified as authors of this work has been asserted by them in accordance with the Copyright, Designs and Patent Act 1988.

The right of Frank Decker to be identified as the author of the editorial material, and of the author for his individual chapters, has been asserted in accordance with sections 77 and 78 of the Copyright, Designs and Patents Act 1988.

All rights reserved. No part of this book may be reprinted or reproduced or utilized in any form or by any electronic, mechanical, or other means, now known or hereafter invented, including photocopying and recording, or in any information storage or retrieval system, without permission in writing from the publishers.

Trademark notice: Product or corporate names may be trademarks or registered trademarks, and are used only for identification and explanation without intent to infringe.

British Library Cataloguing in Publication Data
A catalogue record for this book is available from the British Library

Library of Congress Cataloging in Publication Data
Heinsohn, Gunnar.
 [Eigentum, Zins und Geld. English]
 Ownership economics : on the foundations of interest, money, markets, business cycles and economic development / by Gunnar Heinsohn and Otto Steiger ; translated and edited with comments and additions by Frank Decker.
 p. cm.
 1. Money. 2. Interest. 3. Property. 4. Capital. 5. Economics. I. Steiger, Otto. II. Title.
 HG218.5.H4513 2012
 330–dc23

2012023433

ISBN: 978-0-415-64546-1 (hbk)
ISBN: 978-0-203-07746-7 (ebk)

Typeset in Times New Roman
by Wearset Ltd, Boldon, Tyne and Wear

Contents

Ownership economics: An introduction – by Frank Decker   xvii
Preface to the first German edition of Ownership
Economics *– by Gunnar Heinsohn and Otto Steiger*   xxvi

1 Possession and ownership: Use of goods versus economic activity   1

   1.1 Economic activity as distinguished from mere material reproduction 3
   1.2 Material reproduction in de facto *possession-based systems 5*
   1.3 Economic deployment of de jure *possession in an ownership-based society 10*

2 The blindness of the great schools of economics towards ownership   16

   2.1 Classical economics 17
   2.2 Neoclassical economics 20
   2.3 Keynesian economics 29
   2.4 Conclusion on all three schools 52

3 The economic core of the ownership system: Interest, money and property assets   54

   3.1 Burdening, hypothecation and enforcement 55
   3.2 Ownership premium and interest 57
   3.3 Money of account and money proper 66
   3.4 Money and net wealth 72
   3.5 Money creation by the private note-issuing bank 74
   3.6 Money creation by the central note-issuing bank 83

4 The market as the result of the ownership-based economy 100

4.1 The entrepreneur as an economic agent in his own right and the establishment of markets 100
4.2 Monetary price setting versus adjustment to relative prices 107
4.3 Accumulation, business cycle and crisis 113

5 Issues associated with ownership in developing and transformation countries 126

5.1 The unabating poverty of developing countries 127
5.2 Successes and mistakes of countries transforming from state socialism 133

Editor's glossary of ownership economic terms and concepts 139

Editor's summary of the role of property rights in the modern ownership-based economic system 142

Notes 144
References 167
Index 185

Ownership economics
An introduction – by Frank Decker

The publication of this first English edition of *Ownership Economics* (*Eigentumsökonomik*) represents the completion of a research project that Gunnar Heinsohn and Otto Steiger (12 December 1938–17 January 2008) started in the late 1970s and that was comprehensively presented to the German-speaking public with the publication of *Ownership, Interest and Money: Unresolved Mysteries in Economic Theory* in 1996 (*Eigentum, Zins und Geld: Ungelöste Probleme der Wirtschaftswissenschaft*, Heinsohn and Steiger 1996). The first German edition of *Ownership Economics* followed in 2006 (Heinsohn and Steiger 2006b). It provided an improved and more concise version of *Ownership, Interest and Money*.

While a number of articles summarizing core elements of Heinsohn and Steiger's theory have appeared in English over the past three decades,[1] the broad scope of the theory has made it difficult if not impossible to convey a sufficient level of detail within the size limitations of a journal article. For the first time, this edited translation of *Ownership Economics* makes a full account of the ownership theory of money and interest available to an English-speaking audience.

Heinsohn and Steiger's works are relatively well known in the German-speaking area, with *Ownership, Interest and Money* at the time of writing in its seventh German edition and *Ownership Economics* in its second German edition. In 2006, Otto Steiger received the K. William Kapp prize of the European Association for Evolutionary Political Economy (EAEPE) and William Kapp Foundation for his work on ownership economics and new institutional economics (Steiger 2006a). Both Heinsohn's *Private Ownership, Patriarchy, Monetary Economy* (*Privateigentum, Patriarchat, Geldwirtschaft*, Heinsohn 1984 [1982]) and Heinsohn and Steiger's *Ownership, Interest and Money* were selected for a dictionary of economic works (Herz and Weinberger 2006) that provides summaries of the most important 650 economic works of all times.

In 2008 Heinsohn published an essay (Heinsohn 2008a; see also Heinsohn 2008b) on the global financial crisis in the *Frankfurter Allgemeine Zeitung*, one of the leading German newspapers, and in 2010 Heinsohn and Decker's explanation of the global financial crisis was selected as one of the introductory articles in Kolb's book on the crisis (Heinsohn and Decker 2010; Kolb 2010).

Heinsohn and Steiger's work is a radical and important contribution to both monetary and economic theory, and it can be argued that the authors have been the first to recognize the profound economic importance and impact of ownership and security rights. In contrast with prevailing economic theories, money is neither conceptualized as a commodity that facilitates barter exchanges nor as a debt instrument issued by the state in order to make payments and to receive taxes. Rather, Heinsohn and Steiger argue that in all well-functioning monetary systems both past and present, money has been represented by a documented claim over property that is created when a creditor, such as a note-issuing bank (private or central), issues notes to a debtor (for example, a producer) as part of granting a loan. Hence money must be backed by valuable property, because the creditor (bank) has to underwrite the issued notes with capital and the debtor (producer) must provide collateral in order to receive the money-creating loan.

Money thus presupposes property rights, and property backing implies that in each act of money creation, property is temporarily burdened (creditor) or hypothecated (debtor). This creates a temporary loss to the note-issuing creditor and the note-receiving debtor, both of whom can no longer freely dispose over their burdened or hypothecated property during the period of the money-creating loan. Heinsohn and Steiger hence argue that all unburdened property carries a premium – the ownership premium. The temporary loss of ownership premium suffered by the note-issuing creditor must in turn be compensated by interest, while the debtor's loss is compensated by the liquidity of the received money notes (gain of liquidity premium).[2] This provides the long-awaited explanation of the rate of interest.[3]

The debtor-producer must now engage in production to acquire the means to refund the contractually agreed loan principal with interest. The requirement to realize a nominal money sum greater than the initial outlay creates the impetus for growth, innovation and technical progress and is the reason for the characteristic dynamic of ownership-based economies.

Heinsohn and Steiger met in 1968 in Berlin, and their joint research began in 1974 with seminars on population theory at the University of Bremen. Their first joint publication was 'The Significance of "The Wealth of Nations" for an Economic Theory of the Production of Population' (Heinsohn and Steiger 1977). The work on ownership economics appears to have started in the same year with a letter from Steiger to Heinsohn.[4] Heinsohn was in Eilath (Israel) at the time, while Steiger was publishing on the history of Swedish monetary economics and the re-evaluation of Keynes's monetary thoughts as part of the development of a general theory of monetary economics (see, for example, Steiger 1978).

In his letter, Steiger expressed his astonishment that his own economic discipline had not found a satisfactory answer to the question of what money was. Heinsohn was working on the question of how private ownership and patriarchy had originated, a question also regarded as unexplained. Heinsohn's investigation had been triggered by his involvement – as one of the examiners – in Ernest Borneman's PhD thesis 'The Patriarchy'.[5] Heinsohn subsequently developed his own analysis into an article published as 'Origin and Decay of the Patriarchy'[6] (Heinsohn 1976).

Heinsohn, while reading Steiger's letter at the Sinai Oasis Nueiba, conceived the idea that the origins of private ownership and the origins of money could be related and hence that the solution to one puzzle could lead to the solution of the other. Research notes made in Israel were compiled after Heinsohn's return to Germany and developed in March 1978 into a manuscript entitled 'Theory of the Origin of Patriarchies, Deductive Logic and the Requirement for Money – 20 Theses'[7] (Heinsohn 1978). This was the beginning of ownership economics.

Heinsohn's work on the origins of ancient money was further developed in *Private Ownership, Patriarchy, Monetary Economy* (Heinsohn 1984 [1982]). His conclusion was that money could not have originated in an evolutionary process from barter but must have arisen alongside the emergence of societies based on private ownership, the foremost examples being the Greek *polis* and the Roman *civitas*. The universally held 'barter paradigm' had to be rejected. Money was not an invention to make barter transactions more efficient. Instead, Heinsohn argued that money – which began as symbolic representations of claims over security stocks of commodities issued by temples (Heinsohn 1984 [1982], 128, 136) – was created as the consequence of creditor-debtor relations in order to increase social safety and to function as a buffer against future economic uncertainty.

Money became critical, because a society based on free and independent individuals could no longer rely on the social support infrastructure previously provided by tribal or feudal command systems. Heinsohn further concluded that the ancient institution of debt-bondage, where a person – in addition to his obligation to repay the loan principal – temporarily turns over his freedom to the creditor, should be interpreted as a pre-monetary form of interest reflecting the loss of property incurred by the creditor during the period of the loan (here envisioned as a pre-monetary loan in kind). Hence interest was not related to the risk of not receiving the creditor property (loan principal) after the period of the loan, but was due to the loss of access to the lent-out property experienced by the creditor during the period of the loan.[8]

In parallel with Heinsohn's research on the origins of money in the ancient economy, Heinsohn and Steiger developed an important study on the rise of the modern English and German monetary economies and the lack of economic development in socialism (Heinsohn and Steiger 1981a, 1981b). This work concluded that the development of modern-day monetary economies had been triggered by the emergence of creditor-debtor relationships underpinned by free wage labor and the private ownership of land. As in ancient economies, private ownership and money – the latter a 'means of operating newly-arisen debtor-creditor relationships' (Heinsohn and Steiger 1981b, 46) – were interrelated and had emerged at the same time (Heinsohn and Steiger 1981b, 46, 51).

This pioneering work on the origins of monetary economies was followed by a number of publications (Heinsohn and Steiger 1983, 1988, 1989) that placed these findings into a broader economic theory context and advanced Steiger's original project to formulate a general theory of monetary economics (Steiger 1979). By 1989 Heinsohn and Steiger had shown that interest could be explained on the basis of a premium on property and that the defining element of an economy where money is essential was private ownership. Moreover, the classical dichotomy between the theory of value and the theory of money could be overcome by correctly identifying the credit contract as the underlying basis of a monetary production. All prices had to be money prices (Heinsohn and Steiger 1988, 341–349).

In these earlier works Heinsohn and Steiger's definition of money was still relatively broad. Creditor-debtor relations were made operable through money which could take various forms. At the time it was sufficient to define money in the Keynesian tradition as a property asset that minimizes carrying costs, has the highest of degree of liquidity and is used in creditor–debtor contracts as the money of account (Heinsohn and Steiger 1988, 347).

This definition of money as money of account necessarily included material variants of 'money' such as barley and silver alongside immaterial variants such as promissory notes (claims over such property as commodities and land) and nominal coins (see Heinsohn and Steiger 1981b, 46, 51; Heinsohn 1984 [1982], 136; and Heinsohn and Steiger 1989, 194–195). While Heinsohn and Steiger had always regarded commodities (e.g., wheat, barley and silver) as money only in the early pre-monetary phases of economic development, the space left for 'material' variants remained unsatisfactory, as it had long been argued that the essence of money was of an abstract nature (Knapp 1924 [1905], 2; Riese 1983, 79; see also Laum 1924, 159–160). For example, full-bodied coins can trade with an agio above their intrinsic metallic value (Stadermann and Steiger 1992) and the scarcity of commodity money can be undermined by its increased production, while bank money can always be kept scarce.

The breakthrough on this issue was presented in *Ownership, Interest and Money* (Heinsohn and Steiger 1996; see also Heinsohn 1995) and was later described as 'a most original attempt to define in a rigorous fashion the essence of money ... as being completely distinct from any kind of material good' (Graziani 2008, 69–70). Now Heinsohn and Steiger defined money as an abstract claim over the property of the note-issuing creditor. But unlike in previous works, the economic role of ownership rights and security rights were explicitly identified in the context of the money-creation process. Money understood as a claim over assets in this way was a right against the asset owner holding the title to the assets, and was not tied to any physical possession of the assets or possession of previously accumulated goods. Money was a derivative of an abstract non-possessory legal right that had no physical existence. Hence money was of an abstract nature.[9]

The transition in focus from a theory of interest to a theory of money is also visible in the history of the underlying manuscript. The first version was begun in October 1992 and released on 12 February 1993 under the title 'The Mystery of Interest'[10] to the first set of reviewers. The second version was released on 17 May 1993 using the title 'Interest: Creating a Foundation of Economic Theory',[11] which was also maintained for the third version released on 10 September 1993. From the fourth version, released on 1 June 1994, the title was changed to 'Ownership, Interest and Money: Creating a Foundation for Economic Theory'.[12] The ninth version was the basis of the 1996 publication with the title changed again, this time at the request of the publisher. Versions of the manuscript were used in lectures at the University of Bremen in the summer semester of 1993 and the winter semester of 1993/1994. The final version of the manuscript of *Ownership, Interest and Money* introduced the important concept of the ownership premium on property and separated it from the Keynesian liquidity premium on pre-existing money.[13]

Development after 1996 can be considered as consolidation and refinement. Steiger's joint work with Stadermann (Stadermann and Steiger 1999, 2001a, 2006) led to a full appraisal of the work of James Steuart, who had already identified the property-based nature of money in 1767. The publication of *School Economics*[14] (Stadermann and Steiger 2001b) delivered a masterful review of the history of economic thought on the matters of money, interest and security rights. The conclusion was that, perhaps with the exception of Steuart and Bagehot, the economic importance of ownership and security rights had been overlooked. Hence economic theory had to be rewritten. Another strand of work became the analysis and critique of the new European central banking system (the Eurosystem) and the introduction of the Euro (Heinsohn and Steiger 2002b, 2011, Spethmann and Steiger 2005). Unlike many other economists, Heinsohn and Steiger very early on identified the inherent weaknesses in the design of the Eurosystem, the consequences of which would only become apparent a decade later in the context of the European debt crisis.

Heinsohn and Steiger's subsequent work introduced and refined a number of important concepts, culminating in the publication of *Ownership Economics* in 2006: the distinction between creditor's and debtor's money; the full conceptual separation of ownership and possession; collateral and (own) capital; the role of the market in an ownership-based economy; and ownership and security rights as the preconditions for economic development (Heinsohn and Steiger 2006b, Steiger 2006a and Steiger, ed., 2008).

The idea to translate *Ownership Economics* into English was mine and was suggested to Steiger in e-mail correspondence in 2002, after I had noticed the success of de Soto's book *Mystery of Capital* (Soto 2000, which includes an explicit reference to and endorsement of Heinsohn and Steiger's work). I did not know at the time that it would fall to me to execute this task some four years after Steiger's death.

Heinsohn's brief to me was not only to carry out a translation but to edit and 'improve' the text. Moreover, his request was to carry out the editorial process and translation as if *both* of the authors were no longer alive.

The basis of the translated text is Heinsohn and Steiger, *Eigentumsökonomik* (2006b), with some input from their article of the same year (2006a). The text was first translated, edited and furnished with explanatory and other editorial comments. Next, the translated and edited text was reviewed by Heinsohn, who suggested corrections and additions. It was up to the editor to add, modify or discard Heinsohn's comments and additions. As part of this process, some of the editor's comments and additions originally placed in footnotes were elevated on Heinsohn's request into the main body of the text. These are identified as such.

Editor's notes are enclosed in braces: {}. Most material changes have been identified, but numerous smaller changes were simply integrated into the translated text. To help the reader I have added a glossary of important ownership economic terms, together with a table summarizing the role of property rights in the modern ownership-based economic system, at the end of the book. My commentary and additions have focused on improving the readability of what is a fairly complicated and technical German text, and enhancing and strengthening some of the arguments based on my own research on ownership economics over the past 10 years. This has focused on many areas, including but not limited to:

- property law;
- ownership premium and liquidity premium;
- money creation and commercial banks;
- secured lending and banking;
- price setting;
- interest rates and growth;
- the differences between money and debt;
- the global financial crisis of 2008 and the European sovereign debt crisis;
- additional references on the origins of ancient money.

The changes that I have made to the legal and related economic terminology require some further explanation. I have adjusted and tightened the definition of money and the various legal terms used by Heinsohn and Steiger based on my research on property and security law (Decker 2008, Decker 2013) and my interpretation of Heinsohn and Steiger's theory of money in a common-law context (Decker 2010). In turn, this interpretation has been further developed as part of the present work.

The translation of the most important German word for the book, the legal term 'Eigentum' (the most comprehensive right over a thing in German civil law) involves some complexities. First, it can be translated both as property and ownership. This is due to the fact that in English law the term 'property' can identify both the thing owned and the right of ownership.[15] Second, the German civil law of things more clearly distinguishes between the thing, which is the subject of property rights ('Sache', Roman law 'res'), and ownership, which is a right over the thing ('Eigentum', Roman law 'dominium' or 'proprietas'; see Wolff 1923, 144 on rights versus things and Kaser 1981, 93 on the corresponding Roman law terms). Third, ownership when defined as a bundle of rights typically includes possession. This is despite the fact that legally ownership is distinct from possession, as it can be retained without possession (see for example Hepburn 2001, 31; also Wolff 1923, 147). Fourth, the common non-legal use of the term 'Eigentum' in German can refer to an asset ('Vermögen') as well as the right of ownership. To complicate things even further, assets can also be referred to as possessions ('Besitz'). Similarly, in everyday English, objects owned can be referred to as possessions and the term 'possession' is frequently used when reference should be made to 'ownership' (see the discussion in Nicholas 1975, 108). A case could be made that this ambiguity in terminology

1.1 Relationships among property rights

Legal system	Object subject to property rights	Strongest right	Occupation or control	Security rights	Examples of other property rights
English common law (law of property)	property	ownership/property/legal title	possession	pledge, mortgage, equitable charge, lien	easements
Roman law (law of things)	res	dominium (also proprietas)	possessio	fiducia, pignus	servitudes
German civil code (law of things)	Sache	Eigentum	Besitz	Pfand, Hypothek	Dienstbarkeiten

Notes
See Wolff (1923), Nicholas (1975), Kaser (1981), Goode (2004), McCracken (2004).

and undue emphasis on possession still reflects the influence of feudalism to this day. The term 'ownership' only dates back to the sixteenth century (Pollock and Maitland 1898, II, 160). English medieval feudalism as a command system was governed by the concept of 'seisin' (possession, to sit on land), and hence the emergence of the term 'ownership' must have been linked to the rise of the ownership-based economy in early modern England (see also Decker 2013).

In the following text, the term 'ownership' signifies a concept of ownership that is separate from possession. Following Goode, ownership is defined as 'the residue of legal rights in an asset remaining in a person ... after specific rights [such as possession] have been granted to others' (Goode 2004, 31). It is the strongest property right. An example is the title to land through entry in a land titles register, which does not require possession. As a consequence, property rights are generally classified into ownership ('Eigentum'), possession ('Besitz', Roman law 'possessio') and other more limited property rights. The latter include security rights ('Pfandrechte', e.g., mortgage, pledge, charge, lien; Roman law 'fiducia' and 'pignus') and easements (e.g., Roman law servitudes). These relationships are summarized in Table I.1.

Heinsohn and Steiger's original German text uses the German civil law term 'verpfänden' – to pledge. However, the English common-law pledge transfers possession. Because Heinsohn and Steiger were particularly interested in security rights that leave the possession with the debtor, which are economically the most important, I have chosen the Greek term 'hypotheca' for the taking of security over property assets. This term originates from *hypotheke* ('the object put down'), a security right in ancient Greece that left the possession of the assets with the debtor (similar also to the more frequent *prasis epi lysei* – 'sale on condition of release'; see Finley 1951, 29, 31). In Roman law, security that left the possession with the debtor was implemented as a transfer of ownership subject to an agreement to reconvey (*fiducia*; Kaser 1981, 123, Nicholas 1975, 151) or by a 'pledge without possession' (*pignus obligatum* or *hypotheca;* Kaser 1981, 125 and Nicholas 1975, 152). In English common law this type of security right is implemented through mechanisms such as the equitable charge, the equitable mortgage or a legal mortgage where possession is returned to the debtor (see, for example, McCracken and Everett 2004).

When reference is made to 'ownership economics' an emphasis on non-possessory rights is implied. This is also the reason why the term 'ownership economics' is used rather than the term 'property economics'. The latter term was used in previous English-language publications with reference to the Latin *proprietas/dominium* (see for example Heinsohn and Steiger 2006a, Steiger 2006a and Heinsohn and Decker 2010). While technically correct, this choice – with the benefit of hindsight – was not very helpful, as it made it more difficult if not impossible to articulate the core message of the work. It should be noted that the English translation of the German civil code also translates 'Eigentum' as 'ownership' (German Federal Ministry of Justice, 2010), which supports the terminology chosen for this work.

I would like to thank Sheelagh McCracken (Faculty of Law, University of

Sydney), Robert Phillips (Newcastle, New South Wales), Hans-Joachim Stadermann (Berlin) and Karin Steiger (Bremen) for their support, and Gunnar Heinsohn (Bremen) for his generosity in inviting and accepting comments and additions to his own work. Once again I am indebted to Sonja Stewart and our children Klara and Bruno for enduring my passion to work on yet another 'money book'.

Frank Decker
Sydney, 15 September 2011

Preface to the first German edition of *Ownership Economics*[1]

Ownership Economics[2] replaces the book *Ownership Theory of Economic Activity versus Economic Theory without Ownership: Supplementary Volume to the new Edition of 'Ownership, Interest and Money'*,[3] which was published in May 2002 by Metropolis, Marburg. That book had 113 pages and was published with a print run of 550 copies, which were sold out in spring 2005.

The original edition of *Ownership, Interest and Money*[4] was published by Rowohlt in June 1996. Despite a print run of 3,000 copies, a large number for a specialist economic theory text, the book had already sold out in June 1999. A second, revised edition was published by Metropolis in May 2002 with a print run of 800 copies. A third edition, once again revised, was published by the same publisher in November 2004.

Since 1996 several individual reviews and three separate collections of articles have been published on our ownership theory of interest and money. In further developing our approach, beginning with the *Supplementary Volume* of 2002 (Heinsohn and Steiger 2002a, and then Heinsohn and Steiger 2000a and 2006a), we have explicitly taken the objections of our critics into account. With *Ownership Economics* an improved, more precise and more concise version of *Ownership, Interest and Money* has been made available.

A register of all critical reviews and adoptions of *Ownership, Interest and Money* from 1996 and the *Supplementary Volume* from 2002 is included in the appendix of this book.[5] The reading of *Ownership, Interest and Money*, however, is still recommended, because that book covers aspects of economic history and the history of economic thought in much more detail than *Ownership Economics*, which has been deliberately kept short and concise. Its expanded English edition[6] is in preparation under the title *Property, Interest and Money: Foundations of Economic Theory*. The book will be published by Routledge in London at the end of 2006.

As in the second and third edition of *Ownership, Interest and Money* (2002 and 2004), foreign language quotes appear in their original language in the footnotes.

While objections may provide more insights than agreement, we permit ourselves at this point to quote a joint book review of *Ownership, Interest and Money* and the *Supplementary Volume* that represents praise for our work:

With their book *Ownership, Interest and Money*, published in 1996, the authors achieved what is commonly referred to as a 'ground-breaking achievement', or perhaps even as a 'book of the century'. In the meantime the second edition has appeared, as in 'classic' textbooks with extensive prefaces and introductions and a carefully developed page concordance table.... The reading of the book is not easy. It not only requires a comprehensive knowledge of the history of economic thought, which might be expected, but also requires a detailed knowledge of the controversies that have taken place over the last two decades on this subject.... However, in contrast to many economic theory texts, the book also provides enjoyment and education, because the authors excel in dealing with sources and examples, and in the presentation of surprising insights and conclusions'[7] (Busch 2003, 86, 88).

We thank Nadine Kröger (University of Bremen) for the careful review of the text and the creation of the name and subject index.

Gunnar Heinsohn and Otto Steiger
Bremen, 10 December 2005

1 Possession and ownership
Use of goods versus economic activity

Ownership economics[1] deals with one of the core questions of economics: what is the underlying loss that is compensated by interest?[2] The answer given here differs fundamentally from the theories of interest presented by the great schools of economics. Ownership economics argues that the existence of interest cannot be explained by the temporary loss of profit (classical economics), the temporary loss of consumption (neoclassical economics) or the temporary loss of money (Keynesian economics).

Rather, ownership economics argues that the rate of interest results from the temporary loss that is suffered when the *owner* imposes a burden[3] on his property as part of the *money-creation* process.[4] This loss is not a temporary loss of *possession*[5] but a loss resulting from the sacrifice of an immaterial yield arising from *ownership* – the *ownership premium*.[6]

What is the difference between ownership and possession? This question is central to ownership economics but has never been asked by the great schools of economics. Mere de facto possession, without the associated right of ownership arising from a property law framework, implies the mere *command over goods and resources* according to specific *rules*, which are determined by power relations or coercive orders and not by legal rights. However, once de facto possession has become *de jure* possession and has been complemented by ownership, the somewhat arbitrary rule- and power-based deployment of goods and resources is transformed into the economic deployment[7] of goods and resources. The latter are now denominated in money and turned into commodities and assets. Commodities and assets become examples of property that can not only factually and legally be possessed (the *possessory aspect*[8] of property) but can also be owned and hypothecated (the *ownership aspect*[9] of property). Multiple property rights over the same asset can be exercised by different people.

The ownership aspect provides the owner with economically important rights and powers over commodities and assets. These include the power to *sell*, the power to *burden*, the power to *hypothecate* and the power to make property available to satisfy claims in debt *enforcement* actions. Economically of greatest importance is the ability to burden property by reserving it to back money when created, or by hypothecating it in order to secure credit. While assets can generally be burdened, commodities can only be burdened in exceptional circumstances.

The possessory aspect of commodities and assets comprises the rights available to a possessor. The *de jure* possessor does not need to be the same person as the owner. Rights of possession determine by whom, when, where, how and to what degree commodities and assets can be used physically. The *de jure* possessor generally cannot, for example, sell or hypothecate the property. Nor can he transfer the property to fulfill claims arising from debt recovery actions. These abstract, legal and non-physical powers are generally reserved for the owner.

In contrast, the rights arising from the ownership of (or title to) property provide the powers that form the basis of economic activity: (1) the *burdening* of property to back the creation of money in loan contracts against interest; (2) the *hypothecation* of property to obtain money as capital; (3) the transfer of title through *sale* or the transfer of possession through *rental/lease* agreements; and (4) the *enforcement* of contracts and rights against specific assets. When property rights are created, traditional, non-economic rules for the use of goods and resources are transformed into *de jure* possessory rights over commodities and assets. In contrast to rules governing use, *de jure* possessory rights are property rights and are governed by property law.

The notion that the rate of interest results from a loss of an immaterial yield is also present in the three great schools of economics. In classical economics, the rate of interest compensates for a sacrificed profit opportunity with due consideration of the investment risks involved. Interest arises because the 'money capitalist' does not take the same risk as the 'entrepreneur capitalist'[10] when the latter uses the borrowed funds from the 'money capitalist' to invest in means of production. The rate of interest is explained as the difference between the available profit yield on the investment and the risk premium of the entrepreneur. In neoclassical economics, the rate of interest compensates for the sacrifice of the consumption of present goods, as these carry a higher premium than goods consumed in the future. In Keynesian economics, the rate of interest compensates for a sacrifice of the liquidity premium yielded by money because it can liquidate obligations at any time.

Ownership economics argues that interest does not compensate for the temporary loss of profit opportunity, the loss of present consumption or the loss of liquidity. While all three opportunities for incurring losses exist, they do not provide an underlying explanation for the existence of interest. Interest is not an interest yielded by non-invested (classical economics) or non-consumed (neoclassical economics) goods,[11] but always an interest yielded by money.[12] This insight helped Keynes advance beyond classical and neoclassical economics. He, however, overlooked the fact that money is only created against interest. Money can thus only be lent (and can only give rise to a liquidity premium) after interest has already come into existence through a money-creating credit contract. It is the interest that arises when money is created that economic theory must explain.

Moreover, not only is money created against interest, but its creation also requires the burdening of assets and therefore presupposes the existence of property rights. As long as property is not burdened, it carries the immaterial yield of an ownership premium. Unlike the other schools of economics, which in their essence explain interest from a lending operation involving goods, ownership economics identifies the interest-generating act not in a lending operation but in the act of imposing a burden on property. Property is burdened when money is created, as a documented claim over the property of the money-creating creditor, in a loan contract with a debtor. In this contract, the money-creating creditor loses ownership premium, because the note issue imposes a burden on his property.[13] He is compensated for this loss by an interest payment from the debtor.

The burdening of creditor property in the money-creation process and the interest payment for the associated debt implies that economic activity has begun. Economic activity in a genuine sense arises from the activation of property titles, not from either an initial endowment of goods or an initial endowment of money. While *de jure* possession is economically utilized once money exists, without ownership and the associated security rights, neither such money nor genuine economic activity can be generated. Genuine economic activity only arises when the right of ownership[14] is added to mere de facto possession (i.e., use) of physical goods and resources by enactment. While rules governing the use of goods and resources have always existed and are even found in the animal kingdom, only the right of ownership can transform goods and resources into commodities and assets. The abolition of ownership is therefore not only the demise of the ownership premium but also the cessation of economic activity; as a consequence, production and allocation by customary rule or coercion return.

1.1 Economic activity as distinguished from mere material reproduction

An economic theory worthy of that name has been lacking because economists, unlike the jurists of ancient Rome, never made a distinction between possession (whether *de jure* or de facto) and ownership. Because economists have not been interested in the fundamental difference between these two rights, they have mainly been concerned with possession and have incorrectly identified it as the main attribute of property rights. In particular, neoclassical economists believe in an eternal *homo economicus*, who, since the stone tools of the Neanderthal, has been driven to economic production based on mere (de facto) rights of possession. They are convinced that the barter paradigm is the principle under which utility-maximizing agents, constrained only by the scarcity of resources, develop everything that makes up economic activity in an evolutionary process. As the laws of physics govern the movement of the planets, they want to derive economic laws that govern economic agents at all times and places; however, they confuse the agent with a mere user of goods. This proudly-pursued universalism can only have validity for de facto rights of possession, which are indeed mandatory for any material reproduction of living organisms.

Such a universalism does not contribute anything to the understanding of ownership, which is created by man and is always codified in a system of law, and its central role in the economy. It is argued here that only the replacement of the barter paradigm with the ownership paradigm – first formulated in 1982 as the private ownership paradigm of money (Heinsohn 1984 [1982], 120) – allows the development of an economic theory worthy of that name. Ownership economics is the attempt to create this theory.

Mankind knows not one but three (generalized) types of system[15] that to this day impose radically different rule sets on material reproduction. The term reproduction includes production, distribution, consumption and at times the accumulation of goods. The three systems are:

1 A tribal community that regulates production, distribution and consumption based on mutually binding *customary* rules (following the principles of reciprocity) imposed on its dependent members collectively. In this community, transactions related to reproduction are altruistic. Independent institutions of law or codified law which could make rules of reciprocity and associated behavior formally enforceable do not exist.

2 A command system or feudal/socialist seigneurie[16] that regulates production, distribution, consumption and – sporadic – accumulation through coercive mechanisms, which despite their usually codified form are often explicitly identifiable as arbitrary in nature. A ruling class extracts dues and services from serfs or serf-like workers and justifies its position, religiously or ideologically embellished, through the loyalty-securing provision of stored supplies in emergencies (even though these provisions were previously collected through dues and services). State socialism, with its central plans, provides a modern version of such a command system. As in a system based on reciprocity, there is no independent law that could be enforced against the rulers themselves.

3 A society of free individuals based on property rights replaces rules based on reciprocity, custom or coercive orders with *enforceable contracts*. This revolution is identified in the western cultural tradition with figures such as Theseus of Athens and his 'state without a king', or Romulus, who, when dividing feudal estates into the legendary Roma Quadrata, allocated equally-sized plots of land per ballot to his fellow revolutionaries. An ownership-based society regulates production, distribution, consumption and accumulation through *ownership* (on the basis of which property is burdened or hypothecated), *interest* and *money*, none of which are available in the other two systems.

Pure de facto possession-based systems (such as the tribal, feudal or socialist systems) are systems of survival and at the same time social safety networks, although at a low material level. In contrast, the economic operations of ownership-based societies do not create a social safety network from within. However, the comparatively high production yields allow a social policy providing support at a much higher level than possession-based systems. Besides war, the typical crisis for a possession-based system is an exogenous event like a starvation (or harvest) crisis. Such a crisis cannot be resolved internally and can, in extreme cases, result in destruction (tribal system) or revolt (feudal system). The typical crisis in an ownership-based society is endogenous to the system. It is characterized by a lack of ability or lack of desire to burden property. This crisis can be resolved internally only in a limited way. Based on these socio-institutional differences, de facto possession-based systems tend to enlarge their territories and are therefore always ready to engage in war. In contrast, an ownership-based society generally cannot enlarge its wealth by simply adding territories,[17] and is, therefore, less prone to cross-border aggressions against other ownership-based economies (see in more detail Steiger 2005a, 170).

The differences between systems based on reciprocity and command on the one hand and systems based on property rights on the other are of a fundamental nature and not just differences of degree. Genuine economic activity can only be found in an ownership-based society. Because neither tribal nor feudal systems recognize property rights, their operations are limited to the de facto possession or use of goods and resources. Both systems are therefore caught *qua* custom or order in a system where mere command regulates material reproduction. This command system, however, remains limited to providing orders that transform resources into goods and that regulate their production, including stores and occasional accumulation, as well as distribution and consumption. Thus the command over reproduction by rule or orders leads to more or less efficient transactions involving goods and resources, but not to economic activity. The scarcity of goods, which in neoclassical economics is the basis of all economic activity (following from the assumption of an initial endowment with scarce resources), is an obvious element in both de facto possession-based systems. However, neither system develops genuine economic activity. The understanding of both types of de facto possession-based system, in fact, does not even require an economic theory at all. A sociological analysis is entirely sufficient to explain the maintenance and impact of different loyalty- and rule-based mechanisms employed for the utilization of resources.

1.2 Material reproduction in *de facto* possession-based systems

Tribal and command systems are based on rules about de facto possession. Ownership is unknown in these systems, as leading economic ethnologists like Bronislaw Malinowski, Richard Thurnwald and Marshall Sahlins have repeatedly emphasized. 'It is especially a grave error to use the word ownership with the very definite connotation given to it in our own society' (Malinowski 1922, 116). Indeed, '[t]his right of private possession ... does not affect the elementary necessities of life.... A claim to the private ownership of special pieces of land within the "clan" district is generally not recognized' (Thurnwald 1932, 186). Economic ethnologists know that neoclassical economists are misled when they assume that *homo economicus* exists in tribal communities:

The hunter, one is tempted to say, is 'uneconomic man'. At least as concerns nonsubsistence goods he is the reverse of that standard caricature immortalized in any *General Principles of Economics*, page one. His wants are scarce and his means (in relation) plentiful. Consequently he is 'comparatively free of material pressures', has 'no sense of possession', [and] shows 'an undeveloped sense of property' (Sahlins 1974, 13).

While all three researchers insightfully highlight the absence of ownership in tribal systems, they nevertheless remain imprecise in their choice of terminology. The terms 'ownership', 'property' and 'possession' are used arbitrarily and interchangeably as a stylistic device. As an unintended consequence, in the view of these researchers, tribal systems do not even have the de facto right of possession, which in fact they certainly have.[18]

In line with the absence of ownership, economic ethnologists cannot find a *market* derived from barter exchanges or *money* in tribal systems: 'There is no regular market, hence no prices, hence no mechanism of exchange – *still less for money*' (Malinowski 1935, 45, emphasis added; see also the discussion in Heinsohn 2005).

The lending of goods exists in a tribe, but the return of the goods is neither guaranteed nor secured by collateral. Romans, who recollected their tribal past, knew to differentiate between interest (*fenus*), governed by the *ius civile* of a credit contract in their ownership-based society; and the interest-free loan to help neighbours (*mutuum*), governed by the *ius gentium* of their tribal past. In the tribal system nothing equivalent to interest or loan security can be found. Cattle breeders do not even request the calves of the stock lent to their fellow tribesmen as a compensation for the foregone milk or beef consumption: 'it is remarkable that not a lot of emphasis is placed on the interest or amount of interest payment. The focus is entirely on the [cattle] capital lent' (Laum 1965, 60).[19]

Given all this unequivocal evidence, it is no surprise that economic ethnology cannot prove that barter exchanges are prerequisites for the emergence of money:

> Barter, in the strict sense of moneyless market exchange, has never been a quantitatively important or dominant model of transaction in any past or present economic system about which we had hard information.... Moneyless market exchange was not an evolutionary stage ... preceding the arrival of monetary means of market exchange.
>
> (Dalton 1982, 185, 188)

In tribal communities, as Polanyi already knew four decades earlier,

> the idea of profit is barred; higgling and haggling is decried; giving freely is acclaimed as a virtue; the supposed propensity to barter, truck, and exchange does not appear. The economic system is, in effect, a mere function of social organization.
>
> (Polanyi 1944a, 49)

'When money is encountered in tribes it mainly originates from the contact with ownership-based societies' (Pryor 1977, 166).[20]

As well as markets and money, tribal communities also lack money prices. Even unique and identifiable relative prices, expressing rates of exchange and valuation of goods, postulated by the barter models of classical and neoclassical economics cannot be found: '*The characteristic fact of primitive exchange is indeterminacy of the rates*. In different transactions, similar goods move against each other in different proportions' (Sahlins 1974, 281; emphasis added). Moreover, it is not even possible to compare the value of one good with that of another:

> In fact, the narrow range of exchangeable articles and the inertia of custom *leave no room for any free exchange*, in which there would be a need for comparing a number of articles by means of a common measure.... Moreover, what is more important still, we see ... that the character of the exchange does not admit of any article becoming money. Certain things, no doubt, ... are frequently exchanged, and against a wide range of articles, and in economic considerations they may serve us as measures of value, but they are not regarded or purposely used as such by the natives.
> (Malinowski 1921, 14; emphasis added)

The search for money, interest and credit, as well as markets and prices, in the study of command systems has been as intensive as in that of tribal systems (based on reciprocity), although no search has been undertaken for loan security. The results are equally sobering. Mycenaean-Greek feudalism, for example, famous for its mighty castles and its extensive usage of gold and silver, had no comprehension of the economic operations that would later dominate the Greek city-states; operations that still present a mystery to economic historians today: 'The manner in which loans became so mighty a machine is mysterious' (Starr 1977, 183). What can be identified about the material reproduction of Mycenae

> is the activity of the palace; which exacts produce and no doubt much else from the king's subjects, and doles out rations and materials when something has to be done with exact notes of what has been received or issued, and what should have been. There is no reference to anything outside the palace system, and it may well be that this covered the whole country. *There is no suggestion of money, or of any standard by which values might be compared, items just being counted, weighed, or measured as they stand.* Nor is there any direct reference to foreign trade which must have involved some kind of exchange; and we may reasonably suspect that the palace, which controls so much, would control this also.
> (Andrewes 1967, 29; emphasis added)

Interestingly, ancient writers already knew that gold was only used as money after the fall of Mycenaean feudalism, as is evidenced in the famous words of

Lucretius (99–55 BC): 'Later [after the Kings established citadels] came the invention of property and the discovery of gold [money], which speedily robbed the strong and handsome of their status' (*De rerum natura*, V: 1113–1114).

The Inca Empire, extending more than 4,000 km from north to south, had feudal structures similar to the Mycenaean system:

> The ruling class is the tribe of the Incas. The majority of the people are obliged to work for the state for nine months; for three months they are free to support their own livelihood. *There is no individual ownership over land, therefore neither poverty nor wealth.* All land is either temple, state or community land. Sick and old people are cared for by the community. There is ... no individual freedom or freedom of movement.[21]

Although the Inca state is 'rich in gold and silver jewellery',[22] and for that reason looted by the conquistadores, money and markets are unknown. The developed system of roads and the breeding of pack animals were set up to aid the transport of troops and dues rather than to support trade. Dues and labor services were registered by a mobile apparatus of state officials and recorded through a mnemonic knot system (Stange 1960, 708).

The former and failed system of state socialism must be regarded as the most sophisticated command system. Here too a search for ownership, interest and money, as well as markets and prices, has been conducted with even higher expectations. However, while the same legal and economic terminology was in use, the terms were empty shells and not equivalent to the corresponding economic operations in societies based on property rights. All that could be attempted in state socialism was their imitation. For example, the terms 'state ownership' or 'ownership by the people'[23] suggested the existence of ownership. Instead, all they represented were giant agglomerations of de facto possession. Titles that allow the burdening, hypothecation, division, lease or sale of property and that can be enforced in debt recovery actions did not exist. Title registration and land title offices, when inherited from a predecessor ownership-based society as in the case of the German Democratic Republic (GDR), were not maintained diligently or were abolished altogether (as in the Czech republic in 1953).

The rulers of the Soviet Occupied Territory in Germany understood, when carrying out the land reforms after World War II, that ownership over property could not simply be handed over to the state or its people. Ownership needed to be stripped of its powers and key attributes. To achieve this, ownership rights were taken from the owners and then transferred into a 'people's property fund'.[24] The fund, however, was explicitly constructed to be 'untouchable' and thus inalienable for the individual member of the socialist collective. An exception was the 'land reform fund',[25] from which small parcels of land (12.5–20 acres)[26] previously belonging to owners of large properties (greater than 250 acres)[27] were distributed to small farmers and farm laborers. However, the 'land reformers' knew that the recipient of the land grants would only receive use, i.e., de facto possessory, rights. All other operations over landed property were explicitly prohibited. For example, Section VI of the land law ordinance of the State of Saxony-Anhalt dated 3 September 1945 stated: 'the farm economies [sic] created on the basis of this ordinance cannot be divided, partially divided, sold, leased or hypothecated' (Grün 1998, 541).[28]

While reference is made to the 'economic use' of the allocated land, the intention was not to fully activate the property, but to merely allocate individual use rights. Moreover, these rights also implied duties towards the rulers that were not unlike those characterizing the relationship between feudal lord and serf. The person who violated any implied duties, such as a potential heir, lost the use rights. In this case the land was returned to the 'land reform fund', which assigned the use rights belonging to the former 'owner' to the socialist farming collective (landwirtschaftliche Produktionsgenossenschaft, LPG), whose individual members were barred from any individual use. Individual de facto possession was thus turned into collective de facto possession, rather than private ownership into state ownership or ownership by the people.

In the so called land reform judgment of the German Federal Court (Bundesgerichtshof, BGH) on 17 December 1998 (V ZR 200/97), German jurists had to demonstrate the insights that have been so distinctly absent from the analysis of socialism by the prevailing schools of economics:

> based on the prohibition of any free disposition [hypothecation, division and sale], the prohibition to lease and the requirement to utilize the property, the right of ownership over the property resulting from the land reform was stripped of the essential meaning of ownership according to the Civil Code.[29]
>
> (BGH 1998, § 2.1. C, p. 8)

The judges, however, lacked the insight that ownership outside the framework of a civil code does not exist. 'Stripped down' ownership is simply de facto possession.

The lack of ownership in socialism was also reflected in the absence of money, interest and credit, together with the inability to hypothecate property. What was called a 'state bank' or 'commercial bank' was in fact nothing but the system of a so-called 'mono bank', in which 'commercial banks' represented mere divisions of the 'state bank'. The state bank did not have to keep assets to regulate its 'bank note' issue or to implement monetary policy. Instead, its assets were non-tradable 'obligations' of government and state-owned companies.[30] Those 'titles', however, did not represent obligations against anything, as they could not be enforced against state-owned companies or the government. The 'credit' of the state bank simply allowed state-owned companies and government divisions access to goods, whose production was dictated by the central state plan. In line with the plan, the state bank created deposit entries through a 'credit' operation. The deposits in turn allowed wage payments and transfers in the form of bank notes to the public. Bank notes and bank deposits were called money. In reality, they were money of an arbitrary nature,[31] simply representing a voucher that provided an unspecific entitlement to goods produced under the central plan. When these vouchers were expended on goods, they were collected by the state-owned companies and returned to the state bank. In this way loans to the state-owned companies were repaid.

Similarly, what was called 'interest' in state socialism was at best an instrument to ensure that state-owned companies produced their goods according to plan, in which case the money vouchers made their way to the state bank on time. Moreover, if the planned return failed, there were few consequences for the state-owned companies. Only the bonus payments for directors and employees could be cut in this instance, which was experienced as 'penalty interest'.

Like their western counterparts, deposit account balances of employees could generate interest. However, the interest rate was set arbitrarily, was not guaranteed, was paid at irregular intervals and typically remained below one percent. The reason for the low interest rate was that the additional amount of money vouchers required for the interest payment did not represent any previously planned goods.

The absence of ownership, money and interest in socialism was matched by the absence of markets and prices. Instead, a system of administrative prices set subsidized prices for basic goods. Here, producers received higher prices than end-consumers paid. The resulting danger of an oversupply of money vouchers was in turn counterbalanced by setting prices for non-basic and luxury goods, retailed in speciality shops, at a much higher retail price than the producer price.

1.3 Economic deployment of *de jure* possession in an ownership-based society

The physical possession of goods and resources remains of central importance for material reproduction in an ownership-based society. However, goods and resources are now seen as commodities and assets. The ownership-based society distinguishes itself from de facto possession-based systems through the addition of the right of ownership and the transformation of de facto possession (rules governing use) into formal rights of *de jure* possession. Property titles embody property *rights* that are protected by independent courts of law. Independent courts transform rules of custom and coercive orders regulating the use of goods and resources – who can use what, when, where, against whom, how and to what degree – into *de jure* rights of possession.

Because the right of *de jure* possession can only exist within the context of a property rights framework, a *de jure* possessor per se does not exist. Either the owner and the *de jure* possessor are the same, or the owner has transferred the *de jure* possession to someone else. Thus every ownership title is generally associated with a title to *de jure* possession. There is no owner per se. While assets can always be possessed (*de jure* or de facto respectively), only the *de jure* possession in ownership-based societies is linked to an ownership title.

Of course, systems without property rights can engage in production. For such a deployment of de facto possession, not even human beings are necessarily required. Bees, ants, beavers and other animals can produce, consume, distribute and defend their de facto possessions; in a limited way this is even valid for plants.

In contrast, rights to property – including the transformed *de jure* rights of possession – only exist among mankind. The most important among these rights, ownership, is not used physically but is activated by imposing or enforcing a legal obligation – in the creation of money, by securing a credit, by enforcing a debt, and in sales, rental and lease contracts.

Land provides a suitable example to illustrate the difference between the mere deployment of de facto possessory aspect and the full activation of a property title. In all three systems – tribal community, feudalism/socialism and ownership-based society – the access to a plot of land can be used to plough, sow and harvest a crop with a tangible yield. The mere use of the land, however, does not represent economic activity. It simply reflects the fact that de facto possession can be utilized for production. The economic activation of the plot of land only takes place when the farmer, as a member of an ownership-based society, must farm the land (i.e., use the possessory aspect of his property) because he has used the ownership aspect of his property to obtain money in a credit contract via hypothecation and has agreed to repay the money obtained with interest. It is the capacity to burden or hypothecate property that transforms a mere thing into an economic asset and that makes the farmland into a valuable production asset.

The *de jure* right to possession in ownership-based societies is radically different from de facto rules of possession in the two de facto possession-based systems (tribe, feudal/socialist system). While de facto possession in the latter systems is put to work by the direct command over goods and resources, *de jure* possession in ownership-based societies is forced into utilization by the act of burdening or hypothecation. This fundamentally changes the way possession is deployed: deployment is now based on contracts that are always denominated in money terms, and mere goods and resources are transformed in this way into commodities and assets. Accordingly, the latter always appear in the economic process as monetary variables, expressed in sums of money.[32] Assets always have a possessory aspect, allowing a physical use, and an ownership aspect, allowing an economic deployment through burdening and hypothecation. Commodities equally have a possessory aspect allowing a physical use, but their ownership aspect is activated only for the impending sale. Obviously, assets, i.e., property capable of being burdened and hypothecated, can also be sold, whereby ownership and possessory aspects are transferred simultaneously.

It follows that economic activity means a great deal more than the achievement of efficiency and a state of optimum allocation. Ultimately, humans in any system of reproduction, and even other living beings, can deploy resources without wastage or, as assumed in neoclassical economics, can achieve the optimal allocation of scarce resources based on individual preferences.[33] Where such optimization processes, necessary everywhere among flora and fauna for each species' survival, are generalized into the central axiom of economic man (*homo economicus*), economic theory misses its subject.

The economy is not a system of advantage-seeking behaviors, subject to the constraint of scarce resources, where mankind is continuously freeing itself from supposed 'chains' of the past. Instead, genuine economic activity only results from the enactment of property rights. The latter protect every person (whether selfish or altruistic) from despotic rule, but impose their own rules and dynamics.

In ownership-based societies, it is not a set of physical goods – the initial endowment of neoclassical economics – that establishes economic activity. Firms must defend themselves against a price decline in their shares and assets and the risk of foreclosure. They do this by implementing continuous innovations in relation to the physical possessory aspect of the firm's assets, where goods are modified and manufacturing processes are revolutionized. Hence, they must invest money in plant, equipment and wages. In order to borrow this money, they must enter into credit agreements with commercial banks, in which they are forced to risk as collateral the very property assets they have to defend.

The right of ownership not only leads – and for the first time – to *economic rules* but also to the *rule of law* and the *freedom* of the individual (*life, liberty and property*).[34] In the same way that freedom cannot be contemplated without the rule of law and the rule of law cannot be contemplated without freedom, genuine economic activity cannot exist without freedom *and* the rule of law. A mere agglomeration of de facto possession does not result in genuine economic activity, freedom or law. It is ownership that provides the foundation of economic prosperity, law and freedom.[35]

The common dichotomy emphasized by economists that links freedom, law and economic prosperity with the private individual, and blames the collective for a lack or deficiency of this trinity, suffers from a simplified view of property rights as rights of (de facto or *de jure*) possession. This view misses the critical importance of the right of ownership altogether. In a similar way, economists who emphasize the (incorrect) contrast between *private* ownership and *state* ownership miss the correct dichotomy between ownership and (de facto *or de jure*) possession. In reality, an ownership-based society represents the individual as a private person and the collective as a contractually bound group of free individuals.

Table 1.1 presents a summary of attributes of and differences between systems based on de facto possession and those based on ownership.[36] What distinguishes a system that is capable merely of material reproduction from a system with economic activity? It is the immaterial law of property that transforms rules of de facto possession, determined by a tradition of coercive orders, into equally immaterial *de jure* rights of possession so that traditional goods and resources become commodities and property assets. The ownership rights over assets then create the capacity of assets to be able to be burdened and hypothecated, a precondition for the creation of money by a note-issuing bank, and

Table 1.1 Summary of attributes of and differences between possession-based systems and systems based on ownership

De facto possession-based systems with mere reproduction	Ownership-based society with economic activity
De facto possession is the **basis of material reproduction** in animal systems, as well as in human systems based on reciprocity (tribal community) or command (feudal/socialist seigneurie), in which ownership is missing. *Only* de facto possession exists. Informal or arbitrary rules determine who, in what manner, at what time and place, to what extent and by exclusion of whom, may *physically use goods and resources* and change their substance and form.	**Ownership** is the immaterial **basis of material reproduction** in the ownership-based society (at times labeled as 'capitalism', 'market economy', 'monetary economy'), where rules of de facto possession become *de jure* rights of possession. Ownership exists in *addition to* possession.
De facto possessory rules refer to the *non-legal* material use or control of goods and resources including the returns thereon and their alienation. Alienation here does not mean exchange in the form of sale and lease, but only gifts, transfer and – occasionally – inheritance. Per se, these rules are not capable of generating genuine economic activity, with interest and money as its most obvious characteristics. Ironically, mainstream economists apply the term 'property rights' to mere de facto possessory rules and see the key factor in the distinction between common (shared) and individual (exclusive) use.	**Ownership** is a *de jure* **right within a system of property law** and provides owners with the powers that form the basis of economic activity: (i) *burdening* of property to back the creation of money against interest; (ii) *hypothecating* property to obtain money as capital; (iii) transfer of title through *sale* or transfer of possession through *rental/lease* agreements; and (iv) the *enforcement* of contracts and rights against specific assets. Where property rights and ownership are created, traditional, non-economically determined rules for the use of goods and resources are transformed into **de jure possessory rights** over commodities and assets. In contrast to rules governing use, *de jure* possessory rights are property rights and governed by property law.
	Property rights transform goods and resources into saleable commodities and saleable and rentable assets.
Means of regulating material reproduction: production, distribution, consumption and occasional accumulation. Inborn instincts (animal kingdom), custom and reciprocity (tribal community), and command or plans (feudal/socialist seigneurie) exercised in *power* relations over *'unfree'* persons are the non-legal rules of reproduction. Independent courts of law are absent.	**Means of regulating material reproduction:** production, distribution, consumption and accumulation.
	Credit, sales, lease and employment contracts form a legally determined network of rights between *free*, private individuals on markets necessary for reproduction. Independent courts of law overrule custom and power relations.

continued

Table 1.1 Continued

De facto possession-based systems with mere reproduction	Ownership-based society with economic activity
Burdening and hypothecation of property titles, interest and money, assets and liabilities, credit and banks, prices and markets **are absent**, as is the advantage-seeking *homo economicus*. The **rules of reciprocity** (tribe) or **command** (nobility, 'proletariat's avant-garde') determine the production of goods and their distribution for individual consumption, for common storage, and – occasionally – for collective investment in means of production. Therefore, *storage and accumulation require previous savings* or a lower level of individual consumption. Exchange of goods is not the primary aim. When goods are exchanged at all, they serve to strengthen *loyalty*. *Interest-free* intertemporal lending of goods to overcome individual difficulties is bound to the obligation of mutual assistance. Common difficulties are resolved by handing out rations that are to be replenished later, either voluntarily (tribal community) or by command (feudal seigneurie).	The **power to burden and hypothecate property** offers an immaterial yield, the *ownership premium*. By burdening property as part of the issue of *money notes* – documented claims over property – in a credit contract, both creditor and debtor have to give up their respective *ownership premium*; that is, they temporarily lose the freedom to burden, hypothecate or sell it. The **hypothecation** of the debtor's property secures the creditor's claim, and thereby supports the *circulation* of the money notes. The **burdening** of the creditor's own property, his capital[1] or net worth, enables him to withdraw notes from circulation or to redeem his notes. The creditor is compensated for the burdening of his property – i.e. for the loss of *ownership premium* – with *interest*; the debtor is compensated for the hypothecation of his property with the *liquidity premium* inherent in the obtained money notes. The liquidity premium arises from the ability of the money notes to finally settle contracts. They obtain this capacity to either buy/sell or redeem property because they are backed by the property of the creditor. During the period of the loan, creditor and debtor continue with the physical or non-physical use of the possessory aspect of their now burdened property assets. Because money is a *derivative of property assets*, accumulation can start without previous savings of material goods.
De facto possession-based systems have inbuilt **social safety nets** of reciprocity or emergency rations, albeit on quite a low material level.	Ownership-based societies do not create **social safety networks** from within. They have to build them separately.

Notes
1 {Original: Eigenkapital.}

thereby for economic activity. The right-hand column in Table 1.1 summarizes the fundamental operations of an ownership-based society, which are presented in Chapter 3 in detail. Before beginning this discussion we have, however, to deal with the question of why the three major schools of economics – classical economics, neoclassical economics and Keynesian economics – have missed the economic importance of ownership and have therefore not been able to deliver an explanation for interest, money and the reasons behind economic activity.

2 The blindness of the great schools of economics towards ownership

The inability of economists to differentiate between possession and ownership has prevented them from realizing that only ownership-based societies are characterized by genuine economic activity. And it is this lack of insight that is responsible for the absence of a genuine economic theory to this day. This claim may sound presumptuous. However, it can be argued that it has found the support of Harold Demsetz, one of the founders of new institutional economics. While Demsetz ambiguously identifies the ownership-based society with capitalism, he notes: 'Although our theoretical ideas about capitalism have improved as mainstream economics developed, they have never matured into a theory of capitalism' (Demsetz 1998, col. 144a).

While ownership economics shows that economists have completely disregarded ownership, new institutional economics complains that classical and neoclassical economics have not sufficiently considered property rights:

> What has mainstream economics been doing for 200 years if it has not been studying capitalism? From Adam Smith and David Ricardo to Alfred Marshal and Léon Walras, economists directed their efforts toward understanding micro and macro operations of the price system. The property rights system, however, is only implicitly involved in the theory that emerged. This theory ... takes the property rights foundation of capitalism for granted. It does not investigate the role of property rights arrangements.
>
> (Demsetz 1998, col. 144a)

In this chapter, ownership economics takes up Demsetz's question and examines carefully what economists have done over the past 200 years when studying capitalism. In order to answer Demsetz's question, the three great schools of economic theory – classical economics, neoclassical economics and Keynesian economics – are briefly examined. This examination will initially not include the school of mercantilism. This is not because mercantilism has been assessed as 'pre-scientific' since the advent of classical economics but, on the contrary, because it had already articulated important economic insights in relation to ownership. This school of thought reached its peak in James Steuart's *An Inquiry into the Principles of Political Oeconomy* (1767), a work which has been neglected to this day.[1]

Ownership economics and the three great schools of economics all study the same economic system. All explicitly acknowledge that money and interest exist and that these fundamental economic categories are in need of explanation. All schools use the terms 'property', 'ownership' and 'possession' in one way or another. However, the present analysis thus far has shown that these schools have neglected and consequently not explained the key economic role that ownership plays. They resemble a fish that can only understand water after it has been thrown on to the land. The unique and critical attributes of ownership in providing the powers to burden and to hypothecate property, and to make property the subject of debt execution, have been missed by all three schools. It is argued that, as a consequence, they have all failed to provide a satisfactory explanation of interest and money.

2.1 Classical economics

'Private property', i.e., property in private ownership, is positioned at the center of classical economics. There is hardly a term that receives a stronger emphasis. It is the core element of 'capitalism' – either praised as a blessing or considered a devilish curse. Adam Smith could not comprehend a society without property – not even in the 'early and rude state', as in a tribal 'nation of hunters' (Smith 1776, 47). What he regards as property at a more advanced stage is merely transformed from 'common property' to individual or 'private property'. For Smith, profit and rent of land are the specific characteristics of private property and emerge as new sources of income along with wages, the latter assumed as a *reproduction wage* that has always existed:

> As soon as stock has accumulated in the hands of particular persons, some of them will naturally employ it in setting to work industrious people, whom they will supply with materials and subsistence, in order to make a profit by the sale of their work. ... As soon as the land of any country has all become *private property*, the landlords, like all other men, love to reap where they never sowed and demand a rent even for its natural produce.
>
> (Smith 1776, 48; emphasis added)

Classical economics is fixated on a view of 'private property' as individual control over physical resources, which is to be contrasted with collective control over 'common property'. The former allows the exploitation of people who have no access to resources. The interesting aspect of private property for classical economics is hence the *power* of appropriation, which is thought to be immediately exercised by anyone with the opportunity to do so. Classical economics argues that because not all people could acquire private property following the decay of common property, only a minority of people could capitalize on this power advantage. Induced by the natural greed inherent in mankind, in turn, private proprietors exploit the people without property, a view providing fertile ground in particular for Karl Marx. Classical economics overall, therefore, delivers not an economic theory but a social theory, taking the shape of a *theory of domination* over goods and resources. Existing economic categories – especially private ownership of property, profit and rent – are to be explained based on power relations.

The history of man, conceptualized as *homo economicus*, is of interest to classical economics only as far as it relates to the evolution of control over resources. Property is assumed to have existed from the very beginning and enabled at an early stage, in the form of common property, a system where everybody was a ruler. Income could only arise in the form of wages for labor. However, at a developed stage, the class of private property owners, the 'capitalists' (Ricardo 1817) and the landlords, began to rule. This allowed the extraction of profits and rents. For both stages, classical economics only considers the use of goods and resources: in the early stage governed by a collective, and in the second developed stage governed by a class of ruling individuals. The important attribute of 'private property' in the classical context therefore refers to *possession*, the factual use and control, and not ownership, the strongest legal right. Therefore, the term 'possession' in its proper sense is unknown to classical economics and confusingly the term 'property' is used, sometimes with imposing vigor. 'Capitalism' (Marx 1867) – understood as a *system of domination* – provides the decisive characteristic of the economic system from a classical economists' point of view.

In classical economics the economy is understood as an *actual barter exchange economy*. This barter exchange economy, in its raw form, shaped the early stage of 'common property'. Barter arises from the 'propensity in human nature ... to truck' (Smith 1776, 13). Barter, in turn, creates the division of labor, a mighty productive force that is only limited by the size of the market. However, the market in this analysis appears as an incidental location permitting the reproduction of capital with surplus, which is the primary objective of the capitalists. The latter have control over the means of production and can therefore extract a profit. On the market, the value of labor appears as a 'natural price' (Smith) that determines the exchange value or relative prices of all commodities. Actual market prices only fluctuate around this price. However, this labor theory of value – the cornerstone of classical economics – is based on an assumed reproductive wage. Therefore, the natural price is not explained but simply presupposed (Stadermann and Steiger 2001b, 95). We will show later in Section 2.2.1 below that a similar problem occurs in neoclassical economics, where relative prices are explained based on marginal utilities.

Coins perform the function of *money*, and are minted out of the existing stock of precious metals, i.e., already existing goods. Therefore, money in classical economics is, unlike actual money, not created in credit contracts and destroyed after the contracts have been fulfilled. Even though some classical economists – especially Ricardo (1817, 365) – were aware that money (in the form of bank money or paper money) was only created against sound loan security and at market interest rates, the credit-based creation of money remained for Ricardo without consequences for the scale of economic activities. Nor did Ricardo consider the taking of loan security or the execution against assets in debt recovery actions. Consequently, the fear, found even among wealthy capitalists, of losing any of their property put up as loan security in debt recovery actions, does not feature in Ricardo's work.

The wealth of a capitalistic society, according to Ricardo, is comfortably explained by the pre-existing stock of 'capital' (means of production). Classical economists are aware of paper money and the associated bank operations and also see that the whole quantity of paper money does not have to be redeemable in precious metals. However, money is never viewed as an active economic variable that drives the production process through the provision of credit. Classical economics only mandates that the quantity of paper money is to be regulated according to the value of a monetary standard in the form of precious metal, for example, gold. This is believed to be necessary in order to avoid either inflation or deflation. The credit that is enabled through paper money simply serves as a means to better mobilize the stock of precious metals as circulating capital. This avoids transaction costs that would occur if metal itself was used. Simply stated, for classical economists, money exclusively facilitates barter. Money is a special good that can resolve the problem of the double coincidence of wants. This good also serves as the unit of account and is seen as the universal measure of value in all dealings.

Similarly, classical economics does not view *interest* as a driver of economic activity. At the stage of 'common property' no interest existed. Interest only emerged at the advanced stage of 'private property' in association with rents on land and profit. The latter are based on individual control over land and resources. In the classical view, interest and the bartered commodity, money, have no relationship. This follows from the explanation of interest as a derivate of profit. Profit arises as a yield on previously saved goods. The latter are accumulated and form capital goods. Profit arises when previously saved capital goods are deployed. The entitlement to profit is thus linked to the exclusive command and control exercised over capital goods. Control is possible because capital goods are 'private property'. Those capitalists – the masters of production – who have to raise a money advance in order to invest in capital goods in turn have to provide the 'monied class' (Ricardo 1817, 89) – the masters over the money stock – with a part of their profit as interest. The 'monied class' does not desire to directly take on the risks associated with accumulation, and therefore lends out money to others to invest. The loss that is compensated by interest in classical economics is therefore the profit opportunity that is forgone by the 'monied class' by not directly engaging in profit-making itself.

Classical economists were aware that, at the time, *credit* provision was based on the discounting of sound commercial bills (*real bills*). The bill of exchange, however, was viewed as a title to already produced goods and not as what it legally represents – a claim to the assets of the parties to the bill (drawer, drawee/acceptor and indorsers). This incorrect view led to the real-bills doctrine of the banking school, originated by Adam Smith, according to which an over-emission of bank notes is not possible because the amount of banknotes is always limited by the amount of bills, which in turn are secured by already-produced goods of the seller. The mistake inherent this view, the so called *real bills fallacy*, is not – as often argued in the literature – the equating of credit (based on bills) with money. The key oversight is, as pointed out in particular by Joseph Schumpeter, that bank notes are emitted typically for yet-to-be-produced goods. Looking for the reasons that money is advanced on the basis of yet-to-be-produced goods, Schumpeter, however, resorts to the idea that money is created for innovative production ideas 'out of nothing'[2] (Schumpeter 1926, 108).[3] He notes: 'It is entirely clear that purchasing power is created that initially is not matched by *new* goods.... The system of credit not only transcends the existing stock of money but also the existing stock of goods'[4] (Schumpeter 1926, 147).

While Schumpeter correctly rejected the view that money is based on pre-existing goods, it must be argued against Schumpeter that classical economics was right to raise the important question of the underlying backing or anchor for the money supply. It was only the self-imposed limitation to search only among assets classified as goods that led to a poor result. Actual money is not secured by possessory titles over goods but by ownership rights that exist beyond and in addition to goods. Schumpeter and the classical economists suffer from a common mistake: a bill of exchange is not convertible into money because the underlying transaction is based on goods. In contrast, the assets of the drawer (the buyer of goods), the acceptor and all indorsers who are liable for the ultimate payment of the bill represent the property backing of the money created in this process. A quantity of goods does not feature in this money-creation process.

2.2 Neoclassical economics

Like classical economics, neoclassical economics does not deal with the differences between possession and ownership. Neoclassical economists believe that they capture the essence of ownership when they simply refer to *property rights*. In turn, property rights are viewed as rights of possession, even though the actual term 'possession' is cleverly avoided. This is demonstrated nicely by quoting the early neoclassical economist Irving Fisher:

> But what is meant by owning wealth? We answer: to have the right to use it. To have a right is called property or, more explicitly, a property right ... The right of a person to the uses of an article of wealth may be defined as his liberty, under the sanction of law and society, to enjoy the services of that article.
>
> (Fisher 1906, 18, 20)

2.2.1 Pure neoclassical economics

The general equilibrium theory as the most modern version of neoclassical economics does not differ from Fisher in its incorrect equating of property rights with possession. This can be shown using the leading representative of this school, Gérard Debreu, who considers 'private ownership economies' as 'economies where the consumers *own the resources* and control the producers' (Debreu 1959, 78, emphasis added).[5] However, it is clear that the phrase 'own the resources' really refers to possession, because in Debreu's model the sale of resources by the consumer to the producer provides the producer with the right to enjoy the physical use of the resources.

Like classical economics, neoclassical economics analyzes the economy as a barter exchange economy based on transactions with real goods. The difference from classical economics is, however, that the market becomes the strategic center where individual optimization decisions are realized. For this reason, neoclassical economics is not interested in the different stages of command and control over resources but in the establishment of markets. Indeed, neoclassical economics has turned the term 'market economy' into a worldwide trademark.

The neoclassical market has no natural prices. The exchange values of goods are not determined by the value of labor (*à la* classical economics) but through marginal utilities, or more specifically the ratios of marginal utilities. In this way, neoclassical economics overcomes the contradiction between exchange value and use value of a commodity present in the classical theory of value. A good with a high use value – like water – has a low exchange value because its marginal utility (the utility derived from the last increment) is small, as there is plenty of it. In contrast, a good with a low use value – like diamonds – has a high exchange value because even the last increment is highly sought after (high marginal utility), as diamonds are scarce. The relative price between water and diamonds is assumed to be determined by the ratio of their respective marginal utilities, which are set when individuals, after receiving an initial endowment of goods, maximize their total utility according to their individual preferences. However, it can be argued that this model gracefully overlooks the fact that the assumed optimization is only possible if the people involved know the prices beforehand. Neoclassical economics cannot, therefore, explain prices based on the ratio of marginal utilities, but has to assume that individuals adjust their relative marginal utilities in this optimization process based on predetermined relative prices (Heinsohn and Steiger 1996, 49; Stadermann and Steiger 2001b, 221–251).

Neoclassical money, like classical money, is again a special good. In contrast to early classical economics, money is no longer equated with a precious metal, a produced good, but instead is an intrinsically valueless substance that remains outside the economic process (*outside money*). The substance is a stock of fiat money, which can be produced without any underlying backing by a central bank acting as a monetary authority. The supply of fiat money, which takes the form of central bank notes and central bank deposit balances, is then controlled through open market purchases of, most importantly, government bonds. As in the classical view of money, central bank operations are considered to remain largely external to the economy (Axilrod and Wallich 1992, col. 75a). At times, central bank money is simply defined as a state debt instrument (Friedman 1992, col. 252b).

The burdening of property, as it occurs in the actual money-creation process, is never the subject of neoclassical analysis. Like classical economics, neoclassical analysis does not acknowledge that the credit-based creation of money enables a production process that is not limited by a pre-existing stock of goods and resources. As a result, no attempt is made to consider money as an active variable that drives the economic process.

Money creation is only of concern to neoclassical economics insofar as it creates distortions of the production process through inflation and deflation. The producers should be supplied with an appropriate quantity of money not unlike the 'well-regulated paper money' of classical economics. Money should be *neutral*. Like classical economics, neoclassical economics sees the advantage of money in the reduction of transaction costs when the allocation of scarce resources is optimized in barter exchanges. Money in the form of an intrinsically valueless standard good or *numéraire* allows the determination of the relative prices of all goods. However, in the Arrow-Debreu model of Walras's general equilibrium, the most developed model of the neoclassical barter exchange economy, the existence of money is neither required nor desired. This issue presents the 'most serious challenge'[6] to neoclassical economics.

Even monetarism, the dominant neoclassical theory of money, treats today's central bank money with a surprisingly high degree of caution:

> Since 1971 ... high-powered money consists solely of fiat money – pieces of paper issued by the government [*sic*].... Such a worldwide fiat (or irredeemable paper) standard has no precedent in history. The gold that central banks still record as an asset on their books is simply a grin of a Cheshire cat that has disappeared.... The current system is so new that it must be regarded as a state in transition. Some substitute is almost sure to emerge to replace the supply of species as a long-term anchor for the price level, but it is not clear what that substitute will be.... We are in unexplored terrain.
> (Friedman 1992, col. 251b and 262a; see also Friedman and Schwartz 1986, 45)

Friedman cannot find the existing modern anchor because he can only envisage a monetary anchor as a stock of goods, which can be physically possessed. Property titles as a monetary anchor are consequently completely outside his view. Moreover, Friedman does not realize that in reality, gold never represented a stock of goods with special properties, but was simply one of the many variants of property that could back a note issue, for example, by its early substitution with commercial bills.

What then, in neoclassical theory, is the loss that is to be compensated by interest? What is the answer to the core question of economic theory? As in classical economics, interest in neoclassical theory is not tied to money in any genetic way. However, it is no longer explained by the profit opportunity forgone by the money capitalist. Rather, following the neoclassical theory of time preference, interest arises as compensation provided to the consumer for the sacrifice of an early consumption of goods, which the consumer views as more valuable than a consumption in the future. The consumer demands a premium for this act of *saving* for someone else. In this view, the consumer could realize this premium by lending the saved goods to a producer in a (loan) contract for the future delivery of goods (expressed in money terms but in its essence representing a contract over goods) against interest. The producer now invests the loan proceeds in capital goods. Because capital goods are productive, more goods are produced than originally borrowed. The neoclassical rate of interest is therefore set by the productivity of capital goods, with capital representing a form of transformed savings. Consequently, interest is an 'interest yielded by capital'.[7] The additional output of goods from the additional capital invested realizes the premium and services the required interest payment.[8]

Keynes's attack on the neoclassical theory of interest in his *General Theory* (1936) is based on his own explanation of interest as arising from the uncertainty of the future level of interest rates. This criticism was quickly rebutted by neoclassical economists:

> If we ask what ultimately governs the judgements of wealth-owners as to why the rate of interest should be different in the future from what it is today, we are surely led straight back to the *fundamental phenomena of productivity and thrift.*
>
> (Robertson 1940, 25; emphasis added)

Neoclassical theory has never again departed from this position. Keynes's vague terminology, such as *loanable funds* or *liquid resources*, provides unintended support to the neoclassical position, because these terms can be easily interpreted as the supply of resources that are merely expressed in monetary terms. From a neoclassical viewpoint, loanable funds arise from current savings (out of current resource incomes), the early liquidation of savings (based on existing stocks), the hoarding of money balances and additional bank credit. In this model, hoards are defined as resources that are merely dressed-up in monetary terms.

The modern version of the theory of loanable funds assumes that savings are exclusively realized through the purchase of bonds, and that investments are exclusively financed through the issue of bonds (Horwich 1997). In its simplest formulation as an equilibrium of stocks and flows of funds, the market for stocks of funds and the market for flows of funds are in equilibrium at the same real rate of interest: (1) the market for flows of funds based on real savings and real investment; (2) the market for stocks of funds based on the supply and demand of real money stocks and already-existing bonds. In this theory, an increased demand for investment represents an increased demand for loanable funds. If this demand is not satisfied out of current savings (sacrificed consumption), the supply of bonds has to be increased, which decreases their prices and increases their yields. The increased yield (interest) in turn motivates owners of existing assets to hold more high-yielding bonds and fewer non-yielding cash balances. Assuming a constant total output, this dishoarding increases the price level, and the value of real cash balances falls until the market rate of interest increases to its 'natural' level, determined by investment and savings or productivity and thrift, respectively. The belief in the existence of hoards links neoclassical economics with its challenger Keynes. The idea of a treasure or hoard, as will be shown shown in Section 2.3.1 below, is the underlying reason why Keynes failed to formulate a successful theory of money and interest.

In actual fact, the 'fundamental phenomena' (Robertson) of thrift and productivity have always existed but have not resulted in the emergence of interest during most of mankind's history. The neoclassical theory of interest has asserted that the level of interest rates is correlated with the level of thrift and productivity. However, in an ownership-based society, as the only system of reproduction with interest, interest rates generally do not increase with an increase in thrift and productivity. On the contrary, periods of high productivity and high levels of saving are more likely to be characterized by low rates of interest, whereas periods without technical progress and with low levels of saving correspond to high rates of interest.

The fatal consequences of a fixation on the domain of goods are also visible in the neoclassical treatment of credit markets, which are treated like markets for goods. The neoclassical credit contract is fundamentally based on the lending and borrowing of goods, where the latter are merely expressed in monetary terms. The fact that, in reality, a creditor-consumer requires loan security from the debtor-producer is left in the dark and never becomes a subject of inquiry. Like classical economics, neoclassical economics is not aware of the proprietor's fear of losing his property in debt recovery actions. Moreover, it is clear that in reality a credit contract does not involve a sacrifice of goods. The actual sacrifice imposed in a credit contract, in which either money is created or existing money is lent, is the loss of the free disposition over property on the part of the creditor and the debtor. Both sacrifice their ownership premium. Because no sacrifice in consumption is suffered, it does not need to be compensated by interest.

From the early 1870s until the 1980s, the neoclassical theory of credit markets did not consider the taking of loan security (collateral), even though it was well known to be mandatory for most credit contracts (Heinsohn and Steiger 2008). Instead, neoclassical analysis of the credit market maintained for 110 years that the interest rate was determined in the same way as the price of goods in goods markets, by the rate at which the supply and demand of credit is brought into equilibrium. As in goods markets, excess demand is equalized by an increase in price in the short run and by an expansion of supply in the long run, which in turn leads to a reduction in prices.

The neoclassical analysis of the credit market moved on from the supply and demand theory as outlined above when it adopted the principle of 'credit rationing' suggested by Joseph Stiglitz and Andrew Weiss in 1981, who stressed the importance of information *asymmetry* between creditor and debtor. While incorporating this information-based approach, neoclassical economists have, however, viewed this theory as simply a refined version of a theory of credit markets based on goods. Stiglitz and Weiss are new Keynesian economists, and their approach will be discussed in detail in Section 2.3.1.

2.2.2 New institutional economics

The incorrect equating of property rights with the right of possession, i.e., the right to the physical use of goods, reappears with little modification in new institutional economics. The aim of this school of economics is to extend the neoclassical model by incorporating a property rights framework as an attempt to lift the neoclassical theory to a more acceptable level of scholarship without having to modify the core of the neoclassical barter model: 'Because NIE [New Institutional Economics] considers choices to be embedded in institutions, it has a much broader reach than neoclassical economics.... But unlike old institutional economics, NIE does not abandon ... neoclassical economic theory' – especially not its 'orthodox assumptions of scarcity and competition' (Ménard and Shirley 2005, 2).

Along with Demsetz, Armen Alchian is regarded as one of the founders of new institutional economics. What is his definition of a property right? 'A *property right* to a good is a right to select among its, and only its, feasible *physical uses* or conditions' (Alchian 1992, col. 223a; last emphasis added).

Like classical economists, Alchian and Demsetz draw a line between common and state property rights one the one hand, and individual or private property rights on the other. Private property rights differ because, in contrast to common property rights, they are linked to a specific individual. The 'right has the consequent income and wealth assigned to a specified person, who can alienate the right to others in exchange for at least similar *rights to* other *goods*' (Alchian 1972, col. 223a; emphasis added; see also Demsetz 1998, col. 154b).

Demsetz, regardless of his passionate dissatisfaction with the insufficient treatment of property rights in mainstream economic theory (quoted above), does not really deviate from Fisher or Debreu when he equates property rights with 'rights of use' (Demsetz 1998, col. 151b). However, he at least acknowledges without digression the difficulty in identifying the true core of property rights. In his view, property rights 'designate the owner as that person or group, as compared to others, that exercises the most important subset of exclusive, alienable, and presumptive rights. There is no easy way to generalize "important subset"' (Demsetz 1998, col. 146a). Because Demsetz focuses all his attention on what is in reality possession ('rights of use') he cannot find what he should be looking for: ownership, and the associated powers of the owner to burden or hypothecate his property and in that way to deploy it as an economic asset.

Neither Demsetz nor any other representative of new institutional economics, to the best of our knowledge, even comes close to identifying the burdening and hypothecation of property as the all-important economic consequences of ownership that trigger the dramatic difference between mere reproductive systems and the ownership-based system with economic activity. Moreover, the fear of losing hypothecated property in debt recovery actions is again never a topic. It could be argued that this promising branch of neoclassical economics should have labelled itself as an 'economic school of possessory rights' and should have left the analysis of property rights to those who focus their analysis on the economic consequences of the burdening and hypothecation of property.[9]

The inability of new institutional economics to distinguish between ownership and possession is most clearly reflected in Demsetz (1998, col. 145a–b; see Steiger 2008 for more details). In addition to acknowledging the difficulty of identifying the core attribute of property rights, in his analysis of the ownership of land he appears surprised to find that 'to have property rights in the land is not necessarily the equivalent of having the land'. For example, he notes that having the right to till the land 'is not equivalent to having all rights in the land'. Speculating about this feature makes him conclude that the proper identification of asset ownership and control is difficult. Subsets of rights can be 'possessed and owned' by different persons, and in consequence the 'owner' of an asset should be defined as the person or group 'owning' the 'most important subset' of rights; though as mentioned above, it is not obvious how to characterize this subset (Demsetz 1998, 146a).[10]

However, it can be argued that the ownership of land is not a total set of rights that can be arbitrarily divided into subsets. While multiple types of use rights can be granted, these are subordinate to ownership.[11] Demsetz overlooks the fact that, in simple terms, all property assets have, as a basic common attributive, both an owner (the holder of title) *and* a possessor (the user and the party exercising factual physical control over the asset). This becomes especially apparent when ownership rights and possessory rights are exercised by different people. For example, the owner of land can appoint a tenant who as a leaseholder becomes the possessor but not the owner of the land.

One would expect that at least where the term 'possession' is itself the subject of inquiry, its difference from ownership will be clearly shown and possessory rights will no longer be subsumed under ownership rights. The *New Palgrave Dictionary of Economics and the Law* is to our knowledge the first economics work that has allowed for a separate entry for 'possession' (Epstein 1998). Where does this lead us? Is it understood that the right of possession generally excludes the power to burden property? There is not even a hint. On the contrary, possession is defined 'as the source of all property rights' (Epstein 1998, col. 62b). This statement confirms once more that new institutional economics merely considers property rights from the point of view of possession: 'People own property so that they may possess it, just as they possess it, so that they may *use* it' (Epstein 1998, col. 68a; emphasis added).

In Epstein's ambiguous statement, any opportunity to distinguish between the fundamentally different attributes of ownership and possession is lost. Consequently, the separate nature of ownership and possession is only discussed in the context of the wrongful dispossession of an owner and voluntary transfers of possession by gift or sale (Epstein 1998, col. 62b). The economically important difference between an ownership title that can be subject to a burden (or be the subject of hypothecation) and a mere right of possession enabling physical use is never within the view of Epstein's inquiry.

It is therefore no surprise that new institutional economics never distinguished between (1) tribal systems and command systems (feudalism or socialism) of reproduction, characterized by rules governing the use of resources; and (2) ownership-based societies, characterized by private (*not individual*) and shared (*not collective*) ownership rights in addition to possessory rights. For this reason, new institutional economics sees ownership operating without exception in tribal communities, feudalism and socialism. The impact of individual and collective rules about the use of resources are analyzed, but rules about use are misinterpreted as rights of ownership (typical examples are Bailey 1998; Libecap 1998; Pistor 1998).

The mix-up between ownership and possession, i.e., the disregard of the economic consequences resulting from the non-physical burdening and hypothecation of property assets and the undue emphasis placed on the physical use of resources, also dominates the thinking of such neoclassically educated economic historians as Douglass North and Robert Thomas. These authors have searched for the reasons for economic growth at different stages of history and believe, with reference to new institutional economics, that economic growth 'will occur if property rights make it worthwhile to undertake socially productive activity' (North and Thomas 1973, 8).

Again, North and Thomas view the difference between common property and private property as the all-important consideration, not the difference between ownership and possession. A 'common-property *resource*' is blamed for stagnation as well as decline because 'each *user* has an incentive to exploit the resource without regard to other *users*, which results in continual deterioration of the *resource*. ... Since no one owns the resource there is no incentive to conserve the resource or to improve efficiency in its *use*' (North and Thomas 1973, 19; emphasis added). Efficiency increases can only be achieved if 'property rights' are transitioned from a collective to an individual use.[12]

This transition is alleged to have occurred in a 'race to claim' assets based on the principle of 'first possession':

> Behind nearly every system for establishing property rights lies the basic notion of first possession. This rule grants an ownership to the party that gains control before other potential claimants.... By excluding others from access, property rights grant their owner a valuable claim on the rents available from efficient utilization of the resource.... Property rights eliminate overexploitation.

This, in turn, leads to an 'optimal resource use' (Lueck 2003, 200 and 203). However, what is described here is in reality only the creation of territories of possession that can also be found in fauna and flora. Property rights are thus interpreted as simply providing a delineation between individual and collective possession. The theoretical interest is focused solely on structures that allow a better utilization of resources. Consequently, the deployment of property assets through burdening or hypothecation remains completely unmentioned.

In reality not even the acquisition of possession is created through a 'race'. On the contrary, de facto possession is allocated through custom or coercive order. In societies based on property rights, possession is linked to ownership and is acquired through grant, purchase, rent or lease. In defense of new institutional economists, they of course envision the European settler, who coming from an ownership-based society creates new ownership rights by conquering tribal or feudal territories. Settlers can do this because they have the backing of the legal systems of their home country, which are implanted over the existing de facto possession-based structures of the conquered territories. Therefore, the creators of *claims* cannot explain the origins of their property rights because they are the descendants of nations based on property rights. The act of conquest as such does not do anything in relation to ownership. Therefore, victorious tribal or feudal warriors do not create ownership when overrunning new territories of similar legal structure, but merely expand their area of de facto possession.

The way new institutional economics conceives of property rights creation does a disservice not only to ownership-based societies but also to de facto possession-based systems. The assertion that lack of efficiency is caused by a lack of 'ownership', in the sense of a lack of individual possession, has no justification. Both tribal and feudal systems, which are systems with little growth, have individuals as well as collective structures that exercise highly exclusive possession and defend the over-exploitation of their *claims* by all means. The origins of efficiency and growth can therefore not be argued from the alleged superiority of individual over collective possession. Individual possession has been known since the Neanderthal, who possessed his very individual stone tool.

The confusion of ownership with possession and the misconception of possession as the core attribute of property rights were already embedded in the core component of neoclassical economics (without institutions), in the neoclassical theory of value and price; or, to be more precise, in the concept of an individual who optimizes an initial endowment of goods and resources based on his preferences. While this individual is (incorrectly) identified as the owner, he is required in the neoclassical model to be a possessor only. Nevertheless, neoclassical economics, within its paradigm of optimal collection with respect to the physical use of goods, advances beyond classical economics with its non-economic paradigm of the rule over resources.

Neoclassical theory at least attempts to face the challenge of a genuine economic theory, in that an acceptable theory must not resort to mechanisms of rule or control in its explanation of economic activity. The neoclassical confusion of ownership with possession prevents this theory from explaining the mechanisms that force individuals to relentlessly deploy their resources in economic activities. The neoclassical ad hoc assumption of an initial endowment of resources that are deployed in economic activities because resources are scarce is invalid. Ultimately, all goods and resources are scarce in any production system, but scarcity does not generate economic activity in all systems. Scarcity is a necessary but not a sufficient condition for economic activity. The economic deployment of resources must therefore have other causes than a possession-based endowment of scarce goods and resources.

2.3 Keynesian economics

New institutional economics provides an approach that at least aims to underpin the central neoclassical model with a solid foundation by incorporating a property rights framework. While it is clear that the new institutional reformers have not succeeded in their aim, their theory nevertheless surpasses Keynesian economics, which never attempted to integrate property rights into its model. The Keynesian economic schools, regardless of *couleur*, are 'devoid of all political institutions or postulates of property' (Bethell 1998, 30).

2.3.1 Keynes; standard and new Keynesianism

Neither ownership nor its link with hypothecation or debt enforcement plays a role in Keynes's work. This is all the more surprising because very early on, Keynes (1919, 12) realized that 'permanent relations between debtors and creditors ... form the ultimate foundation of capitalism'. Moreover, in his theory of investment (part of his *General Theory*) Keynes appears to believe that he is the first author who has treated the risks involved in credit contracts, and he even touches on loan security (Keynes 1936, 144–145). In his analysis, Keynes differentiates between the risk of the entrepreneur, or borrower risk, and that of the lender, the bank. While the entrepreneur's risk is driven by the uncertainty of earnings, the risk to the bank arises from 'moral hazard' or 'the possible insufficiency of the margin of security, i.e., involuntary default due to the disappointment of expectation [of the borrower]'. However, Keynes overlooks the fact that the risk to the creditor is of a general nature and does not only materialize when the loan security of the debtor is insufficient. A credit contract is generally only entered into if the debtor can hypothecate property at least to the amount of the loan. In addition, the creditor has to reserve a portion of his capital[13] to back the loan. Thus, *both* the creditor and the debtor are owners of property, whose different *risk exposures arising from the credit contracts* must be brought into equilibrium through the hypothecation of debtor property.

Moreover, Keynes overlooks the fact that the security provided by the debtor is only insufficient if, due to the 'disappointment of expectation', the entrepreneur's assets and the associated loan security have been devalued. As protection against this market risk, a situation where the enforcement proceeds from loan security and the entrepreneur's other capital is insufficient, a bank must hold sufficient capital. Keynes overlooks this requirement for bank capital.

Instead, Keynes limits his discussion to highlighting the special features of the creditor risk as compared to the debtor risk. In Keynes's view the entrepreneur will seek to compensate for his exposure to risky investments by setting a higher margin between the interest demanded by the lender and the minimum prospective earnings required for an investment. At the same time the lender requires a wider margin[14] 'between what he charges and the pure rate of interest.... The hope of a very favourable outcome, which may balance the risk in the mind of the borrower, is not available to solace the lender' (Keynes 1936, 145). In any case, as we will show below (p. 34) based on the example of new Keynesian economics, a higher rate of interest cannot address the fundamental lending risk of a bank.

While Keynes, before his *General Theory*, vehemently argued against the barter paradigm of classical and neoclassical economics in his uncompleted 'Monetary Theory of Production' (Keynes 1933), he did not advance to find ownership as the alternative paradigm in this theory torso. The lack of an alternative paradigm is particularly evident in his thoughts about *money of account* in his *Treatise* (1930). He defines it in clear contrast to the monetary unit of neoclassical economics, which is bound to a specific good (*unit of account* or *numéraire*), and relates it to a *money proper*.

One institution exists in Keynes's monetary theory – the state (for more details see Stadermann and Steiger 2001b, 285–295 and 2010, as well as Steiger 2005b, 170–177). The importance that he attributes to this institution results from his adaptation of the state theory of money, developed by Georg Friedrich Knapp (1905). Because money of account, according to Knapp, is legally enacted by the state as the standard for debts, the money proper must always be *compulsory legal-tender money*, money that the state accepts in payments or money that the central bank exchanges for central bank notes. Keynes (1930, 4) calls this money 'state money':

> The State ... comes in first of all as the authority of law which enforces the payment of the thing [money proper] which corresponds to the name or description [money of account] in the contracts. But it comes in doubly when, in addition, it claims the right to determine and declare *what thing* corresponds to the name.
>
> (Keynes 1930, 4; emphasis in original)

According to Keynes, state money has existed for millennia, although for long periods only in the form of 'commodity money'. The further development of commodity money only occurred in the early modern period, when it was discovered that private 'acknowledgements of debt', denominated in the state's money of account, could act as a substitute for money proper (state money) in the settlement of credit contracts. Keynes equates 'acknowledgements of debt' with 'bank money' and emphasizes that they must not be confused with money proper (state money; Keynes 1930, 5). In his view, the discovery of 'bank money' resulted in a revolution in finance, when states in the eighteenth century declared their own debts as legal tender money: 'the State may then use its chartalist prerogative to declare that the debt itself is an acceptable discharge of a liability' (Keynes 1930, 5).

Keynes's reference to the paper money of the French revolution (assignats) in this context (Keynes 1930, 13), which he classifies as *representative money*, is therefore only consistent. Assignats as a form of state money triggered a scandal because they were emitted without any backing by sound collateral (Stadermann and Steiger 2001b, 73). Keynes, untroubled because apparently unaware of the fact that money creation requires backing by such collateral, concludes:

> A particular kind of bank money is then transformed into money proper – a species of money proper which we may call representative money. When, however, what was merely a debt has become money proper, it has changed its character and should no longer be reckoned as a debt, since it is of the essence of a debt to be enforceable in terms of something other than itself.
>
> (Keynes 1930, 6)

Keynes's statement in relation to the 'essence of a debt', and with it the difference between a debt and money, is certainly correct. Nevertheless, he makes a hair-raising mistake in his analysis of bank money that to this day has not been corrected in mainstream monetary theory. He confuses the mutual set-off of money obligations, which requires no money proper, with the substitution of money by private debt titles, which he misleadingly calls *bank money*. However, debt titles cannot replace actual *money*.[15] Instead, in the above payment process, *the payment of money is substituted by a process that mutually sets off the obligations*. This differentiation may appear as an attempt to split hairs, but is important because the lack of differentiation between money and debt makes it impossible for Keynes to distinguish between *creditor money*, guaranteed not by the issuer of debt titles but by a purchaser who voluntarily redeems the money; and state-issued *debtor money*, underwritten only by the debtor state and represented by self-emitted debt titles. It is this confusion that must have lured Keynes into the assertion that representative money originated in the same way as private bank notes: 'The evolution of bank money in the shape of bank notes was showing the way towards representative money' (Keynes 1930, 14).[16]

Consequently, it is not surprising that Keynes falls victim to an adventurous intermingling of central bank money with state money and 'bank money': 'Central bank money ... may be on the same footing as State money or as member bank money' (Keynes 1930, 9). Here, Keynes views state money as a central bank asset which forms the basis for the creation of central bank liabilities, which are provided to member banks as 'bank money':

> The State money held by the central bank constitutes its 'reserve' against its deposits. These deposits we may term *central bank money*.... This central bank money *plus* the State money held by the member banks makes up the reserves of the member banks, which they, in turn, hold against their deposits. These deposits constitute the *member bank money* in the hands of the public, and make up, together with the State money (and the central bank money, if any) held by the public, the aggregate of *current money*.
>
> (Keynes 1930, 8–9)[17]

His double error – the assumption that private debt titles are equivalent and transformable into private bank notes without formalities and (analogously) the equivalence and transformability of state obligations in the form of representative money into central bank notes – Keynes never realized. He confuses existing debt titles that are supplied by a creditor out of his stock of assets, with debt titles that are offered to the market directly by a debtor.[18] While assets of a creditor are always liabilities of a debtor, only the creditor and not the debtor can use the debt title as a substitute for the payment in money proper, or can present the debt title for rediscount at a central bank to obtain money. In contrast to Keynes's assumption, a mere acknowledgment of a debt is no substitute for actual money. Rather, an acknowledgement of debt or promissory note provides the underlying basis for money creation in a credit contract with a money-issuing bank, which may discount the note.[19]

In contrast to his *Treatise*, Keynes did not pursue his state theory of money in his *General Theory*. Though problematic, the assumption that the 'quantity of money' is established exogenously by a 'monetary authority' suffices (Keynes 1936, 172, 206).

Keynes's unawareness of the economic importance of ownership also takes its toll in his theory of interest. This theory is superior to the neoclassical explanation of interest based on goods because it links interest directly to money and not to the deferred consumption of goods, i.e., a saving for capital investments: 'The rate of interest is not the "price" which brings into equilibrium the demand for resources to invest with the readiness to abstain from present consumption' (Keynes 1936, 167). For a given level of consumption, saving does not mean a sacrifice of consumption goods, but saved money. The latter gives the holder three options: (1) hoarding, providing an intangible return in the form of the liquidity premium; (2) direct investment in capital assets, providing an expected profit; and (3) investment in interest-generating bonds:

> [T]here is always an alternative to the ownership of real capital-assets, namely the ownership of money and debts.... For the rate of interest is, in itself, nothing more than the inverse proportion between a sum of money and what can be obtained for parting with control over the money in exchange for a debt for a stated period of time. Thus, the rate of interest at any time, being the reward for parting with liquidity, is a measure of the unwillingness of those who possess money to part with their liquid control over it.
>
> (Keynes 1936, 212 and 167)

This measure reflects the 'potential convenience or security' of holding money, does not create anything tangible 'in the shape of output', and is defined by Keynes as the 'liquidity premium' (Keynes 1936, 226).

Keynes's unawareness of the economic importance of ownership and his lack of insight into the burdening of creditor property as part of the money-creation process forces him to presuppose the existence of exogenous money, which in turn can be lent out against interest. However, the latter step in his thought process also forces him to simply assume the existence of interest-bearing debt titles and with them the existence of interest as a given. One could interpret Keynes's passage above on the 'parting with control over the money in exchange for a debt for a stated period' (Keynes 1936, 167) to suggest that once money has 'arrived' as alternative to 'real capital-assets', interest-bearing debt 'for a stated period of time' emerges as an option for money use. Debt titles allow third parties to acquire money. Without the sudden appearance of debt titles for always presupposed (exogenous) money, the option to use it to acquire interest-bearing debt would not be available. Because Keynes cannot comprehend the burdening of property as the generator of interest, but at the same time cannot afford to leave unanswered the question of what potency it is that can be transformed into interest, he attempts to locate this potency within money itself. Consequently, Keynes creates the concept of a liquidity premium that he assumes to be attached to money itself.

As Keynes cannot deliver an explanation of money, his explanation of interest must also fail. Only the interest arising when already existing money is on-lent is in his view. But in reality, even this interest does not arise from the properties of money itself. Rather it results, like the original interest that arises as part of money creation by a note-issuing bank, from the sacrifice of ownership premium for both the commercial bank creditor and the non-bank debtor in a credit contract in which the money of the note-issuing bank (e.g., the central bank) is 'on-lent'.

Money is still assumed as an exogenous variable in the interpretation of the *General Theory* by the IS/LM model, developed by John Hicks in 1937 and forming the basis of standard Keynesianism. The model is characterized by a conflicting amalgam of the neoclassical interest yielded by goods[20] (investment/saving, the IS-curve) and Keynes's interest yielded by money[21] (liquidity preference/money supply, the LM-curve).

Hicks must eventually have sensed the inconsistency of applying two different theories of interest. He realized 30 years later that the bank creditor *rations* the supply of loans, and does not change this policy even when confronted with potential debtors offering interest at high amounts (Hicks 1965, 285). Hicks explained this unwillingness as coming from the bank's concern for its assets in the event of the insolvency of the debtor. As Hicks was not aware of the actual role of loan security, which provides the bank with direct access to assets in order to compensate loan losses, he searched, apart from the rationing of credit, for other ways to protect the bank. This search culminated in a rather curious theory that seeks to explain the level of interest rates payable by a debtor by assuming that rates must be above the central bank rate so that bad loans can be funded from this margin.

A further 15 years later, Hicks finally discovered loan security. Revisiting his standard interpretation of the *General Theory*, he concluded that the neglect of loan security represented a significant flaw of the IS/LM model:

We now know that it is not enough to think of the rate of interest as a single link between the financial and industrial sectors of the economy; for that really implies that a borrower can borrow as much as he likes at the rate of interest charged, *no attention being paid to the security offered.*
(Hicks 1980–1981, 153; emphasis added)

Hicks's remark on the importance of loan security, i.e., hypothecated property that can be directly accessed in a loan enforcement action, has remained without resonance in standard Keynesianism. Even Hicks has not further pursued his thought.

Only a few months after Hicks's article appeared, the role of loan security became the focus of new Keynesianism in Stiglitz's theory of credit rationing (Stiglitz and Weiss 1981). As for Keynes, money is presupposed as a money stock ('supply of credit') or in Robertson's terminology as 'loanable funds' (Stiglitz and Greenwald 2003, 45–46).

Nevertheless, Stiglitz is convinced that he has found, due to his allegedly new and original[22] focus on loan security, '[t]he first theoretical justification of true credit rationing' (Stiglitz and Weiss 1981, 394; see also Jaffee and Stiglitz 1992). The approach, as later discussed in Stiglitz and Greenwald (2003, 26–42), can be summarized as follows: the credit market is different from a goods market in that a surplus of demand over supply of credit is not adjusted by an increase in the price of credit, i.e., by rising rates of interest. Interest is not a conventional price, which is immediately paid, but a *promise* to pay that can be broken. Higher interest rates typically result in lower-quality applicants, and each applicant is likely to take higher risks, increasing the likelihood of debtor defaults and bankruptcies. A bank must expect lower returns and an increased risk of becoming bankrupt itself. Thus the equilibrium in a credit market is different from that in a conventional goods market and is characterized by *credit rationing* and not price adjustment. The '"equilibrium" interest rate' (Stiglitz and Greenwald 2003, 27) is the rate where the lender's expected return is maximized, even if the demand for credit is higher than the supply.

According to Stiglitz and Greenwald, credit rationing requires the classification of debtors according to credit risk. The assessment is based on information about the debtor's assets, the same assets over which loan security is taken. Why is loan security demanded? For Stiglitz, loan security overcomes the problem of incomplete and *asymmetric information* between creditors and debtors. The bank always knows less about the debtor's repayment capacity than the debtor himself. Good loan security compensates for the missing information.

However, it can be argued that the default of a debtor is not a particular characteristic of credit markets alone. Even the much more perfect commodity markets experience credit risk. If a seller suspects that a buyer may not pay, payment in advance is requested. While Stiglitz occupies himself with the analysis of the asymmetric information between the debtor and the bank, he overlooks the fact that loan security provides the bank with a property right. The omission of loan security in the credit contract, regardless of information asymmetries, results in an *asymmetric distribution of risk* between the creditor (bank) and the debtor. Thus even with perfect information about the debtor, a bank can never relinquish loan security. Without loan security a bank not only suffers from an increased risk of reduced returns, as identified by Stiglitz, but risks its capital[23] and increases its risk of bankruptcy. While Stiglitz and Greenwald (2003, 54) refer to the bank's wish to 'avoid bankruptcy', in their view this is implemented through credit rationing: banks prefer giving credit to debtors where they have the best information. However, the authors fail to recognise that a credit contract is all about ensuring an equal risk distribution between creditor and debtor. It is the hypothecated debtor property that represents this risk equalization and provides access to property when the debtor defaults for reasons beyond those ever identifiable through prior collection of information.

The new Keynesian model of the credit market requires both rationing and compliance with market laws, so that the price always represents an '"equilibrium"' (Stiglitz and Greenwald 2003, 27). However, the authors' use of quotation marks draws into question whether a solution has been found. The fact remains that in the model, market laws are contradicted: not all requests for credit are fulfilled, a surplus credit demand exists, and only rationing can bring the market into a state of '"equilibrium"'. Furthermore, in reality the request for loan security is not a means to ration credit. Loan security equalizes risk positions, and this is the primary condition for the equilibrium of credit markets. In an exceptional case a bank could waive its interest margin, but never the requirement for loan security.

Due to this somewhat shaky concept of credit market equilibrium, new Keynesians are not particularly satisfied with their analysis. Ultimately, the taking of loan security cannot be incorporated into a theoretical model based on barter exchanges, which new Keynesians firmly support. This is because the taking of loan security does not mean that the debtor provides the creditor with the use of the property during the period of the loan. On the contrary, the debtor's right of possession remains unconstrained and he can continue to use the hypothecated property. New Keynesianism's experience with loan security resembles that of neoclassical economics' with money: 'the best developed model of the economy cannot find room for it' (Hahn 1982, 1).

New Keynesians have not acknowledged their cluelessness about the problem of loan security, or about the barely mentioned problem of loan enforcement, to the same degree as they have their cluelessness in relation to money. As a result, they are not able to sufficiently identify and analyze the core elements of economic activity. This is reflected in the fact that their analysis of loan security remains limited to secondary issues. For example, they are interested in deception and false security or the wilful neglect or damage of the loan security by the debtor (Kanatas 1992, col. 382b). Nevertheless, new Keynesians gratefully welcome loan security as a 'healing remedy' in the hand of the creditor, helping to avoid the wastage of loan proceeds by the debtor (Adler 1998, col. 405b). However, as the taking of loan security does not transfer control over the debtor's production assets to the creditor, the latter never obtains oversight or control over the debtor's behavior.

Notwithstanding, new Keynesian economists have felt a degree of discomfort and voluntarily admit that the contributions on the topic of collateral have been 'unclear' and contradictory in their conclusions. Some studies 'predict a positive association between observable risk (of opportunistic behavior by borrowers) and the amount of collateral required', while others predict 'a negative relation between the necessary collateral and the borrower's unobservable risk of default'. There is 'little definitive evidence on the relative economic importance of the ... explanations regarding collateral' (Kanatas 1992, col. 382b). What new Keynesianism, with its concern for the manipulation of loan security, is just able to recognize is the simple fact that possession of the property used as loan security remains with the debtor. However, new Keynesianism fails to generate the insight that the debtor suffers a special, even if immaterial, loss in ownership premium as a result of the burdening of his property through hypothecation.

2.3.2 Post-Keynesianism

The post-Keynesian school (founded by Paul Davidson, Hyman Minsky and Sidney Weintraub), while committed to the work of John Maynard Keynes, has never sought to seriously challenge the monetary theory of the master. In particular Davidson (1994 and 2005) simply varied Keynes's thesis formulated in the *General Theory*, according to which, as a consequence of the uncertainty of future expectations in a monetary economy, '*the importance of money essentially flows from its being a link between the present and the future*' (Keynes 1936, 293). The corresponding need to hold money creates the highest degree of security but also evokes the danger of unemployment.

Challenging the exogenous determination of the quantity of money in the *General Theory*, post-Keynesianism has insisted on an endogenous explanation of the supply of central bank money. This was most profoundly developed by Basil Moore (1988). Moore sharpens the credo of endogenous money by pointing out not only that money had to be explained endogenously but also that the money supply could not be controlled by the central bank: 'Central banks typically *supply cash reserves automatically on demand* at the minimum lending rate. In such cases the money supply function is clearly horizontal' (Moore 1988, 112; emphasis added).

The fact that a central bank limits its money supply by requiring collateral from commercial banks when providing credit, as emphasized by ownership economics, remains foreign to post-Keynesians (Steiger 2005b). Collateral allows a central bank to guard itself against nonperforming loans, and in this way avoids the potential loss of its capital or even its own bankruptcy. The difference between creditor's and debtor's money is also unknown to post-Keynesians.

It is the view of the central bank as a monetary authority, following Randall Wray's state theory of money, that post-Keynesianism holds as its guiding star. Here, Keynes's state theory of money remains the foundation of all developments. Wray expressly views the chartalist approach underlying Keynes's state theory as the alternative to the barter paradigm. However, while Keynes discards the barter paradigm, he does not replace it by his state theory of money. In addition, post-Keynesians believe more strongly than Keynes that state money, regardless of its role as legal tender, is money as soon as it is accepted in the payment of taxes:

> In summary, with the rise of the modern state, the money of account ('the description') is chosen by the state, which is free to choose that which will qualify as money [proper] (the 'thing' that answers to the description). This goes beyond legal tender laws – which establish what can legally discharge contracts – to include that which the state accepts at its 'pay offices'.
> (Wray 1998, 31–32; see the quotation from Keynes 1930, 4 above)

Wray, like Keynes, creates a peculiar amalgamation of state money and the money of a note-issuing bank. This is best demonstrated in Wray's analysis of US government expenditure, where he equates US Treasury debt titles with the notes of the Fed (Federal Reserve System):

> When a modern government spends, it issues a cheque drawn on the Treasury; its liabilities increase by the amount of the expenditure and its assets increase (in the case of a purchase).... When the recipient 'cashes' a Treasury cheque, a bank will convert reserves to currency – which is always supplied on demand by the Fed, which acts as the Treasury's 'bank', converting one kind of Treasury liability (a cheque written to the public) to another kind (coins or an IOU to the Fed, offset by the Fed issuance of paper money).
> (Wray 1998, 77–78)

In this instance, Wray basically repeats what Keynes proposed in the *General Theory* (Keynes 1936, 200) as a way to finance public works (Stadermann and Steiger 2001b, 310–320). The difference is merely that Keynes lets the state directly submit its debt titles to the central bank. In contrast, Wray uses the commercial banks as agents dealing with the central bank, as in the German empire during World War I (see Section 4.3). Nevertheless, the transaction remains a direct monetization of state debt by the central bank: as in Keynes's approach, debt titles are transformed into debtor's money and do not represent creditor's money. If checks drawn by the Treasury were to be transformed into creditor's money, the Treasury would need to offer these as interest-bearing securities in the open market. After the market purchase of such titles by a bank, which would turn the bank into a Treasury creditor, creditor's money is created if the bank in turn sells the titles to the Fed or obtains Fed notes by using the titles as collateral in a Fed discount window operation. The reality is precisely characterized by these steps, which are taken into account by the Fed when US dollar notes are created. For post-Keynesians, this reality remains *terra incognita*.

As a result, post-Keynesians simply consider central bank money creation as part of government expenditure: 'It is only because the central bank's purchases of government bonds ... are not counted as part of government spending that it can appear that persistent government surpluses are possible' (Wray 1998, 79). Whoever questions the identity of central bank money, a creditor's money, with a state fiat money, a debtor's money, is reminded by Wray that he cannot see through a supposedly simple trick: 'In a sense, this is nothing more than an accounting gimmick – the government keeps two books, the Treasury's book and the central bank's book, and runs a surplus on one and a deficit on the other' (Wray 1998, 79).

Post-Keynesians, like Keynes, lack any insight into why the taking of loan security, which can be enforced in the case of default, is necessary for central bank money creation. While Wray admits that central bank loans are not granted completely without conditions, he nevertheless believes that the granting of loans by the central bank largely occurs automatically in response to the wishes of the public:

> To some extent central bank provision of reserves would be automatic so that if the public wanted to hold more fiat money, the central bank would ensure that banks would be able to convert deposit money to fiat money. However, the central bank *in practice* imposes conditions for such loans on banks. For example, the central bank requires *collateral*'.
>
> (Wray 1998, 84; emphasis added)

Why central banks require collateral 'in practice', for example as a safeguard against credit risks as for a commercial bank, is discussed nowhere.

The conditions for the granting of loans when creating money is not a topic of discussion for post-Keynesians, even though Hyman P. Minsky, in a text fundamental for the post-Keynesian school (Minsky 1975, 106–116), took up the difference between creditor and debtor risk again, an issue for the first time identified by Keynes (1936). In contrast to Keynes, who identified the difference in the fact that banks, unlike entrepreneurs, could not take comfort in the expectation of higher returns but required higher interest when confronted with insufficient security, Minsky (1975, 110) believes that creditor risks are not expressly listed in contracts but merely reflected indirectly in a number of countermeasures: 'Lender's risk shows up in financial contracts in various forms: higher interest rates, shorter terms to maturity, requirement to pledge specific assets as collateral and restrictions on dividend payouts and further borrowing are some of them'.

Minsky, however, overlooks the fact that a contract between a bank and an entrepreneur would not be submitted for signature if collateral, along with term and interest, had not been specified. The property over which security is taken does not just reflect the creditor's risk indirectly, as alleged by Minsky, but in fact has to directly correspond to the loan amount. Higher interest and other measures, at least as understood by new Keynesians, cannot remove creditor risk. Also not specified in the loan contract is the capital[24] required by the bank, which Minsky also overlooks. This represents, next to loan security, the second core safeguard against creditor risk.

Similarly deficient is Wray's analysis of credit provision by commercial banks. Following Stiglitz and Weiss (1981) he establishes the 'rationing' of credit. However, he reverses the asserted asymmetry of information between banks and non-banks without being clear about what this is meant to achieve:

> Clearly, large segments of the population are 'quantity rationed' in the sense that banks do not meet their demand at the going interest rate. There can be several reasons for such rationing. Banks might be worried about *default risk of borrowers*, but might not be able to raise interest rates sufficiently to cover default risk – so that quantity rationing is superior to price rationing. Often, banks probably have better information than do borrowers about such risks.
>
> (Wray 1998, 110; emphasis added)

Nothing here suggests that in reality a commercial bank lowers *its* credit risk by requiring good loan security from a debtor, thus avoiding a loss of capital and with it the potential for its own bankruptcy.

With its neglect of fundamental credit risk techniques, post-Keynesianism is in good company with modern theories of bank management. While the latter openly regret their neglect of credit risk in their efficiency analysis of banks, an inclusion is deemed problematic from a methodological point of view. This is so because credit risk is to be considered as 'an undesired output of bank production (*wastage*)' (Varmaz 2005).[25] In this theory, missed loan repayments in the business of 'bank production' are interpreted as analogous to wastage, for example as occurs in the production of machine tools. However, the machine tool producer experiences wastage as a technical problem, which may force product price increases to compensate for the losses, but which ultimately can only be solved technically. Contract defaults experienced by the 'producer' bank, however, cannot be mitigated technically, but require the enforcement of loan security and the availability of sufficient bank capital. The bank does not experience *wastage*, but unfulfilled payment obligations that no interest increase is going to compensate for.

2.3.3 Monetary Keynesianism

In this section, the monetary Keynesianism of Hajo Riese's Berlin school is treated in more detail than other Keynesian schools of economics because this school has been more determined in its attempt to free itself from the barter-theory elements of neoclassical economics than Keynes and the post-Keynesians. Monetary Keynesianism correctly assumes that individuals can only have goods and resources at their disposal when they have obtained money *beforehand*. For this reason the economy is called a *monetary economy* and not a market economy. The monetary system is at the center. Monetary Keynesianism views stocks of goods for which no money is available, such as surplus and unused resources and in particular the unemployed, as economically irrelevant. It correctly accuses neoclassical economics of not having advanced beyond a theory of possession because it has been entangled in a world of bartered goods.

In monetary Keynesianism, the ability of an entrepreneur to dispose over goods and resources is determined by the willingness of a 'possessor of assets', a commercial bank, to give up money. This 'possessor', who in actual fact is an asset owner, is the main actor in monetary Keynesian economic analysis. His sacrifice of money advances economic activity, while his failure to sacrifice curtails economic activity. The bank's sacrifice of liquidity occurs in the *financial market*[26] only against interest, the latter reflecting the price of money based on its scarcity. In contrast to the neoclassical credit markets, this market is not simply analyzed as another goods market but as a market that dominates the goods market. Money made available in this market, without which entrepreneurs cannot engage in production, results in the creation of incomes that must return a profit corresponding to the interest payment. The requirement to return a profit in turn advances economic production. However, this model immediately raises the question of how the money that enables commercial banks to provide funds to entrepreneurs enters the world.

What is the answer provided by monetary Keynesianism? Its undisputable superiority over neoclassical economics stems from the fact that it does not consider money as a good: neither as a bartered good, as a store of value nor in particular as a standard good. Rather, money has an attribute that is lacking in goods: the capacity for final settlement of creditor-debtor contracts. Money is in its essence understood as a *means of payment*. Here, the central bank as the only producer of money has to guarantee the liquidity of commercial banks as the *lender of last resort* (LOLR), a topic not discussed in neoclassical economics. Moreover, in comparison with neoclassical economics, monetary Keynesianism is also more advanced due to its insight that money is not simply exogenously created by a central bank acting as monetary authority, but is always created endogenously based on credit against interest.

What does the central bank sacrifice when it creates money against interest? Riese, the inspiring leader of monetary Keynesianism, answered this question in his first debate with ownership economics by stating that the central bank sacrifices nothing, as 'money arises *out-of-nothing*'[27] (Riese 1999, 153; emphasis added; see Heinsohn and Steiger 1999a). He moved the interest-based nature of credit, of great importance to him in previous works, to the fringe of his analysis. The focus since 1999 has been solely on the role of the central bank as the guarantor of liquidity.[28] This comes at a cost, because the central bank is now understood less as a bank and more as a monetary authority or, indeed, a utility.

In order to follow this theoretical turnaround one has to accept Riese's surprising discovery of the existence of two fundamentally different types of credit. The agreement between commercial bank and non-bank is, as in the teachings of neoclassical economics, an income-creating 'resource credit', representing 'a *transfer of the disposition over goods and services* from the creditor [to] the debtor'[29] (Riese 1999, 152; emphasis added). In this type of credit, the commercial bank, based on an independent individual assessment,[30] has indeed to insist on loan security to balance the risk that the loan principal might not be repaid. In contrast, the 'money credit' between commercial bank and central bank only safeguards the liquidity of the commercial bank and is not creating income. Accordingly, the need for an independent individual assessment that would have otherwise resulted in the requirement for loan security does not exist. Rather, central bank claims against the commercial bank correspond to a money balance of the commercial bank debtor, the former providing the latter with a 'payment opportunity'[31] (Riese 1999, 152).

Here, Riese makes the assumption that the central bank as LOLR can create money *without limit* to ensure the functioning and the liquidity of commercial banks. As briefly mentioned above, Steuart, as the founder of the theory of the note-issuing bank, knew already that unlimited money creation contradicts the fundamental rules of the art of banking. For Steuart, the ability to create money is limited by the availability of collateral from the bank's counterparties and by the capacity of the bank's capital to absorb loan losses.

It is Riese's major achievement to have been the first in the German debate to develop the linkage between the 'elasticity of the money supply and the avoidance of liquidity crises',[32] reflected in the LOLR function, with the associated 'payment difficulties of a central bank'[33] (Riese 1993, 412). Such payment difficulties have always resulted: for example, in the case of the Bank of England under Peel's Bank Act of 1844, when the central bank money supply was limited by the volume of specified assets. In the Bank of England case, the limiting asset was gold. The payment difficulties of the central bank are not overcome by simply abolishing the money supply limitation imposed by gold but by 'satisfying *every* credit based demand for money'. The only remaining question is 'at what *price* [the demand] is satisfied'[34] (Riese 1993, 453; emphasis in original). Or, expressed differently, the installation of a central bank as a LOLR results in the suspension of the imposed gold limit on the note issue. This, in turn, guarantees the payment capacity (liquidity) of the central bank '*securing the functioning of the economy*'[35] (Riese 1993, 444; emphasis in original).

This assessment of the beneficial impact of central banking after the abolition of the gold standard is, however, based on the idea of a central bank's unlimited capacity as a LOLR. This assumption is not only shared by monetary Keynesians. However, the leading theorists of the note-issuing bank, besides Steuart, Henry Thornton (1802), Walter Bagehot (1873) and Ralph Hawtrey (1932) (for more details see Steiger 2002, 54–60) have rejected such an idea, though not always with sufficient reasons. For them, the central bank's ability to act remains restricted by the availability of commercial bank collateral and the capacity of central bank capital to absorb potential losses.

What statements does monetary Keynesianism make in relation to loan security and bank capital? Practically none! While Riese (1993, 451 and 455) mentions Bagehot's second rule, to provide unlimited credit against good collateral in a liquidity crisis, he does not provide any further comments, and downplays its importance

42 The great schools' blindness to ownership

by assessing it as a 'strict conservative course of action' having the mere purpose 'together with a high rate of interest to act as a market barrier against a rush into liquidity, preventing the domino effects of a liquidity crisis'[36] (Riese 1993, 455).

Good loan security is also irrelevant in Riese's theory of a LOLR. It is thus no surprise that the capital of a central bank, like the role of loan security for money creation, is not mentioned once. This is reflected in Riese's discussion of the interactions between three sectors – central bank (Z), commercial banks (B) and the public (P) – and how these are reflected in their respective balance sheets. Out of eight scenarios, two examples are shown in Figure 2.1: (1) the sale of central bank money; and (2) multiple money creation; see Riese (1993, 430; see also 435).

Riese succeeds in demonstrating the '*decoupling of money demand and credit demand*'[37] (Riese 1993, 434) by assuming that the holding of money balances[38] is carried out by both the public (balance sheet entry 'C') and the commercial banks (balance sheet entry 'R'), which results from 'the *risk of asset losses*'[39] (Riese 1993, 433). However, the corresponding entries for (equity) capital are missing, as is a specification of to what degree claims on the asset side are secured by collateral of the debtor. In scenario (2), for example, the bank with claims against the public of $F_P=3,000$ and total liabilities of 3,200 against the central bank ($V_Z=1,200$) and the public (D=2000) cannot simply secure its claims by keeping a reserve of R=200. Rather it requires an amount of assets that exceeds its liabilities ($R+F_P$). Banks therefore must acquire additional reserves in the form of asset holdings so that a surplus of assets over liabilities results: i.e., the existence of capital.

Capital is also missing in Riese's central bank balance sheet, where, unlike with commercial banks and the public, he never raises 'the *risk of asset losses*' as a topic. In a later work Riese explicitly excludes central bank losses, as we will show below (p. 45).

The weakness of monetary Keynesianism in its analysis of the emission of bank notes is also found in Riese's student Peter Spahn's (2001, 49–52) discussion of reputational issues for private note-issuing banks. Thornton's observation

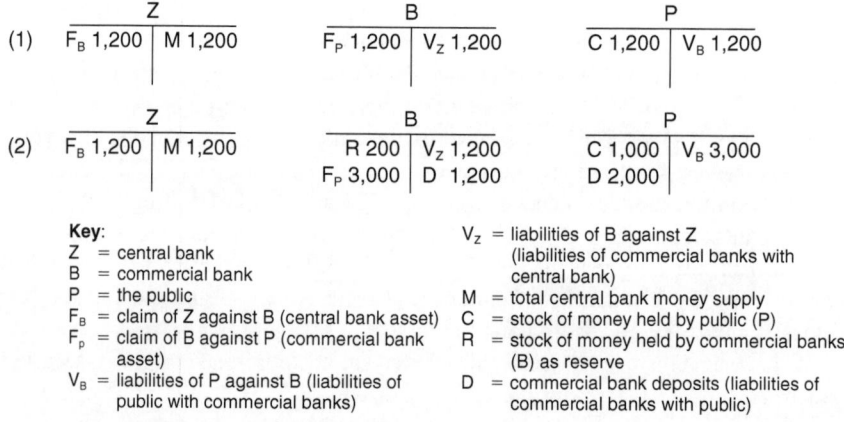

Figure 2.1 Balance sheets à la Riese.

(Thornton 1802, 188) that the poor reputation of note-issuing English *country banks* in the late eighteenth century was caused by their insufficient capital is not realized by Spahn. This can be shown based on Spahn's bank balance sheet structures (Figure 2.2).

Spahn claims that a bank of issue with low reputation is one that issues 'worthless paper money' because it does not possess an 'asset reserve', only 'resources'. In contrast, 'reputable banks possessed an asset reserve consisting of precious metals (for example gold). Their *business of attracting deposits* is taking in coins and bullion which then is acknowledged by credit entry or issue of notes' (Spahn 2001, 50).

Like Riese, Spahn does not realize that the reputation of a bank does not improve if it turns its resources into gold. Gold as such is indeed a property asset but is not an asset reserve. It only becomes a reserve when the note-issuing bank purchases gold with its profit. Profit is obtained, for example, from the interest proceeds of credit contracts through which bank notes are issued. With these profits a bank can then increase its capital in the form of gold assets. In the latter case the bank does not issue additional notes, even though the notes it obtains from its debtors as interest and that in turn are used for the purchase of gold cannot be distinguished from the notes it issues when providing loans.

Unlike Riese, Spahn realizes that the note-issuing bank is confronted with a liquidity problem, without, however, understanding the underlying reasons. This problem, he claims is caused by the redeemability of bank notes. He does not understand that a private note-issuing bank, like a central bank *without* the obligation to redeem its notes, can become illiquid from a lack of capital. 'Today nearly all currencies in the world are issued without the right of redemption of their bearers' (Spahn 2001, 62).

Spahn uses the historical fact that the right to redeem bank notes was abolished as an opportunity to criticize the assumption – emphasized by ownership economics – that loan security is required for the creation of money as 'absurd': 'Backing money by property is neither necessary nor sufficient for attaining ... a "true", "genuine" or "good" money' because 'the *value* of private-property assets depends ... on the quantity of money' (Spahn 2001, 62). Spahn overlooks the fact that the abolition of the historical gold backing merely removed the linkage to a *specific* type of property asset. Today's central bank is free to choose which '*secure* property assets it purchases with its notes'[40] (Stadermann 2002, 53), but it cannot dispense with demanding security altogether.

Spahn disregards the undisputable fact that the price of the loan security submitted to the central bank can fluctuate, and also the fact that a central bank that

Private note-issuing bank		Non-bank	
+ gold	+ deposits/notes	./. gold coins + deposits/notes	+ deposits/notes

Figure 2.2 Balance sheets à la Spahn.

waives the requirement for loan security will risk losses that will endanger the stability of its currency. Fluctuations in the value of loan security are never a sufficient argument against the taking of security. Reputable central banks have always responded to this risk: in the past by utilizing the self-liquidating nature of sound commercial bills, and today by their focus on repurchase (repo) agreements. In both cases the submitting commercial bank bears the risk. Moreover, Spahn misses the central role played by the provider of loan security for the functioning of a currency system. His approach 'does not see that the decision about *what* should be the currency foundation[41] determines *who* in a currency region can create or limit production and income'[42] (Stadermann 2002, 113). The parties are the central bank *and* its counterparties.

Does the removal of note redeemability solve the liquidity problem of a central bank? Spahn appears not to realize that the removal of the redeemability requirement is a consequence of the tight set-up of today's two-level banking system. Here, the central bank only has commercial banks as counterparties. Therefore it is only non-banks that have lost the right to redeem their notes. In contrast, commercial banks have retained that right. This must be the case to enable commercial banks to have their loan security released after the fulfillment of their contracts. For example,[43] in a repurchase (repo) agreement the commercial bank must supply central bank notes or balances to repurchase the assets underlying the transaction. Central bank notes are thus redeemed by the central bank.

In a scenario where a commercial bank is unable to pay back the borrowed central bank notes and the market price of the provided loan security is below the loan amount, the central bank has to withdraw the outstanding notes with its capital from circulation. If its reserves are exhausted, it has a liquidity problem like any private note-issuing bank. For example,[44] in a scenario where a commercial bank defaults, a proportion of the central bank's assets will be written off while its liabilities (notes and deposits) remain the same. Its capital, or net equity, as the difference between assets and liabilities, is therefore reduced. In order to maintain its target amount of notes it must now reduce its asset holdings further by selling assets to withdraw the surplus notes from circulation. In this transaction both assets and liabilities are reduced by the same amount. As a result of both transactions, the central bank has fewer assets against the target amount of note liabilities.

Very similar views to those of Riese and Spahn on the interaction of central bank, commercial banks and the public, the latter differentiated into enterprises and wealth-owning households, are held by other monetary Keynesians such as Karl Betz (1993, 51 and 2001, 75) and Andreas Hausknecht (1995, 208), as well as Michael Heine and Hansjörg Herr (1999, 332, 337 and 371). In none of these works does capital appear as a variable requiring serious consideration. As a result, enterprises, banks and central banks act in a world without capital.[45]

Ownership economics does not assert that monetary Keynesians are unaware of the fact that enterprises and banks require capital as a security buffer in addition to their assets. Nevertheless, monetary Keyensians believe, together with the majority of other economists (Steiger 2006b), that capital is not a requirement for a central bank: 'The central bank is the only economic unit that *cannot become illiquid* (with respect to domestic money).... A linkage of money creation and property, in whatever way implemented, would be dysfunctional'.[46] A linkage would result in 'quantitatively limiting the central bank money creation and could lead to a situation where the bank cannot exercise its role as the *lender of last resort*'[47] (Heine and Herr 1999, 340 and 377; emphasis added).

The maxim 'that which must not, cannot be'[48] is obviously not a sufficient justification for the proposition of permanent central bank liquidity and solvency. Riese may have had some inkling of this shortcoming and tried to subsequently deliver an explanation in his second debate with ownership economics (see Riese 2000a and 2000b; Heinsohn and Steiger 2000b). Here he goes further than Heine and Herr and argues not only that a central bank can always maintain liquidity in its domestic currency but that this attribute is also a matter of principle. The central bank's potential liquidity problems in relation to foreign currencies could not be compared with those in relation to commercial banks:

> Nothing would be more incorrect than such an assumption. A central bank only has a liquidity problem when it acts as the guarantor of convertibility – a special condition, wherein its counterparties are exposed to the exchange rate changes themselves. In contrast, the liquidity problem of commercial banks is of a principle nature because their liabilities have to be transformable into central bank money [which they cannot create themselves] in any situation.[49]
>
> (Riese 2000a, §31, col. 492a)

Why, according to Riese, can a central bank never have a liquidity problem, which could render it unable to fulfill its payment commitments? Simply, because it can remove the cause of its liquidity problem – the missing money to settle debts – by creating money *without* entering into a simultaneous *liability*: additional central bank liabilities, associated with money creation and matched by assets in the form of central bank claims against commercial banks, do not represent payment obligations but 'the production of liquidity ... asset creation by the central bank'.[50] Why?

> The money supply does not represent, as is still often assumed, a central bank liability in whatever form. What would be the nature of this liability? Formulated ironically, a central bank as producer of liquidity has *ex definitione* no liquidity problem itself; self-fabricated liquidity is transformed into self-fabricated liquidity.[51]
>
> (Riese 2000a, §33, col. 492b)

Nevertheless, Riese is not daring enough to rely solely on his explanation '*ex definitione*' and provides yet another. In his view, a central bank is like a bank, but unlike a 'normal' commercial bank is not subject to any risks. This follows for him from the assumption that money creation is asset creation, money being an asset the disposition over which the central bank can sacrifice in favor of the commercial banks: a central bank

> as the universal producer of liquidity is not subject to any *creditor risk* and cannot be subject to payment difficulties in the case of asset write-offs. The risk-free nature of its business forces the bank to take particular care when granting credit.... *However, the critical factor is that the holding of money turns into asset creation* – reflected, due to an accounting technicality, in the booking of its money emission as a liability. This reflects, in analogy with net equity, the *sacrifice over the asset 'money'*.[52]
>
> (Riese 2000a, §39, col. 493b; emphasis added)

By using the term 'sacrifice' Riese unavoidably postulates that the central bank has the option to dispose of its money without further complications. Only based on the existence of such an option can money be sacrificed. The central bank is thus placed in the same position as any holder of money, who indeed has the option of holding or giving up money. Riese does not recognize that the central bank in reality only has a choice between the following two options: (1) it can create money in a credit contract with commercial banks which are liable for their obligations; (2) it can abstain from creating money for commercial banks. A power associated with central banks to sacrifice the 'asset' money does not exist. This would only be possible if a central bank had the choice between (a) holding money that it has issued itself, and (b) abstaining from holding its own money. However, a central bank can never hold its own notes, in particular not as assets.[53] Even the layperson can recognize this from the fact that central bank notes for very good reasons appear, and not just due to an 'accounting technicality', in the central bank balance sheet as liabilities rather than assets.

A central bank can of course profit from its note issue business, predominantly from its interest income, as shown above in the discussion of Spahn. Interest can originate from money-creating credit contracts with commercial banks. Similarly, a central bank can purchase income-bearing securities (*outright*), which commercial banks sell to the central bank against newly created money. In this case commercial banks do not obtain money in a credit contract, which would have required the payment of interest; they lose, however, the interest income arising from the securities sold to the central bank. In turn, the central bank can sell securities through which the issued money is again withdrawn, i.e., destroyed. The securities purchased *outright* can also remain with the central bank until due. The money created through the purchase of securities in both cases only flows back to the central bank when the securities are sold by the bank or when the original issuer of the income-bearing securities, such as a finance minister, fulfills the payment obligation with central bank money.

A central bank can (1) transfer the money arising from interest incomes to its owner, in Germany the Finance Minister. It can (2) increase its capital, i.e., assets that can be used to fulfill obligations, with its earned bank notes, even though these were originally created for commercial banks. In this case the bank uses its notes to purchase securities, denominated in the domestic currency unit, which will appear on the asset side of its balance sheet. It can (3) also increase its holding of assets through the purchase of gold and foreign currency with the earned notes. In all three cases, the central bank does not issue new money, even though the money used for the purchases was originally created by the central bank.

In contrast, central bank notes that are repaid by commercial banks are not earned by the central bank. Consequently, these notes are *uno actu* destroyed as money when returned. The destruction does not mean that the returned notes are transformed from a central bank liability to a central bank asset. The return means that the notes are extinguished as money.[54] They represent merely printed forms that can only turn again into money when re-issued in new credit contracts between the central bank and commercial banks or in outright purchases of interest-bearing securities or gold.

Why can Riese fall for the idea that a 'nothing kept scarce'[55] represents an asset at the same time? He appears to be unaware that commercial banks need to fulfill not just one but two conditions in order to enable the central bank to successfully perform its function to uphold the liquidity of commercial banks and at the same time maintain control of the money supply: (1) interest and repayment obligations; (2) liability with their property to the amount of the debt. Riese deals with only the first condition and not with the second. The second condition is not of interest to him, because in his view a central bank cannot be subject to payment difficulties in the case of defaults. He is convinced of the 'risk-free nature of its business'. Ultimately it only transforms 'self-fabricated liquidity' into 'self-fabricated liquidity'.

Based on this belief, Riese cannot see that a central bank is exposed to the risk of being unable to withdraw its notes from circulation after a refinanced bank defaults without having provided loan security from which the central bank can recoup its losses. The central bank capital, which must now be deployed to withdraw the notes, is, as discussed above, not even mentioned by Riese. Similarly, the property titles of commercial bank debtors that are the property basis of central bank money creation are viewed as insignificant by Riese. From this, it follows that for commercial bank debtors Riese's money creation out-of-nothing represents a wealth creation out-of-nothing. Commercial banks do not need to bring their property to bear. Riese can only conceptualize money as arising out of nothing by neglecting the fact that the creation of genuine money is tied to (1) the property titles of commercial banks guaranteeing the return of the issued notes to the central bank; and (2) the capital employed by the central bank compensating for the performance shortfalls of its commercial bank counterparties.

Commercial bank assets, or more precisely their holdings of fixed-income securities or securitized assets (nominal assets eligible as central bank collateral), consist consequently of property titles, which as part of a temporary or permanent purchase are *assigned a price* by the central bank.[56] The money issued against property assets, however, is *not* turned into an asset through this price-setting process. Money is not directly an asset but a derivative of the ownership aspect of a property asset. Money is a note that a commercial bank obtained from a central bank in return for assets delivered as part of a credit contract, and represents the right of the commercial bank to have the asset released according to the terms of the contract.

The central bank does not, as Riese believes, sell money against the mere commercial bank obligation of repayment and interest, while having no obligations itself. Rather the central bank buys 'assets that it [cannot] create itself' (Stadermann 2000, §13, col. 536b) and which it has to return after repayment and interest obligations are met.

Unlike Baron Münchhausen,[57] a central bank cannot escape from a swamp by lifting itself up by its own hair, as would be the case if it could 'fabricate' additional liquidity, i.e., additional 'assets', as Riese suggests. On the contrary, in a case of unforeseen losses it must, like a commercial bank or any other actor in a monetary economy, use retained earnings in the form of capital as compensation.

The central bank of monetary Keynesianism is not a note-issuing bank that emits creditor money suitable for the money market. Rather, it resembles a 'state bank', or a note-issuing bank with deficient central bank constitution, that issues more or less valueless debtor's money. Such a bank indeed buys 'non-tradable debt instruments, whose quantity can be arbitrarily increased'[58] (Stadermann 2002, 46), directly from their originators as part of its note issue. This is unlike a genuine note-issuing bank, which will never purchase debt titles directly from an issuer but will instead purchase titles from third-party creditors in the open market.[59] This monetary Keynesian 'state bank' also does not need capital because it is *in no way* obliged to redeem or to accept back its own notes.

Riese, in his theory of central banking, must have somehow sensed that his daring separation of central bank 'money credit', requiring neither loan security nor bank capital, and common 'resource credit' provided by commercial banks, requiring both security and capital, is untenable. He therefore ventures into a further radicalization of his approach and does not hesitate to refer to Milton Friedman's metaphor of the money-dropping helicopter as an 'outstanding achievement in the history of economic thought' because it 'avoided the market theoretical perplexity of linking credit and money'.[60] Previously, he had criticized this metaphor as a 'dichotomization of money market and goods market'[61] (Riese 1999, 154).

Hence, Riese makes two remarkable blunders in one stroke:

1   A 'resource credit' does not exist in a monetary economy. The credit contract between commercial bank and central bank is always about the transfer of money or the disposition over money, and never about resources and services. This contract is always a money credit. The fact that the non-bank usually purchases or produces goods and services with the borrowed money does not turn a money credit into a resource credit. Whatever the non-bank debtor wants to do with the money, including maintaining liquidity, which

Riese had previously acknowledged (Riese 1993, 354–356), the money is only obtained against good loan security and interest.

2 The contract between commercial bank and central bank deals with the transfer of money and the disposition over money alone. The fact that central banks predominantly guarantee the liquidity of commercial banks does not turn this 'money credit' into a special form of credit that could equally be performed through the exogenous control of the money supply by 'helicopter or furnace'. Obviously, commercial banks can also refinance themselves at the central bank for income-generating purposes, for example, when they improve their interest income by expanding credit to non-banks or by purchasing securities. Whatever banks intend to do with the money, they only obtain it against good loan security and interest.

Even though Riese's central bank cannot suffer any loss, it nevertheless demands interest. As a consequence, he lapses into a central bank theory of interest. Its money, created out-of-nothing, can only serve as a generally accepted 'medium to fulfill contracts',[62] if it is a 'nothing that *is kept scarce*'[63] (Riese 1999, 153; emphasis added). The central bank thus had to invent a form of interest that is specific to its operations and ensures the scarcity of its money. However, Riese is also aware of the ordinary interest arising between commercial bank and non-bank or generally between actors that hold money and those who want to obtain money. For this type of interest Riese refers back to Keynes's liquidity premium: for Keynes the ability to always settle debts immediately and definitively. When money is given up, i.e., in the sacrifice of money in a credit contract, liquidity premium is lost and therefore must be compensated for with interest. This second explanation of interest presupposes the existence of a type of money that is kept scarce by the central bank interest. Riese thus oscillates between two types of interest: the interest that makes money scarce[64] and the interest that is directly attached to money and results from its liquidity premium.

If someone mixes up money credit and goods credit[65] and in addition confuses explanation and postulation, then indeed 'apocrypha'[66] (Riese 1999, 145) are created, becoming a feature not only of theology but also of economics. Riese, who attempts to 'rescue' ownership economics through the above lines, senses of course that this critique of his theories of interest cannot be rebutted by his beautiful metaphor of apocrypha. Therefore, he makes – as shown – a daring attempt to extricate himself[67] from this difficulty by proposing that a central bank sacrifices its 'disposition over the asset "money"'[68] (Riese 2000a, §39, col. 493b). This alleged sacrifice, in Riese's view, is the loss for which the central bank must demand interest (see Heinsohn and Steiger 2000b, §19, col. 518a–b).

Riese, in his reply to the critique of this last of his theories of interest by ownership economics (Riese 2000b), did not repeat this honorary rescue of the monetary explanation of interest *à la* Keynes. However, he also did not explicitly distance himself from this theory (Riese 2000b). While Riese in the outline of this theory (Riese 2000a) promotes the central bank from a money creator to a creator of assets, which can demand interest because it is giving up its disposition over 'the asset "money"', he states once again in line with Keynes – but in ambiguous words – that the rate of interest 'is the price, determined in an individual experiment, for the temporary giving up of the disposition over money ... by the asset owner'[69] (Riese 2000b, §3, col. 546a). Here, the rate of interest follows from a preference-based calculation by asset owners who reduce the scarcity of money by money creation and increase its scarcity by money destruction. Therefore, interest is 'the price for scare money as determined per market experiment'[70] (Riese 2000b, §3, col. 546a).

The 'authority' of a central bank, previously absolutely indispensible for Riese, now merely appears as a (possible) substitute (curate) of the asset owner, noted modestly and inconspicuously in a footnote (Riese 2000b, col. 546a, fn.11). However, this step does not advance Riese beyond Keynes, as Riese, like Keynes, forgoes the explanation of money creation, which is associated with the note-issuing bank and not with an arbitrary 'asset owner'. As a consequence, Riese must also forgo the opportunity to find the explanation of interest, as interest emerges at the same time that money is created by the note-issuing bank. He has to drop the project to integrate the emergence of interest with the process of money creation like a hot potato, because he cannot rebut the argument put forward by ownership economics that a central bank can never freely dispose over the money it has created. Instead, Riese makes the unfortunate attempt to accuse this school of having blamed Riese for something it never has. Ownership economics had – 'completely and senselessly' – held the view against him that 'the central bank' and not the asset owner was 'prepared' 'to pay a price for the disposition over money that is kept scarce'[71] (Riese 2000b, §16, col. 550b). Ownership economics, however, said something completely different: the central bank demands interest because it suffers a loss of ownership premium and not because it suffers from a loss arising from an alleged sacrifice of its own money, represented as a sacrificed asset.

Riese (2000b, §§16–17, col. 550b) would also like to escape the criticism that he has not overcome the weakness of Keynes's monetary explanation of interest. Keynes, according to Riese, 'interpreted interest as reward for the dishoarding of an exogenously fixed money supply' (Riese 2000b, §16, col. 550b), that is, 'as the reward for the giving up of liquidity'[72] (Riese 2000b, §17, col. 550b). In contrast, in Riese's theory, interest is determined 'as (payable) price for the disposition over money'[73] (Riese 2000b, §17, col. 550b). At the same time, however, Riese also wants interest to be 'the price for the temporary sacrifice of the disposition over money'[75] (Riese 2000b, §3, col. 546a). Solely the choice of words distinguishes him from Keynes. On the one hand interest is offered for the disposition over money, while on the other hand it is demanded for the sacrifice of the disposition over money. *However, the money that is to explain interest is always already present.* This cannot even be obscured by the fact that for Riese, in contrast to Keynes, money is not fixed exogenously but is created in a money credit, about the conditions (good loan security and capital) of which Riese however remains silent. But even here Riese is not consistent. He concurs finally with the view of ownership economics, but Riese formulates this acknowledgement not in a direct reply to the two founders but concealed in a response to another critic, who supports the position of ownership economics that money cannot be created without hypothecated property: 'I have the same opinion as Hans-Joachim Stadermann (apart from a few details of interpretation)'[75] (Riese 2000b, §17, col. 550b; see, however, Stadermann 2000).

The above comment shows that Riese, taking into account his understandable defensiveness, has adopted many concepts from ownership economics in the meantime. This can easily be shown by reference to Riese's mockery of the barter paradigm. His comment that 'the existing economic theory as a science hypostasized the inclination to barter as the *motive power* behind the economy'[76] (Riese 2000b, §2, col. 545b) could have been directly taken from Heinsohn and Steiger (1996). Using ownership economics, in an act nothing short of bravado, he wants to show mainstream economics its limits: 'It is not ... acts of barter between individuals that have created the foundation for market price formation. This reveals barter as being an unhistorical and from the view of an appropriate theory formulation a non-theoretical construct. Throughout all of economic history there has *never* (never!) been, at no time and on no occasion, a traffic in goods that has fulfilled the barter theoretical conditions of price formation'[77] (Riese 2000b, §3, col. 546a).

Yet in earlier controversies (for example in 1983) Riese only admitted that ownership economics (Heinsohn 1984 [1982]) had provided a 'social history' at best but not a theoretical explanation. Ownership economics had committed the mortal sin of playing off (historical) reality and theory against each other. Now, in contrast, Riese positions himself courageously next to ownership economics with his proposition that 'the rate of interest is the price category that holds together the world in its innermost folds'[78] (Riese 2000b, §3, col. 546b). For ownership economics, however, the explanation of interest is the core piece of economic theory that one should not leave – as Riese has – in an ambiguous state by having money created 'out-of-nothing'.

In his latest contribution to the theory of the monetary economy, Riese (2006) has refrained from an explanation of interest altogether. He limits himself to rejecting the classical and neoclassical interpretation of interest as a non-monetary variable, but also rejects Keynes's liquidity preference interpretation as untenable. Questioned by ownership economics about the status of his own monetary explanation of interest (Steiger 2001) he replied that this was 'research in progress' (Riese 2001).

It appears almost sensational that Riese, in the same contribution, no longer considers the (macroeconomic) budget limitation of a monetary economy to be based on the scare supply of money (kept scarce via interest) but instead on the '*total value of wealth*, where the values represent the equilibrium asset prices'[79] (Riese 2006 [2001]; emphasis added) and where interest as the reciprocal asset price sets the norm for these prices. This can be found, by anyone who can read, in all its details in Heinsohn and Steiger (1996).

An analysis of money creation reveals in the end that monetary Keynesianism, like classical and neoclassical economics, remains entangled within the world of goods. That may be considered surprising for a school of economic thought that wants to create money out-of-nothing. But this is precisely shown by the fact that this theory can only conceptualize an alternative to the existence of material goods by its absence – the nothing. Because money creation indeed does not involve the sacrifice of goods, Riese, as the leader of the Berlin school, is left to postulate that the central bank sacrifices a nothing that it creates. This nothing, in turn, appears at the commercial bank recipient, miraculously, not as nothing but as a property asset.

An ownership-based society cannot be conceptualized by a contrast between the existence of goods *versus* the non-existence of goods. This society has three entities at its disposal: (1) material possession of goods; (2) immaterial ownership titles; and (3) the real nothing. While the monetary Keynesian critique of theoretical approaches based on the barter of goods tries to take the distinction between ownership and possession seriously, like classical and neoclassical economics, it fails to reveal the critical role of ownership and the burdening and hypothecation of property titles in the process of money creation. This is shown time and time again when the creditor and the owner, and the debtor and the possessor, are equated. It never struck monetary Keynesianism that both parties to a credit contract are represented by owners. As a consequence, this school misses the critical fact that both parties are also possessors. In the credit-based creation of money the possession of goods is indeed not affected. Thus money – not goods – arrives with the debtor. However, in the process of granting credit, property titles are changed in the sense that through their burdening and hypothecation two new titles emerge: (1) property-backed money is received by the debtor; (2) the credit contract, specifying the claims and liabilities of creditor and debtor, is received by the creditor.

By curtailing the economic reality into goods and nothing, the Berlin school cannot advance further than did its mentor John Maynard Keynes. Keynes had at least reversed the goods-theoretical nexus of causality claimed by classical and neoclassical economics that the willingness to *save* determines the level of *investment*, by showing that willingness to invest enabled savings by generating growing incomes in the first place. Keynes could not show what enabled investment. In his model, money is simply exogenously created; obtained from unexplained loanable funds; obtained from liquid resources within the banking system and mysterious 'hoards' held by the public (Heinsohn and Steiger 2005, 69–71); or simply created from state debt without much trouble (Stadermann and Steiger 2001b, 310–320 and 2010).

2.4 Conclusion on all three schools

Our expedition through classical, neoclassical and Keynesian economics leads to the following conclusion: all three schools fail because they try to explain economic activity, especially interest and money, without considering the ownership aspect of property.

Classical economics as a theory of domination does not provide an entry point to the understanding of economic activity. Moreover, by staying firmly within the barter paradigm it overlooks the linkage between interest and money.

Neoclassical economics at least offers reasons for economic activity by postulating scarce stocks of goods and resources. However, it cannot find the reasons for this scarcity. Its adoption of the barter paradigm presupposes scarcity and prevents the linking of interest and money. This cannot be resolved by the extension its models received in new institutional economics because this theory of 'property rights' uses the term property rights as a label only and merely focuses on the rights of possession.

Keynesianism, while attempting to overcome the barter paradigm by explaining interest from money, similarly cannot develop an adequate theory of economic activity. Monetary Keynesianism, as its most interesting variant, tries to explain the scarcity of goods, assumed by neoclassical economics, via production processes that are kept within limits by the available supply of money. Money must be kept scarce and this scarcity enforces economic activity. However, money on the one hand is a nothing kept scarce through interest, and on the other hand is an asset that can be created by the central bank out-of-nothing. This asset can be sacrificed by the central bank, as by any other holder of money, against interest. This daring mixture of an artful invention of interest and a creative merger of money creation and money holding lets the reasons for economic activity once again remain mysterious.

This darkness turns into light as soon as ownership, which none of the three theories has ever made the subject of their analysis, is understood. They remain economic theories *without* ownership.

Classical economists, neoclassical economists and Keynesian economists could raise the objection against this judgment that they do not question the importance of ownership for the economy and that in their works they make every effort to provide comment to that effect. Ownership economics is not denying this. It solely claims that all three schools have never really analyzed ownership as the only institution that leads to economic activity with burdening, hypothecation and enforcement. Whenever the three schools have used the term ownership or property rights they have merely looked at (de facto or *de jure*) possession. Ownership economics is not aware of any other investigation in which the difference between ownership and possession is discussed with a view to determine the relevance of ownership and possession for economic theory.[80] It is indeed imaginable that one day economists will analyze the right of ownership and the associated capacity to burden property titles, and will conclude, in contrast to ownership economics, that this is of no importance to economic activity and economic theory. However, such a controversy is still outstanding.

With their unreflecting use of the word ownership or property, economists in a way resemble the ancient astronomer Ptolemy. This scholar used the terms earth and sun possibly more often than Nicolaus Copernicus did at the beginning of the early modern period. Nevertheless, it was Copernicus and not the great Alexandrian who discovered the correct relationship between the central star and the planets rotating around it, and with it the right theoretical description.

3 The economic core of the ownership system

Interest, money and property assets

A property rights system that includes the right of ownership is not provided by nature. It can only be created by *legal enactment*. This always immaterial step, in contrast to ploughing or harvesting, does not change the object of (de facto or *de jure*) possession physically. Immediately after the creation of ownership titles *out-of-nothing*, these yield the ownership premium. This premium, in contrast to interest or profit, does not need to be earned. It cannot be emphasized often enough that the ownership premium arises neither from the physical use of goods and resources nor from a pre-existing stock of money. It arises from an act of law.

Ownership titles do not replace 'titles' to de facto possession, but are added. In this process, traditional rules governing de facto possession are transformed into *de jure* rights of possession. In contrast to possession, ownership cannot be tasted, heard, smelled or touched. *De jure* possession, as the legal right governing the nature and extent of use, is, like ownership, something created by law. However, *de jure* possession differs from ownership in that its exercise can lead to physical changes. The exercise of (de facto or *de jure*) possessory rights therefore has a *real* impact. In contrast, the activation of ownership, which has nothing to do with any type of use, has no direct real impact.

As immaterial legal creations, ownership titles lead to fundamentally new relationships in the world of goods. If still in existence, obligations that have arisen from relations of reciprocity in tribal communities, or from relations of command in feudal seigneuries, are pushed aside. In brief: it is only from the activation of ownership titles, that genuine economic activity can arise. Through this economic deployment of legal titles, the previously self-sufficient non-economic rules about de facto possession are replaced by new obligations that arise from the asset deployment. These obligations are always obligations of creditors *and* debtors, and are in the first place entered into as part of contracts that create money[1] and contracts that transfer claims to money, i.e., credit contracts. Contracts transferring claims to money[2] have as their consequence sales contracts,[3] which further underpin the obligations of creditors and debtors.[4]

The special characteristic of credit contracts is that ownership premium must be sacrificed, and as a consequence interest must be earned in a countermove.

In order to service the interest entitlement, which arises from the burdening of creditor property, the exercise of possessory rights over goods and resources (now turned into commodities and assets) becomes the subject of a permanent regime of economization. This degree of economization could never have existed while the deployment of goods and resource was still governed by the traditional rules or coercive orders of possession-based systems. With ownership, the mere control over resources gives way to their economic deployment as assets.

3.1 Burdening, hypothecation and enforcement

For the prevailing economic theories, as shown in Chapter 2, burdening, hypothecation and enforcement have no relevance to the explanation of economic activity. From the perspective of ownership economics, the exercise of these powers establishes economic activity. Economic activity results from the powers of *burdening* and *hypothecation*, which are attached only to ownership titles. Both powers secure economic contracts. While burdening refers to an unsecured claim against the general property of an owner,[5] hypothecation[6] provides a direct property right that can, on default, be enforced directly against the specified assets – the loan security – of the debtor.[7] In both cases, an independent institution of law is indispensable for effective *enforcement*.[8]

Enforcement, and the associated execution in debt recovery actions, is always related to a legal claim, i.e., an ownership title, held by a property owner. It cannot be emphasized strongly enough that ownership is a property right that is distinctively different from a mere use right in the sense of a possession-based disposition over goods and resources.

Such a use right, as shown in Chapter 1, determines who may *use*[9] what, when, where, against whom, how, and to what extent. It is irrelevant in this context whether the use right is absolute or has been granted with limitations. The full and final transfer of ownership titles automatically transfers rights to possession. In contrast, during the mere activation of property assets through hypothecation, which exposes the assets to potential enforcement actions, possession is not transferred. Instead, property titles are in a sense temporarily blocked *qua* hypothecation and are therefore removed from further activation.[10]

Ownership, with its associated rights of burdening and hypothecation, exists beyond the sphere of the possession of goods with their typical use rights. The ownership system guarantees, by threatening punishment even against the powerful, protection against any *non-economic* transfer of property to others.[11] The gain as well as the loss of property must, as a matter of principle, only occur through enforceable credit or sales contracts between property owners and can no longer be achieved through rules of custom or coercive orders.

The ownership system protects with its legal powers the right to recover overdue debts out of the property of the debtors, and in this way also protects the property of the creditor. Why? Not only the debtor but also the (note-issuing) creditor is threatened by the risk of bankruptcy. The always popular desire to protect the 'small' heavily-indebted owner from the 'large' and wealthy creditor, for example, as evidenced by the new German insolvency law or the recent debt relief for developing nations, overlooks the fact that the creditor too has something to lose: the property burdened in the credit contract.

Immediately following the commencement of the new German insolvency law mentioned above, a practice against creditors that could be described as fraudulent became widespread. Notably in the construction industry, companies could legally transfer assets into newly-set-up entities before filing for insolvency. Many creditors, especially tradespeople and suppliers, became insolvent themselves because they could not enforce their claims against the newly-founded entities. The debtor in an ownership-based society, however miserable he might feel, must not be confused with a serf, who on non-delivery of his dues is punished by his castellan. The debtor – an owner like the creditor – must also not be confused with the tax 'debtor' confronted by the sheriff, who was sent to him by the taxation office 'creditor'. The 'defrauded' creditor needs the sheriff to avoid the danger of property losses. In contrast, the taxation office employs the sheriff like a medieval castellan, exercising coercive power. The difference between tax collection in a system of feudal rule and in a system of ownership is that the tax 'debtor' in the latter can appeal to an independent court, and in this respect resembles the private debtor.

The legal prohibition of any non-economic access to property by others also ensures that incomes can only be generated either by using the possessory aspect of assets or the ownership aspect of assets (burdening and hypothecation). Thus every owner can personally use the physical possessory aspect of his property. He can, however, transfer possession in a special 'creditor-debtor contract' that is only known in the ownership-based society: the *lease* or *rent* agreement. Here, the ownership aspect of the creditor property is unaffected, while the lessee or rentee benefits from the possessory aspect and makes a lease or rental payment in return.[12]

Unlike the immaterial concept of ownership – implying an enforceable title to property that can be burdened or hypothecated – rights over possession determine rights governing the physical use of things. In tribal communities and feudal seignories, a specific type of use is assigned to members. In contrast, the use of things in ownership-based societies is no longer simply assigned by rules arising from the domination and control over resources, but becomes an economic operation.

The ownership aspect of property assets alone, standing next to their possessory aspect, can establish economic activity. This takes place through contracts between creditors and debtors in the form of *credit contracts*. The activation of property in these contracts has the special attribute that while the assets involved are temporarily blocked from further activation through either burdening or hypothecation, their possession is unaffected. This is different from goods transactions in possession-based systems and from lease or rent transactions in ownership-based systems. Economic agents involved in credit contracts keep and use the possessory or 'goods' aspect[13] of their property assets and continue with their economic activities. In a credit contract, neither possession nor goods are borrowed or lent.[14]

3.2 Ownership premium and interest

Where the lending of goods[15] is encountered in history, for example in the possession-based system of a tribal community, neoclassically educated economic historians are puzzled about the absence of interest in these transactions. Where jewellery, clothing, tools or food are not exchanged but lent, 'the borrowing against interest is not possible'[16] (Heichelheim 1938, 62). Moreover, loan security is not demanded. Even unlucky members of a tribe, who have failed repeatedly to return their borrowed items, can be confident of receiving further loans: 'The readiness to provide impoverish herdsmen with animals was at times so great that the wealthy lender, by gift or loan, depleted his large herds to a very small number of animals or sometimes lost the whole herd'[17] (Laum 1965, 47).

Possession-based systems have the inbuilt social safety nets of reciprocity (tribe) or emergency rations (feudal seigneurie). In contrast, the members of the ownership-based society find themselves without a *social safety net*. They attempt to overcome this predicament by deploying their property in a particular way. The result is not an inbuilt social safety net but economic activity achieving yields at a scale never before possible. Out of theses surpluses, taxes can be drawn to finance public safety nets.

How can the first step to economic activity be imagined? For this purpose, let us consider the founding heroes of *polis* and *civitas*, who abolished feudal rule and divided the land to create Theseus' 'state without King' or Romulus' 'Roma quadrata' (see Heinsohn 1984 [1982]).[18] The first harvest provided some of the co-revolutionaries, advantaged by a more favorable allotment, with plenty of stores, while others could barely maintain their existence. The individuals under threat could obtain neither help on the basis of blood relationship, *à la* tribe, nor support from feudal masters through rations, *à la* feudalism. However, they still had their allotment of land and conceived the idea of *requesting* credit from the more successful members of the society. This credit must not be confused with the lending of goods in tribal societies, and had completely different characteristics. Initially, this credit was unavoidably in kind – 10 bushels of barley received, but 12 months later 11 bushels of barley returned. However, the provision of repayment and interest in kind resulted in immediate storage costs, which was soon addressed through switching from credit in the form of physical goods to money, i.e., claims to the creditor's non-physical ownership titles over barley fields or cattle pastures.

The excellent storability of barley, its weight stability and divisibility, together with its suitability for consumption (food) and capital good (seeds), became decisive factors for its use in the first credit contract:[19]

> due to their irregular weight, grains of wheat are not suitable for the purposes of weighing. I have weighed a set of 60 grains and determined a

weight of 3.08 g. In contrast, a different set weighed only 2.99 g. However, 60 grains of barley weighed 2.81 g and a different set of 60 again exactly 2.81 g. Accordingly, 180 grains of barley have a weight of 8.43 g. The Siklu [shekel] of the so-called light Babylonian mina of 504 g weighs 8.4 g and this was without doubt the basis of the Babylonian silver currency.[20]

(Willers 1909, 4)

The use of barley in early credit contracts has nothing to do with the intertemporal barter of goods *à la* neoclassical economics. The provider of credit as an individual – without a social safety net apart from his land allotment – loses, as a consequence of the transfer of barley for 12 months, the extra safety buffer that this barley would have provided if it had remained with him. Such an immaterial yield and its sacrifice in the credit contract is unknown to neoclassical economics and its concept of loans based on goods. For this loss of social safety the creditor demands interest, the eleventh bushel of barley. Indeed, the deferment of consumption *à la* neoclassical economics is not his problem, as the harvest was abundant. His concerns, therefore, relate to the loss of social safety, for example in the event that something happens to him in month six, but the debtor is only obliged to repay after month twelve. This loss of social safety exists beyond the repayment risk and must be compensated with interest.

In addition to the concern over the loss of social safety, the free farmer turned creditor is also concerned about repayment risk. This is addressed through the provision of loan security by the debtor. The loan security must not be identical with the borrowed goods. Loan security too plays no role in neoclassical economics. Only the recently allotted parcel of land is suitable as loan security, because the non-payment of barley cannot be protected against by barley. *In the process of hypothecating the debtor's allotment of land, both debtor and creditor, in turn, comprehend ownership.* In practice, the debtor can continue to farm the allotted land and at the same time use it as security for the borrowed 10 bushels – plus 1 (interest) – of barley. The creditor on the other hand experiences that his barley is absent for 12 months but that he has obtained a documented security right over the debtor's allotment without, however, having permission to use the debtor's land himself.

The transition from *credit* in kind, not the neoclassical goods-based loan, to the money credit is based on the understanding of the double and simultaneous employment of the allotted land as arable field (possession) and loan security (ownership) for the barley repayment. Very quickly the creditor learns to work with two different documents. He does not lend barley by weight, but instead a document no. 1 (money), a claim against his land allotment that places a burden on his land (ownership), which he continues to use (possession), i.e., by sowing and harvesting. He records this procedure in document no. 2 (credit contract), in which the debtor, the loan security, the amount of credit and the interest are recorded. The immaterial ownership aspect of the creditor's property is now activated too. In the previous barley credit, i.e., *prior* to the money credit, only the debtor's property was activated by being put up as collateral.

The economic core of the ownership system 59

Property owners, in contrast to the de facto possessors in tribal or feudal systems, experience not just one but two types of yield: (1) as in possession-based systems, a *material* yield arises in ownership-based systems from the physical use of possessory rights over goods and resources; (2) in contrast to possession-based systems, an *immaterial* yield from the ownership aspect of resources (now assets) arises in ownership-based systems in addition to the material yield. Only the immaterial yield establishes the operations underlying economic activity and is defined by ownership economics as *ownership premium*.

What is the significance of this premium on ownership? It is a nonphysical yield reflecting the capacity to enter into new contracts (the ability to burden and hypothecate property and to take on debt) and is associated with property assets as long as they have not yet been activated through burdening or hypothecation for economic activity. The premium allows property owners to enter into legally binding contracts, especially credit contracts. In relation to such contracts, the premium is a measure of the degree to which owners can become creditors *and* debtors. Only property assets that are neither burdened nor hypothecated can produce this premium.

Unburdened property allows *identifiable* individuals, partnerships or corporations to *create claims against their general property* in the form of documentary intangibles,[21] or money *notes*,[22] by employing a second document – the credit contract – (discussed as documents no. 1 and no. 2 above). What is the significance of the documentary intangible, the money note? As the link between ownership and possession, it establishes the starting point of economic activity because its issuer sacrifices ownership premium and now has to accept claims against his property. *The notes imply claims against the property of the issuer as soon as they are originated via the credit contract document.* For the set-up of the second document (the credit contract), other property owners are only prepared to take on the debtor role because the execution of the credit contract coincides with the burdening of creditor property. A property owner can only become the issuer of notes if he, through a sacrifice of ownership premium, establishes the general right to redeem the notes against his property. This obligation is underwritten in the first instance through the credit contract with an identifiable debtor and not yet by the money notes themselves.

The ownership premium expresses the capacity to create money but also the capacity to borrow money. Only through the burdening of property and the loss of ownership premium can someone become a (money-creating) *creditor* in a credit contract. Similarly, only by accepting claims against property by putting it up as loan security can someone become a *debtor* in a credit contract. The acceptance of such claims signifies that the creditor has been provided with legal rights that will allow him to enforce his claim against debtor property in the case of contract default. For precisely this reason, debtor property must be made available and is blocked *and* hypothecated. Unavoidably, during the period of the credit contract, the debtor loses ownership premium.

In all credit contracts, creditors *and* debtors are property owners. These contracts can be divided into *pure* credit contracts and contracts of *sale*. Pure credit contracts specify – along with repayment terms and interest – temporary arrangements for the taking of loan security. Possession is not transferred for the term of the loan.[23] Contracts of sale, on the other hand, supply the required means for the discharge of the loan, i.e., the fulfillment of the credit contract. Contracts of sale are therefore subsidiary to credit contracts. Without credit contracts, contracts of sale would not exist.

Contracts of sale are between creditors and debtors. The seller of property receives a claim to money, i.e., takes on the role of the creditor, while the purchaser enters into an obligation to pay money and therefore takes on the role of the debtor. As in the credit contract, interest is due if the money obligation is not settled immediately. Prior to payment, the purchaser is liable with his general property and loses the corresponding ownership premium,[24] because the liability for payment creates a burden on his property.

The crucial difference between credit contracts and contracts of sale is that in contracts of sale both ownership and possession are transferred. Thus the new owner immediately obtains the potential to burden or hypothecate the acquired property, its ownership premium, *and* the opportunities associated with the the possessory rights over his new property. In contrast, pure (money-creating) credit contracts are not concerned with the *transfer* of possession. They deal with the *burdening* of creditor property and the *hypothecation* of debtor property for a period of time, i.e., the sacrifice of ownership premium by both parties. Hence, credit contracts are not only about the claims of the creditor for principal repayment and the payment of interest by the debtor. They are also about the implied obligations of the creditor, resulting from the burdening of his property, to redeem claims against his property. Moreover, credit contracts also deal with the creditor's rights against the debtor, which, as the result of hypothecation, include the right to commence enforcement actions involving the loan security if required.

While a credit contract always specifies the debtor, specific loan security (collateral) may not always be specified.[25] However, this does not support a theory of credit where loan security is subsidiary or optional.[26] In fact, contracts without specified collateral typically suggest a particularly strong property position of the debtor.[27] This is reflected in the very definition of a sound debtor, which states that the quality of his assets is not subject to any doubt. However, as Hawtrey (1932, 126) noted, anticipating Stiglitz's theory of asymmetric information, even a creditor who is absolutely confident in the high credit standing of his debtor will not often waive the requirement for loan security: 'It is not ordinarily possible to examine in detail the entire assets of an applicant for a loan.... But the furnishing of security makes scrutiny of the general solvency of the borrower unnecessary'. It should be added that ownership economics shows that in reality loan security is taken because it provides a more equal risk distribution between creditor and debtor (see the discussion of Stiglitz in Section 2.3.1).[28] Even if the creditor is willing to waive the requirement for specific loan security, he will never waive the right to enforce his debt in a recovery action. This holds even in the case of a first-class debtor.

When property assets are burdened or hypothecated, possession remains with the creditor and the debtor. If the burdened property is land, both can continue to use the field unhindered for agricultural production. Credit contracts never transfer the possession of goods for the purposes of their use over a period of time. The creditor does not sacrifice goods, nor does the debtor receive these.

It has to be emphasized once again that credit contracts do not transfer property assets.[29] This holds also for the money-creating credit contract and not only for the credit contract that deals with claims to already existing money. In the former, the issuer of money notes burdens property assets and gives up ownership premium because part of his property has to be made temporarily available to redeem the notes or become the subject of enforcement actions. Only a successful enforcement action would actually transfer ownership and possession in one act.[30] The act of enforcement therefore resembles the redemption of money notes by third parties as well as a contract of sale. In the credit contract with existing money, ownership and possession of goods are jointly transferred from the seller to the buyer *for* a money payment. In the case of the redemption of money notes, ownership and possession of creditor property are transferred to the third party redeeming the notes, while the money notes are destroyed or booked out.[31] In contrast, an enforcement action against a debtor is carried out *because* money, which has not been repaid with interest, continues to circulate and could potentially be presented for redemption against the issuer. Here, ownership and possession of debtor property are transferred in one step to the creditor.

In relation to the question of what loss has to be compensated by interest, it can already be noted at this point that neither possession nor ownership are lost for the period of the loan. Rather it is the free disposition *over* property that is lost when the property is burdened or hypothecated, reflected in a loss of ownership premium. The money-creating credit contract accounts for this loss of ownership premium through a particular claim to money: the claim to *interest*. This claim is added over and above the repayment obligation of the sum of borrowed money. Interest as a percentage on the borrowed sum of money is therefore inevitably a *monetary* interest,[32] an interest yielded by money, and never an interest yielded by goods.[33] Moreover, interest does not arise from the sacrifice or the *giving up* of money, i.e., the loss of the liquidity premium on money. On the contrary, interest arises in the creation of money *for* and *issued to* a debtor. The money-creating creditor cannot create this money for himself and, in turn, sacrifice this money like a creditor who on-lends already existing money. Therefore, interest originates in the creation of money and not when already existing money is on-lent.

If a creditor[34] issued notes for himself they would simply be debts, for example represented by a promissory note. In contrast, the issue of notes as part of a credit contract by a net creditor (i.e., a party with positive net worth or capital) implies an independent market valuation of the debtor's loan security, which together with the capital of the issuer ensures an adequate note backing. Moreover, the time limit implied by a loan requires that notes are frequently issued and redeemed, which supports their currency and value. Thus notes issued in a credit contract have special properties distinguishing them from a mere debt.

In the money-creating credit contract not only the creditor but also the debtor loses ownership premium, because for the money the debtor must not only agree to an interest payment but must also hypothecate his property.[35] For the proper understanding of interest it has to be emphasized that the money-creating creditor cannot be compensated for the loss of his ownership premium through the ownership premium of the debtor, because he does not receive full ownership over the debtor property for the period of the loan.[36] If this were the case, the creditor could burden the transferred debtor property for his own purposes.[37] However, this property would have already been hypothecated by the debtor as part of the credit, so that the creditor could not receive any right to hypothecate the debtor's property himself. Hence, the two parties do not exchange full property rights but simply create a security right (hypothec) over the debtor property.[38] As a result, *both* parties lose ownership premium in the money-creating credit contract.

The answer to the core question of economic theory about the nature of the loss that must be compensated by interest is therefore provided as the *loss of ownership premium of the money-creating creditor*.

Interest does not compensate for the temporary loss of goods or consumption, as alleged by neoclassical economics. The creditor continues to use his possession of goods without any hindrance. Therefore, the neoclassical theory cannot be saved by a variant of this theory suggesting that the creditor is entitled to interest because he cannot use the possessory aspect of the hypothecated debtor property during the period of the loan. While the debtor continues with his use, the creditor is perceived to sacifice consumption.[39] This view relates to the institution of *antichresis* (pledge allowing use and occupation) in the monetary economy of ancient Hellenistic Greece. Here the credit contract would indeed specify the right of the creditor to directly use the possessory aspect of the debtor's property, typically the fruits (e.g., seeds and harvest) of farm land. However, the right to the fruits of the land never implied that the creditor gave up interest. Instead, it simply implied the right to set off the creditor's proceeds from the fruits of the land and the interest obligation, which was unaffected by this arrangement.[40] Because the interest to compensate for the creditor's loss of ownership premium was under normal circumstances earned by the debtor out of the productive use of his property anyway, the institution of *antichresis* merely implied that the creditor had a stake in deciding of how the property was used. This was a further protection against negligence on part of the debtor.[41] One could also argue that it must have avoided the need for the debtor to obtain money for his interest payments by selling goods in the market, which would have been subject to price and market liquidity risks.

As has already been shown, interest does not compensate for the loss of liquidity premium on money, which, according to Keynes and monetary Keynesian theory, occurs when money is temporarily given up. In such a loan, money is already presupposed to exist and therefore must have already been created against interest. While the lending of already existing money also transfers the interest payment obligation, this transfer of interest cannot explain interest itself. It can only explain any interest margin charged in this process, which is determined by the ownership premium required by the on-lending party. Moreover, we have shown above[42] with respect to Keynes that, in order to be able to transform liquidity premium into interest, he had to assume the existence of interest-bearing securities. Keynes's theory of interest is based on the postulate of interest-bearing securities, whose origin he does not explain. Therefore, his derivation of interest as the giving up of liquidity premium is in a double sense misleading. It assumes the existence of money, which must have already been created against interest, *and* the existence of interest-bearing securities.

Because Keynes is not aware of the significance of ownership, he also cannot grasp the specific quality of the liquidity premium, the existence of which he at least identified. The potency of money to finally settle money-denominated credit and sales contracts at any time cannot be deduced in a circular fashion from its existence as such. Rather, the fact that creditor's money can create liquidity signifies that intrinsically worthless documents can finally settle contracts and can invoke property transfers only because they imply claims on property themselves (Heinsohn 2005 and 2008a).

The creditor can access the collateral of the debtor not only in the case of an outstanding repayment but also in the case of the non-payment of interest. However, this does not mean that the creditor's demand for the provision of loan security follows from the creditor's demand of interest. A debtor cannot dissuade a creditor from demanding interest by the provision of loan security.

Loan security, serving as collateral in credit contracts, is of course never without risk, and is subject to market valuations and market risk. There is always a ranking of property titles, starting from real estate with the lowest risk, via movable capital goods and tradable debt securities, to contract-based incomes with the highest risk. However, this hierarchy only pays a role in the determination of the *level* of interest rates. The *pure* rate of interest, which is determined by the ownership premium, can be increased by the creditor by adding a *risk*-based premium.

This additional risk premium expresses the fact that a credit contract is never fully underpinned by debtor property. The premium is highest in the case of open (unsecured) credit, where the requirement for loan security is waived.[43]

> Even in this case the business is not conducted without any security, but is backed by the capital of the creditor, who in the case of a breach of contract has to carry the loss or at times becomes liable with his property towards third parties.[44]
>
> (Stadermann and Steiger 2001b, 361)

The finding of ownership economics that the creditor has to give up ownership premium due to the burdening of his capital in every credit contract finds its purest expression in open (unsecured) credit. It makes clear that in an extreme case, the creditor may lose ownership premium, and the creditor has to compensate for the possible loss through a risk premium charged in addition to interest. If the requirement for loan security or property backing is to be given up, this can never occur with respect to the creditor but only with respect to the debtor.

As long as the debtor repays the loan, the risk premium leads to a tangible and increased income at the end of the credit period. The creditor's risk premium is mirrored by the risk premium of the debtor, who compensates for his risk associated with the demanded interest by adding a margin to his expected investment returns. The additional risk of the creditor, which, as Keynes identified (1936, 145), results in a mark-up being added to the interest rate, must not be confused with the ownership premium of the creditor, which, like the ownership premium of the debtor, has nothing to do with this increase in interest. Rather, both ownership premiums show how creditor and debtor assess the risk arising from the burdening and hypothecation of their own property and to what degree this property is already burdened or hypothecated.

The giving up of ownership premium provides the reasons for the creditor's interest demand and the debtor's gain of liquidity premium. Interest and liquidity premium, however, do not lead to the *equalization of risks* in a credit contract. The *credit risk* of the creditor can only be equalized by the taking of security over the property of the debtor. Therefore, even absolutely safe debtor collateral cannot induce a creditor to give up his interest demand. Merely a mark-up may be given up.[45] Conversely, not even the lowest interest rate can induce a debtor to hypothecate his property for credit and take up credit, if there is no certainty that the creditor's notes are backed by the property of the issuer. If notes are not accepted by others, he will be prevented from making the investments necessary to earn the proceeds to repay his loan. At the same time, the creditor can still enforce the security taken over the debtor's property.

Based on Steuart's (1767) discussion of the private note-issuing bank, which issues redeemable bank notes, it can be inferred that the interest-creating ownership premium is lost by both the creditor and the debtor when money notes are created. The non-bank, typically an entrepreneur-debtor, loses ownership premium through the hypothecation of property to the note-issuing bank. At the same time, the note-issuing bank gives up ownership premium through the burdening of its own capital.

The property-owning creditor issues money to earn interest, while the property-owning debtor must hypothecate his property for the money loan and in addition offer to pay interest. The debtor prefers this to issuing his own notes (debtor's money) against his property, which would be interest-free. Why? The answer is that the debtor does not want to be obliged to redeem his own notes. Rather, he wants to profit from the fact that creditor's notes circulate. While he has to hypothecate his property to obtain creditor's money, the possessory aspect of his property remains untouchable and can be used without limitation as long as he fulfills the terms of the loan. Steuart discusses this advantage by using the example of a landlord who is short of coins but wants to consume the commodities offered by a producer and who pays with promissory notes, representing claims over his property matching the value of the commodities. Even this debtor's money, the promissory notes, as long as the operations conclude as planned, does not affect the possession of the land: 'the land ... remained as before, ready to produce anew' (Steuart 1767, vol. I, 365).

The note-issuing creditor has to accept the redeemability of his notes and would lose the possessory aspect of his property if he defaulted on this commitment. Like Keynes, Steuart does not understand what it is that justifies the *interest demand* by the note-issuing bank: the loss of ownership premium due to the burdening of property in the credit-based creation of money. Like Keynes, Steuart encounters money, credit and interest in his observed reality and considers them as extremely useful to society. Like Keynes, he deduces the reasons for interest in a circular fashion by arguing that the economically necessary credit cannot be encouraged without it, and that without interest, money, so useful for everyone, must remain unemployed:

> Forbidding the loan upon interest has the effect of locking up the very instrument which is necessary for supplying the wants of the society. The loan, therefore, upon interest, as society now stands composed, is established not in favour of the lenders but of the whole community.
>
> (Steuart 1767, vol. II, 114)

Notwithstanding this circular explanation of interest, Steuart recognizes that the capital requirements of a money-creating bank, at the time held in form of gold coins, imply a loss that has to be deducted from the – again simply presupposed – interest profit: 'The profits of the bank proceed from the interest paid upon all the securities which have been granted to it ... out of which must be deducted ... the loss of interest for all the coins they preserve in their coffers' (Steuart 1767, vol. II, 151). He does not realize that such a loss is not due to the fact that locked-up coins do not generate interest, but can only result from the burdening of such capital. The loss emerging from the burdening of capital is not to be deducted from the interest proceeds but is the reason why interest must be charged. In Steuart's case, the fact that the economic importance of ownership and the difference between ownership and possession is not in the center of his analysis takes its toll and results in an interest theory based on mere postulates.

At least Steuart is able to identify the advantage arising for the debtor that makes him willing *to pay interest*. It is the ability of creditor's money to circulate effectively that enables the debtor to avoid the risk of having to redeem his own, debtor-issued, money:

> And for what does he [the debtor] pay that interest? Not that he has gratuitously received any value from the bank; because in his obligation [the debt] he has given a full equivalent for the notes, but the obligation carries interest and the notes carry none. Why? Because the one circulates like money, the other does not. For this *advantage, therefore, of circulation*, not for any additional value, does the landed man pay interest.
>
> (Steuart 1767, vol. II, 31; emphasis added)

3.3 Money of account and money proper

The credit contract, through which money notes are created for a debtor as claims against the property assets of the issuer, constitutes *uno actu* a common *and abstract standard of value*. The creditor has no choice but to set this *money of account* standard when he assesses his ownership premium, the loss of which he must express in a rate of interest payable by the debtor. In the central banking literature, this reason for the setting of a common monetary standard by the money creator is not understood. Instead, it is simply assumed that 'the unit of account in a purely fiat system is *defined* in terms of the liabilities of the central bank' (Woodford 2003, 35). The ensuing analysis remains superficial by taking refuge in such factors as the facilitation of economic life:

> The special feature of central banks ... that they are entities whose liabilities happen to be used to define the unit of account in a wide range of contracts ... there is perhaps no deep universal reason why this need be so; it is certainly not essential that there be one such entity per national unit. Nonetheless, the provision of a well managed unit of account – one in terms of which the equilibrium prices of many goods and services are relatively stable – clearly facilitates economic life.
>
> (Woodford 2003, 37)

The moment that the interest rate[46] is set together with the loan principal[47] by the note issuer, the price of the underlying property is set. Fisher's well-known formula to determine the value of an asset $-i = r/R$ – results from exactly this process. Here, i is the interest rate, r the earnings and R the asset value. Assuming constant earnings, changes in the interest rate must inversely change asset values. The valuation of all assets follows this formula.[48] Increases in interest rate reduce asset valuations; decreases increase them. Fisher suspected this in his own way:

> To obtain the value return on the orchard, we must reduce both physical income and capital goods ... to a common standard of value. If the net annual crop of apples is worth $5,000 and the orchard is worth $100,000, the ratio of the former to the latter, or 5 per cent, is a rate of value return.... The important fact, and the one lost sight of in the naive productivity fallacy, is that the value of the orchard is not independent of the value of its crops; and, in this dependence lurks implicitly the rate of interest itself.... It is not because the orchard is worth $100,000, that the annual crop will be worth $5,000, but it is because the annual crop is worth $5,000 net that the orchard will be worth $100,000, *if* the rate of interest is 5 per cent. The $100,000 is the discounted value of the expected income of $5,000 net per annum; and in the process of discounting, a rate of interest of 5 per cent is already implied.... The orchard is the source of the apples; but the value of the apples is the source of the value of the orchard.
>
> (Fisher 1930, 55; emphasis added)

Fisher was unable to draw the conclusion that asset values change with the inverse of the interest rate, assuming unchanged asset earnings. If the interest doubled in his example to 10 percent, the value of the orchard, assuming unchanged earnings of $5,000 for its apples, would be halved ($50,000). Fixated on the value of earnings, the neoclassical theorist missed this.

It is the rate of interest set together with the price of the loan principal that is the source for the determination of the price of the earned goods.[49] The ownership premium as the first valuation step, and the interest rate and loan principal as the 'first price', are established in the money-creating credit contract and nowhere else.[50]

The step from credit contracts to money – and not the other way around – was sensed by Ralph Hawtrey in his statement that '[m]oney must be defined in terms of debts' (Hawtrey 1930, 545). Here, money is understood by Hawtrey as 'money of account' (Hawtrey 1919, 2).[51] Keynes, in a very similar way, sees that a 'money of account comes into existence along with debts'. Moreover, Keynes, by distinguishing between money of account and *money proper*, emphasizes that the former 'is the primary concept of a theory of money' because 'debts ... can only be expressed in terms of a money of account' while the latter 'in the full sense of the term can only exist in relation to money of account' (Keynes 1930, 3).

Based on Keynes's differentiation, it follows that money proper is not a bartered good but a means of payment for the settlement of debts. Moreover, it follows that money of account, as a monetary standard having primacy over money proper, is an *abstract* standard, required to express the ownership premium as a rate of interest. It must not be mistaken for a tangible standard derived from a physical standard *good*. The neoclassical *unit of account or numéraire* measures goods as items of possession,[52] with the aid of a tangible standard good – such as barley or gold – as the unit. In contrast, money of account makes abstract titles of ownership operable, without reference to the associated titles of possession. Neither Hawtrey nor Keynes could see that credit contracts and interest emerge only from ownership titles. As a result, their insightful observations have not been able to overcome the neoclassical dichotomy between (relative) goods prices and (absolute) money prices.

In the neoclassical model of a real barter exchange economy, the standard good receives as the unit of account – not as the money of account – the price of 1 (one). This price serves as a *nominal* anchor for the prices of all other goods. Quantities of goods valued based on utility assessments and exchanged based on their marginal utilities are then measured in the price of the standard good (1). Hence, prices can only be expressed in *numéraire* money. However, with a standard-good anchor, only *relative* prices as ratios of quantities of goods can be determined. The number of barter relations is reduced only by the selection of a standard good.

In contrast, the money-creating creditor in the economy of an ownership-based society does not work with a *goods unit* as nominal price anchor. Instead, he monetizes his property titles. While these always have some aspects that resemble those of goods,[53] the possessory aspect is not activated in the money-creation process. The issuer is not bound by a standard for money based on a selected well-known good. On the contrary, through the credit-based creation of money he *forces* the adoption of all reckoning being in money, i.e., in money of account, and not in goods. Thus, with the estimation of the ownership premium and the associated interest rate calculation the issuer sets the monetary standard. In turn, the monetary standard is used to define in what *monetary units* money proper is issued, credit contracts are written and repayment obligations are entered into.[54]

When a creditor A agrees to provide notes with the value of 100 A-dollars in a money-creating credit contract by burdening 100 square meters of his land,[55] this does not mean that the future redeemer of one A-dollar note issued in the credit contract is entitled to one square meter of A's land. It solely means that he has a claim over A's property for the value of one A-dollar,[56] because the notes represent a claim over the *general* property of the issuer and not a contract for the transfer of a specific area of land on note redemption. The implications on a per-square-meter basis are that the money issuer has to keep the price of his land stable.

It goes without saying that first of all, the measurement in money of account affects the property titles that are burdened in the money-creating credit contract by the issuer himself. In the same process, however, the property hypothecated by the debtor is also measured in this money of account. This signifies that in the case of default, debtor property over the sum of the outstanding repayment and interest payments must be sold as a minimum, with the realized money proceeds falling to the creditor.

The valuation of creditor and debtor property, being a result of the setting of the interest rate, has as its consequence the general market valuation of property.[57] The fact that a note issuer measures the property underlying the note issue in the money of account has, therefore, very important consequences. It means that a note-issuing bank can set the price of the property underlying their discount or repurchase operations (see Heinsohn and Steiger 1996, 265), which influences the prices of all other property assets. The 'causation' (Stadermann 2002, 24) flows from the issued notes, denominated in the selected money of account, to the assets underlying the repurchase or discount operations, which obtain their money prices in this process.[58]

Credit or *financial markets* originate for the reason that from this point on, as a matter of principle, all property, whether offered on a market or not, receives a price in this money of account. Financial markets determine the degree of credit risk implied in the various property titles and set an absolute price or price quotation on this basis. Interest payments and loan repayment are typically serviced by deploying the possessory aspect of assets *qua* production of commodities, of which the associated contracts of sale realize the required money proceeds. From this, it follows that an ownership-based society is characterized by a constant effort to increase the yield of this possessory aspect. The need to strengthen the credit standing, or equivalently to increase the gap between the current net asset position and the threshold value considered as excessive indebtedness, forces property owners into an uninterrupted search for opportunities to increase yields. The results are competition and technical progress (see Section 4.3 for more details.).

As already shown, new Keynesians view credit markets in analogy to goods markets that are characterized by rationing. In contrast, monetary Keynesians view the credit market as the nucleus of economic activity, which dominates and controls goods markets through the liquidity premium and the money sacrifice of 'asset owners' respectively. However, in reality credit contracts are not expressed in terms of a standard good (as in classical and neoclassical economics) that emerges from barter exchanges of goods and exists *ab initio*. Moreover, credit contracts are not determined by an arbitrary standard that is predefined by a monetary authority (as in monetary Keynesianism).[59] Rather, the monetary standard is related to property titles, which must indeed exist to begin with and beyond the sphere of goods. The capacity of these property titles to be able to be burdened and hypothecated, or more precisely the *willingness* to burden or hypothecate these titles, provides the inducement and the limit to economic activity. There is no monetary standard independent of these property titles.

The insight that property titles are required *to begin with* gives the decisive blow to the *real-bills* doctrine of the banking school. This school justifies its rejection of the possibility of an excessive issue of bank notes by invoking the natural limitations imposed by the exclusive discounting of commercial bills. In this view, loan security in the form of commercial bills limits the note issue because commercial bills are based on real, already existing goods. The already-mentioned fallacy of this theory (Section 2.1) is not that it searches for a note-issue limit as such, but that the alleged limitation by real goods cannot resolve the obvious contradiction that this credit creates money for goods that are yet to be produced in the future. Therefore, money creation must be limited by something else. The limit is established by the willingness to burden property as a safeguard against potential redemptions (money-issuing creditor) and the willingness to hypothecate property (credit-receiving debtor). Only such a risky loss of the free disposition over property generates money, which precedes the production of 'goods' and as a consequence cannot be limited by it.

The characteristic feature of property as the only means to back money cannot be derailed by the argument that property assets are subject to fluctuating prices. The reason is that fluctuations cannot lead to a substitution of property for something else. In the money-creation process, these fluctuations are taken into account by issuing money only against property titles with low risk. Accordingly, titles with higher risk are only accepted with a 'haircut' or additional backing provided through other asset reserves of the issuer. The resulting increase in the issuer's own capital signifies that the issuer must increase the surplus of his assets over his liabilities. If money is not backed by low-risk assets then the issuing institution will find itself without assets to withdraw its money from circulation. Its currency will prove itself as insufficiently backed and will be discounted against currencies with better backing.

70   *The economic core of the ownership system*

As shown in Section 3.2, money creation based on credit leads to two separate documents, both denominated in money of account: (1) the interest-bearing document or credit contract, secured by the collateral of the debtor; and (2) the non-interest-bearing document or money proper (money note), which is anchored in the property of the creditor. *Therefore, money is created through credit without becoming credit itself.*

The thesis that money is not credit but is always created through credit is not limited by the fact that money can obviously enter the world by *outright* purchases of property titles by a note-issuing bank. In this case, however, the bank is faced with the problem that titles also have to be regularly sold so that the quantity of the money supply may be controlled. Regular outright sales and purchases, however, resemble the credit-based issue of bank notes, which automatically guarantees the reflux of notes, as in the refinancing operations of commercial banks through sound commercial bills. The latter was, until the mid-1980s, the preferred method of the German Bundesbank. Today, repurchase agreements (also referred to as repos) involving tradable securities are the dominant method. This has the advantage that the price risks associated with the purchased securities stay with the supplying commercial bank. Legally, these transactions are sales and repurchases within a short period[60] and imply a change in ownership. In contrast to secured credit contracts, in which the earnings arising from the securities deposited as loan security remain with the commercial bank debtor, akin to the continued use of the possessory aspect of a real asset, in repurchase agreements earnings must obviously be transferred for a short term to the central bank owner. Nevertheless, the European Central Bank (ECB) regards repurchase agreements as an elegant alternative to secured credit contracts in a monetary union such as the European Monetary Union. The ECB regulations for secured credit transactions take into account the procedures and formalities governing the exercise of security rights and the realization of the loan security in the different national legal systems (European Central Bank 2005, 17).

The mistake of the banking school in equating money with credit is based on a lack of differentiation between the constituting elements of a credit contract and the proper significance of a money note. A credit contract (a claim against the debtor) has to be fulfilled by something different from itself, i.e., by money proper or, in the case of default, by hypothecated property. In contrast, a money note (a claim against a creditor), even though it is created *uno actu* with a credit contract, does not establish a claim against a debtor. That claim is the credit contract itself. The obligation entered into by the issuer does not require a specific contract but nevertheless provides any holder with a valid claim against the creditor.[61]

Hence, money is also not identical with what is incorrectly called 'credit money', with bank deposits or demand deposits as its most visible variants. These are, like credit contracts, simply claims on money, which, however, are payable on demand. In contrast to credit contracts, demand deposits can be used to set off mutual claims. However, demand deposits are not – as commonly believed – a substitute for actual money (money proper). Demand deposits can merely be used to mutually set off claims to money and money obligations with third parties, substituting for the payment in actual money (see Stadermann and Steiger 2001b, 289). In contrast, for the repayment of a loan with actual money, the payer does not require a third party who has incurred an obligation against the payer or with respect to whom the payer has a claim to money.

The interest-bearing document – the credit contract – is a specific title that nominates creditor and debtor. It commits a specified debtor to repay the borrowed sum of money, to pay interest and to hypothecate property to at least the value of the borrowed sum for a specified creditor. In the case of a tradable title – in the form of a bond – the creditor can change while the instrument and the debtor remain unchanged. The bond issuer (debtor) does not have to hypothecate property, but his credit standing and the availability of assets[62] is verified by specialist rating agencies.

The non-interest-bearing document – the money note – implies an anonymous claim to the property of the issuer, to the extent that the issuer is named but the debtor, to whom the money is issued, is not named. The note-issuing bank commits the specified debtor to refund the borrowed sum. However, the bank does not want third parties, who obtained its money notes from the bank's debtor, to redeem the notes, even though they are entitled to do so. The note-issuing bank will therefore do everything it can to keep its notes in circulation, i.e., to secure the *ability* of its notes to *circulate*. Therein, the note-issuing bank has to act similarly to modern commercial banks. These attempt to avoid, through sound business practices, a circumstance in which the right of their depositors to turn their deposits into cash is not exercised by all of the depositors at the same time. Of course, should note-issuing banks or commercial banks suspend the right of redemption, an unavoidable *run* would quickly end their existence.

It is the quality of the property assets that the note-issuing bank burdens for its note issue, together with the quality of the property assets that its debtors provide as collateral, that determines whether the notes will be presented for redemption or not. Every current holder of a money note has the *option* of redemption, but not the obligation. If he exercises the option, he will signal to the creditor that he has doubts about the backing of the money. In contrast, the specified debtor, identified in the first credit contract document, has not an option but an *obligation* to fulfill his liabilities.

While ownership economics uses Keynes's term 'money proper', it in no way identifies itself with Keynes's view that money proper is always *state money*. As shown in Section 2.3.1, the identification of money as state money enticed Keynes to recommend the central-bank financing of public spending programs. This identification is still haunting today's prevailing theories of money, where money is defined as a public debt (for example, Tobin 1963, 415; Friedman 1992, col. 252b; or Richter 1987, 320).

3.4 Money and net wealth

A note-issuing bank that insists on loan security and is furnished with sufficient burdenable property (capital) issues a type of money that ownership economics calls *creditor's money*. On the other hand, if a bank issues notes for a debtor without hypothecating debtor property and without burdening its own property, as is the case when state debts are monetized by a central bank, the issued notes will correspondingly be *debtor's money*. Only creditor's money can control economic activity, because it leads – by triggering production and investment – to the creation of net wealth. Debtor's money – from the perspective of the issuer – is never an asset and is avoided by the public as long as currencies based on creditor's money are obtainable.

In the dominant theory of money – as shown in Section 2.3 – the difference between creditor's money and debtor's money has never been a subject of investigation, nor indeed has the difference been recognized. For example, the standard Keynesian James Tobin (1963, 415) can pronounce without challenge: 'Governments ... can ... create means of payment to finance their own purchases of goods and services'. Tobin has no inkling that his statement makes a case for the money-destroying practice of central-bank-financed state debt, which is of course a prohibited operation for any serious central bank.[63]

By the issue of money notes for a debtor, the issuer burdens his property as the creditor, hence losing the free disposition over his property or his ownership premium, respectively, during the term of the loan. This step signifies that the issuer enters into the commitment – not to be confused with that of his debtor in the money-creating contract – to redeem the notes in property on presentation at any time and by any holder without an additional contract. Whoever issues notes provides a general guarantee that he accepts the enforcement against his property. The issuer's undertaking to burden, to redeem and to accept enforcement are inseparable steps in the creation of money notes.

The existence of two separate documents as part of the money-creation process – credit contract and money note – is not made visible in the balance sheet of the modern note issuer, the central bank. It goes without saying that it classifies bank notes as 'liabilities'. However, this classification does not clarify the central bank's critical obligation, to provide the holder of its notes with property at any time, when the holder, for example a commercial bank, is the counterparty in a note-creating credit contract with the central bank.

This obscurity in the central bank balance sheet has created continuing confusion in the money-theory discussion. In the 1960s it resulted in the formulation of the New View of money, with which, for the first time, John Gurley and Edward Shaw (1960) attempted to disprove the Old View, that money, then understood as 'commodity money',[64] was part of the net wealth of society. Consistent with the representation in the central bank balance sheet, both authors identify money as a liability of the note-issuing bank or as an asset of the commercial banks, respectively, which the commercial banks obtain in a credit operation. From this the authors conclude, by consolidation for the economy as a whole, that the net wealth of money is zero. Against this thesis, Boris Pesek and Thomas Saving (1967, 143) wanted to rehabilitate the Old View: money is not a debt but net wealth: 'bank notes are an item of net wealth leased to the private sector'.

Ownership economics can now show that Pesek and Saving's thesis is correct but incorrectly justified. They consider the credit-based creation of bank notes, which in their view creates a net *nominal* asset[65] analogous to the nominal asset created when a manufacturer leases out a newly produced machine, which increases the net stock of *capital* assets.[66] In their analysis, Pesek and Saving overlook, like the monetary Keynesian, Riese, discussed above, the fact that a note-issuing bank – in contrast to a machine producer – cannot increase *its* net wealth when it creates money.[67] But then, what is the proper significance of the liability of a note-issuing bank? It is not – as already shown – the bank-note document as such that is the bank's liability, but the obligation to surrender its property on presentation to the holder of its notes. In the words of the US Treasury: 'Federal Reserve notes are claims on the assets of the issuing Federal Reserve bank' (US Treasury 2005).[68] Obviously, this statement is only correct if the word 'are' is replaced with 'imply'.

Against this view of a central bank liability, the objection could be made that the money-borrowing commercial bank enters into a liability with respect to the central bank when it adds the freshly created money to its net assets. Doesn't this set the total net wealth back to zero? However, the question posed in this way omits from the balance sheet the commercial bank's assets that it must provide as loan security to the central bank, so that the borrowed money can be created in the first place.

This can be illustrated as follows.[69] In a hypothetical economic system the private sector has one asset, $100 worth of land. Liabilities are zero. The commercial bank and central bank each have $10 of assets (again assumed to be land) but no liabilities, i.e., the total bank capital is $20. The net wealth of this system is $120. The private sector, commercial bank and central bank now enter into a money-creating credit contract. The commercial bank takes a mortgage over the land and creates $100 in bank deposits. It now has a loan asset of $100 (debt to the private sector) and $100 in deposit liabilities. Simultaneously, it enters into a credit contract with the central bank using the title over the debt with the private counterparty (secured by mortgage) as central bank collateral. The central bank creates $100 in notes and now has a loan asset of $100 (debt of the commercial bank) and $100 in note liabilities. The commercial bank has an additional $100 in liabilities reflecting the central bank loan, and a matching asset of $100 in central bank notes. In addition it holds the loan to the private sector (mortgaged land) as an asset, together with matching bank deposit liabilities. The private sector withdraws $100 in central bank notes, reducing bank deposit assets (private sector) and liabilities (commercial bank) to zero. The private sector now holds $100 in central bank notes. The net wealth of the system is unchanged at $120. Both banks have matching loan assets and liabilities that consolidate to zero and a capital of $10 each. However, $100 worth of land and $20 of bank capital were required to create $100 of central bank notes.

74 *The economic core of the ownership system*

Therefore, money is indeed additional wealth because it activates property, which is collateralized and even put at risk, but is not reduced.[70]

Unlike the money notes created in the above process, the net wealth is not eliminated through the repayment of the money credit to the note-issuing bank. In order to be able to repay the loan, the debtor commercial bank must enter into a contract with another debtor. Disregarding financial transactions, this debtor must be an entrepreneur-producer, who, for example, manufactures a machine that is used to extend his capital assets, and can be sold or leased. In any case, net wealth is added to the economy as a whole.

Stadermann (1992, 188–189) has also argued against the view that the 'monetary wealth'[71] for the economy as a whole is zero because it

> provides only a cursory treatment ... of those financial assets that underlie money creation.[72] ... The dominant theory [has] added the total sum of [financial] assets and liabilities to zero ... and has assumed *per saldo* a non-existing monetary net wealth.[73] ... This move is as amusing as if one asserted that the net wealth associated with goods and resources in a society was zero because the quantity of purchases in goods and resources markets must equal the quantity of sales.[74]

According to Stadermann, only the right way of balancing, i.e., the subtraction of liabilities resulting from money creation from the total value of tangible assets that could be eligible central bank collateral,[75] will result in a positive monetary net wealth: 'The remaining wealth is represented by claims, denominated in money, held by property owners against the economic assets of households and entrepreneurs that can be used to further extend the money issue'.[76] This is correct. However, the important point is not to find the indisputably correct way of balancing national accounts but the insight that, while property is burdened to the level of liabilities, it is precisely not reduced. The backing of money, for example, in the form of a mortgage over land results in a title over a nominal asset.[77] Hence, the adding up of all financial assets and liabilities to zero severs the link between money and property and makes the origin of money out of property assets incomprehensible.[78]

3.5 Money creation by the private note-issuing bank

As a matter of principle, every property owner can, as a creditor, issue claims against his property for a debtor as money notes. The qualification of the issuer as the owner of property assets, which are able to be burdened or be used to redeem the notes, and as someone who creates money in a contract with a debtor, whereby the debtor must hypothecate property assets, ensures by itself that not just anyone can create money. Creditor's money can therefore never be 'anyone's money'.[79]

It has been shown already from the first historical stage of the monetary economy – ancient Mesopotamia – that private property owners – not yet acting as bankers – began to create money-like instruments in collateralized credit contracts with interest:

> Credit in its legal form, loan security and interest could not have been practiced first by the [state] temples. *Private contracts are much older than sacred contracts.* We believe that *private individuals, merchants or property owners* were the ones who invented the credit contract ... the temples ... imitated the private capitalists.
>
> (Boegart 1966, 66; emphasis added)[80]

The private origin of money is also suggested by evidence from colonial economies. For example, in the remote colony of New South Wales money first appeared in the form of small merchant notes.[81]

In the next step, arising from the competition between money-creating creditors, partnerships of the strongest property owners developed into the first *credit* banks and at the same time *uno actu* into *money-issuing* banks. We will see – two-and-a-half millennia after Mesopotamia – that in 1833, when the notes of the Bank of England received *legal tender* status, the outstanding acceptability of this money could only be achieved because the bank could raise, through the privilege of incorporation as a limited liability company, a significantly larger total capital than the so-called *country banks*, which could have only a maximum of six fully liable partners (Hawtrey 1932, 131).

During the English financial crisis of 1793, these small note-issuing country banks experienced the rejection of their notes even by their own customers, who requested Bank of England notes instead. Henry Thornton (1802, 188) identified the lack of sufficient capital as the reason for the destruction of these banks in the crisis. He therefore demanded that the 'country bankers should be taught ... to provide themselves with a larger quantity of that *property* which is quickly convertible in Bank of England notes' (emphasis added).

It is plausible that ancient credit banks issued 'notes', which were documented on diverse materials (metal rings or plates, miniature axes and sickles etc., representing the ownership of pastures and grain fields) and were redeemable in their property.[82] The historical research emphasizes that in no way were goods made exchangeable through money. On the contrary, 'money [coinage] did provide a mode of translating immovable assets into reckoning assets' (Starr 1982, 431). For Mesopotamia it has been observed: 'The silver is like the field' (Skaist 1994, 130). Hence, money was equated with landed property and not with the fruits of the land, such as the grains produced from the soil, i.e., not with its possessory aspect.[83]

The barley credit secured with the debtor's land, encountered in the early beginnings of economic activity, as sketched out in Section 3.2, was in the next step extended to include the note of the creditor, which was backed by the land he owned. In this credit, the debtor no longer received natural barley for the equally natural repayment of which he was liable with his land. Now he received notes, for the repayment of which he again was liable with his land. For these notes, however, third parties would sell him just the amount of barley required as seed or animal feed. Notes were accepted because they were backed by the property of the issuer, in whose assets – taking the form of ownership titles over barley fields – third parties could, if in doubt, redeem the notes.

The need to accumulate barley stocks in the granaries of former feudal lords, with the associated losses due to rot and pests, was encountered by the ownership-based society only in its beginnings. Soon, storage costs of natural produce became the problem of specialized merchants that sold cereals as commodities. What has remained are the weights and measures for barley as the names of the first currencies, which as lira, peso or pound have to some extent persisted to this day, and have always remained as weight units close to the 504 grams of the Babylonian mina.

However, mere notes only enjoyed limited acceptability among non-members of the legal system of *polis* or *civitas*. Citizens from other state territories were often not allowed to acquire property in the note-issuing republic. For this reason, they effectively could not redeem the money against the property of these states and therefore would potentially not benefit from the sound property backing. For example, among the Greek city-states, Corinthians could not easily acquire property in Athens. They wanted unconditional certainty about their access to the collateral. This was only achieved by amalgamating the 'notes' and the backing property, as found in *private* coins made from precious metal property; for example, in Mesopotamia as Shamash heads (Silver 1992, 22–23 and Silver 1995, 163–164). The coin, a coined 'money note', made the collateral directly available.[84]

Interest remains unaffected by the difference between a mere note and a precious metal coin. This is because interest originates from property and not from money. Whether one has lost the free disposition (to sell, to burden again, etc.) over a barley field for 12 months because it backs notes, or whether one cannot access the gold property contained in the coins for 12 months, does not make a difference in principle. The issuer loses in both cases the freedom over his property, therefore ownership premium, and demands interest for this loss. However, the limitations of precious metal coinage are immediately apparent: the possessory aspect of the metal property cannot be used during the term of the loan.[85]

The precious metal property circulating in the form of coined notes is immediately exposed to loss by use, clipping and adulteration, etc. This creates acceptance problems. Moreover, a currency based on coins threatens the economic process, when due to a shortage of precious metal only an insufficient number of coins can be made available to debtors with capacity to hypothecate their property. The circulation of money thus collapses unexpectedly. When already indebted enterprises successfully produce commodities and find demand for their products, but coinable metal no longer enters the circulation in sufficient quantity, the way is paved for the state-issued coin.[86]

How can this step be imagined? The state withdraws all precious metal and turns it into what are now state coins with lower precious metal content or the same content but higher denomination. Debtors with a repayment burden over a nominal amount of 100 and coins denominated as 50, hand in the coins, receive 100 in form of state coins, and repay their loans. The creditors are the losers, because they receive less metal than they lent out. However, at least their claims are fulfilled to their nominal amount. The Greeks called Solon, who has been attributed with taking the first step in the creation of a state monopoly for coins, a wise man for a good reason. This step not only enables the fulfillment of credit contracts, but also keeps the economy going, in which the damaged creditors have every interest. The historical evidence locates the first step to state coinage in Greece: 'Coins were probably created by *private individuals* for economic purposes, however pictures like the Lyd. [Lydian] lion and the bee of Ephesus etc. show that the issue soon became the responsibility of the state' (Chantraine 1979, col. 1448; emphasis added).[87]

Incidentally, the state monopoly over coinage also ensured that the 'theft' of collateral through clipping and adulteration is more forcefully addressed, namely with the death sentence. However, the state could now commit theft of collateral itself. Herewith, the path from creditor's money to debtor's money is paved. As soon as the state coin had come into existence, attempts were made in the ancient city-states of Greece to pay for increasing public debts with debased coins; and in this way also to force private individuals, who were no longer allowed to mint coins, to accept these. In order to limit its losses, the public held back the higher-value coins or sold these as bullion in order to obtain a higher nominal amount than the newly enforced denominations.

It was only in early modern times that the property-defending concerns of credit providers found a method to escape the state-induced deterioration of money. The Bank of Amsterdam, founded in 1609, became the most famous in this context (Bagehot 1873, 79–82; Stadermann 1994a, 45–54). In the Dutch capital, foreign merchants offering commodities received bills of exchange from domestic merchants that were meant to be redeemed by the banks of Amsterdam in full value coins. However, if these banks had gone to the Dutch drawers of these bills on the due date, they would have received coins to the required nominal amount, but with a lesser weight, resulting in a loss. This problem was solved by the Bank of Amsterdam by creating a deposit account for the drawers of bills corresponding to the real value of the precious metal content of the supplied coins, and not according to their nominal denominations. In addition, the Bank charged costs for melting down and other management expenses.[88] From now on, a Dutch merchant could only pay with a bill of exchange if he maintained a deposit with the Bank of Amsterdam. These deposits were called 'bank money'. Claims and obligations could now be simply settled by a set-off between deposit holders. Hence, sellers and buyers could enter into contracts of sale without the risk of losing precious metal property in the process.

If – in passing – one wants to understand why tiny Holland (together with Zealand) from 1590 to 1740, with half of all oceangoing vessels, dominated world trade and consequently needed banks like the one of Amsterdam, one needs to look at its '[n]ew ways of financing ship building and ownership'

(Israel 1989, 21). While in the old north European trade centers of Lübeck and Antwerp a maximum of three to four owners partnered in an enterprise, Holland invented small share holdings. Through small holdings a much higher percentage of the national volume of available property was deployed in economic activity than anywhere else in the world. 'Ownership not just of sixteenth and thirty-second, but also of sixty-fourth shares became commonplace.... Typically, the owner of Dutch fluyts were timber dealers, shipbuilders, sailmakers, brewers, millers, and so forth' (Israel 1989, 21).

Holland compensated for its relatively small population and land area by enabling even small tradespeople and farmers, who would have been excluded from participating in large enterprises elsewhere, to risk their small property positions. Because the feudal ties to the Spanish-Habsburg Empire were successfully severed and patrician privileges, such as those enjoyed by the senator families of Lübeck or Danzig, had never been established, small property holders could transform Holland into a nation of entrepreneurs. Its farmers, endowed with small property holdings, entered into the production of butter and cheese for export markets in direct competition with large-scale feudal landholders, who skinned their serfs in cereal and timber production and otherwise cooperated with patrician trade dynasties in Hanseatic or Mediterranean city republics. Although Amsterdam ascended to become the richest of all cities, it achieved this position not through a dominion of the surroundings areas, but indeed because it had to compete with these areas on a permanent basis. Correspondingly, Holland lost its position when it withdrew from a production model based on small property holdings and made itself comfortable in its role as 'Europe's "trade emporium par excellence"' (Israel 1989, 400).[89] This fragile position was easily destroyed by Napoleon's continental blockade.

In turn, England rose to greatness not by effectively conquering the Dutch position of ruler of the seas, but due to its widely dispersed property-owner-based production. The latter created innovations in production and manufacturing processes that were demanded everywhere and brought the, until that time relatively backward, island into a top position (for more details see Section 4.3 below).

But back to the monetary use of precious metals. For lawmakers and bankers, but also for monetary theorists, for example, the great neoclassical economists Léon Walras and Knut Wicksell (Stadermann and Steiger 2001b, 246 and 268), the use of valuable commodities for the coining of money 'notes' remained bewildering for a long time. The very late recognition of bank notes as legal tender, for example 1833 in England and as late as 1910 in the German empire, contributed to this confusion. This holds even more for the statement printed on dollar notes prior to the abolition of the redemption in gold in 1973. Until that time US-Fed notes carried the statement *legal tender*, which was to be redeemable in *lawful money*.

The still commonly accepted notion of commodity money as a type of money that is fundamentally different from an intrinsically worthless paper money (for example, Friedman 1992, col. 251b and 262a) finds its origin in this obscure contrasting of *legal* and *lawful*. The belief that, prior to the abolition of the gold standard, only gold and other precious metals were real money, while bank notes merely represented money because they could be redeemed in a 'money commodity', has been held to this day (Richter 1987, 319). In reality, gold simply provides a *variant* of property. Hence, money can be issued without gold but never without property. Modern central banks that in the meantime have completely dispensed with the use of gold, for example, the Australian and increasingly the Swiss, have to use other assets in the place of gold. The principle remains that money must only be issued against burdened property assets.

In antiquity, as well as in early modern times, it is the credit bank – and not the deposit bank – that evolved into the note-issuing bank. Nevertheless, the popular view still persists that goldsmiths had invented paper money in early modern times. These had issued deposit receipts for deposited gold, which circulated like well-secured bank notes (for example, Dowd 2000, 144). In this view the note-issuing bank emerged from the deposit bank. In reality, this belief obscures the fact that money[90] can only be deposited in a bank after it has been created in a credit contract. The deposit bank is therefore an offspring of the note-issuing credit bank. The 'deposit view' of banking also overlooks the fact that bank deposits are mainly created by loans and not by the deposit of specie. There is evidence that even goldsmiths notes were issued as part of the loan and discount business (see Wee 1977, 351).[91]

It became an important concern for Walter Bagehot in his seminal book *Lombard Street* (1873) to make this sequence of bank development[92] clear and free of any ambiguity and to explain why in his time only England had a money market worth mentioning. Bagehot is the only monetary theorist of the nineteenth century who understands that bank notes are created in credit contracts[93] and not just provided against interest because debtors require 'property they wish to pledge' (Bagehot 1873, 89). Money created in this way neither demands to be redeemed nor hoarded. The public begins to trust the note issuer so much that it deposits the issuer's notes as demand deposits against interest rather than redeeming the notes:

> The way in which the issue of notes by a banker prepares the way for the deposit of money with him is very plain. When a private person begins to possess a great heap of bank-notes, it will soon strike him that he is trusting the banker very much, and that in return he is getting nothing.... The credit of the banker having been efficiently advertised by the note, and accepted by the public, he lives on the credit so gained.
>
> (Bagehot 1873, 87)

Long before Bagehot, Steuart (1767) knew that the first note-issuing banks in early modern times were created as associations of strong property owners. These united the roles of creditor *and* debtor. The money (bank notes) was initially only made available to partners of this owner-based bank:

80   *The economic core of the ownership system*

> A number of men of property join together in a contract of banking.... For this purpose, they form a stock which may consist indifferently of any species of property. This fund is engaged to all the creditors of the company, as a security for the notes they propose to issue. So soon as confidence is established with the public, they grant credits, or cash accompts, upon good security [also to the public].
>
> (Steuart 1767, vol. II, 150)

The credibility of a note-issuing bank is based on the property position of its partners, i.e., its creditors, whose redeemable capital was at Steuart's time gold property in the form of specie:

> In proportion to the notes issued in consequence of those credits, they [the banks of issue] provide a sum of coin, such as they judge to be sufficient to answer such notes as shall return upon them for payment. Nothing but experience can enable them to determine the proportion between the coin to be kept in their coffers [own capital], and the paper in circulation.
>
> (Steuart 1767, vol. II, 150)

For the private note-issuing bank the liability of its partners with their own capital and the right of redemption enjoyed by the note holders are indispensible. The notes are only creditor's money as long as suitable property can be enforced against if required. Of course, the note-issuing bank can indemnify itself against losses from the loan security of its debtors. Third parties, however, will only accept the notes, if they do not have to proceed against the debtors themselves, for whose benefits the notes were created. In Section 3.6 below it will be shown that in a two-tier banking system, with a central note-issuing bank and commercial banks, the liability of a note issuer is partly transferred from the note-issuing central bank to the commercial bank because central bank notes also receive backing from the capital of commercial banks. The latter have to compensate any loan losses (associated with their money-creating central bank loans) out of their own capital before the central bank's capital is utilized.[94]

The *soundness of a note-issuing bank*, which is underpinned by its capital, is extended by the credit standing of its debtors, who are not shareholders, i.e., the public. The evolution of the note-issuing bank from an association of owners to a fully developed note-issuing bank was elaborated by Steuart:

> When paper is issued for no value received the security of such paper stands alone upon the original capital of the bank, whereas when it is issued for value received that value is a security on which it immediately stands, and the bank stock is, properly speaking, only subsidiary.
>
> (Steuart 1767, vol. II, 151)

It is the hypothecated property of the public, which has received bank notes *qua* credit, that secures this credit, as a supplement to the own capital of the note issuer, and in this way enhances the notes' acceptability with the public and secures the circulation of the notes. In the case of debtor default, notes remain in circulation. If the assets taken as loan security are not of the best quality, the note-issuing bank will need to service requests to redeem these notes out of its own capital. This can lead to the insolvency of a note-issuing bank. The bank cannot free itself from this exigency by creating bank notes for itself out-of-nothing. Such debtor's money would merely trigger further note redemptions and eliminate the issuing bank's capital. Again it is Steuart who recognizes this point clearly and rebuts the notion (still popular, for example Riese 2000b, §39, col. 493b) that a note-issuing bank can never become illiquid with respect to its own money. Steuart understands that a note-issuing bank is always liable for its notes with its property – its own capital in the broadest sense including profits:

> I have dwelt the longer upon this circumstance, because many, who are unacquainted with the nature of banks, have a difficulty to comprehend how they should ever be at a loss for money, as they have a mint of their own, which requires nothing but paper and ink to create millions. But if they consider the principles of banking, they will find that every note issued for value consumed, in place of value received and preserved, is neither more or less, than a partial spending either of their [own] capital, or profits on the bank.
> (Steuart 1767, vol. II, 151)

Why did the era of private note-issuing banks[95] come to an end? Banks did not act alone, and while in competition, had to act interdependently of each other. It was the *system* of private note-issuing banks that could be brought down by an individual member, and in the end it was brought down. The research has neglected this topic because it believes that poorly secured note issues of individual banks were punished through a discount of their notes, which made these banks act more carefully. Discounts did certainly exist, but they could not prevent – as is already shown by the frequent banking crises of the eighteenth century – a careless issue of notes becoming a problem for other banks and therefore for the banking system as a whole:

> In those days banks were banks of issue, and ... there was a continuous presentation to each bank of those of its notes which the others received in the course of business. The clearing of notes like the clearing of cheques gave rise to liabilities between bank and bank.
> (Hawtrey 1932, 132)

In 1773 the note-issuing banks of England created the institution of a *clearing house* to avoid complicated and uncertainty-creating settlement procedures wherein every bank was forced to exchange notes with every other bank. Through the delivery of notes from other banks to the *clearing house* it becomes quickly obvious which bank – we name this bank 'D' – had created more notes for potentially bad debtors than others in its credit operations.

Before the establishment of a clearing house, the banks A, B and C present bank D with its notes for redemption. Assume bank D does not have sufficient gold property or notes of banks A, B and C to fulfill their demands. Because this information does not remain secret, a *run* on bank D by non-bank deposit holders of bank D begins. At the same time it becomes obvious that banks A, B and C sit on notes of bank D, which are no longer redeemable. Like bank D, these banks are at risk of becoming insolvent. They have to curtail their lending, and hence they create the impression in the eyes of their deposit holders that they can no longer fulfill depositors' requests for note or deposit redemptions. Banks A, B and C now equally experience a *run* by their depositors. The whole banking system is at the brink of collapse.

In order to avoid such liquidity crises, clearing houses – also in the US since the 1857 financial crisis – took two measures: (1) they declared a suspension from the obligation to redeem notes for all banks; and (2) they created so-called *clearing house loan certificates* for banks A, B and C, which were accepted in business transactions like cash (Gorton 1997, col. 99a–b).[96] With these certificates (akin to notes), banks A, B and C can pay out their depositors so that a general run is avoided or stopped at the last minute.

These newly created *clearing house* liabilities nevertheless do not appear out of nothing, but are only created against loan security delivered by banks A, B and C. Therefore, the *clearing house* functions like the LOLR authority of a modern central bank. Unavoidably, at the same time the *clearing house* develops into a bank supervisor, who keeps banks of the D-type under observation. In the United States, this system still operated until the creation of the Fed in 1913. *Clearing house loan certificates*, created by banks in their own interest, lacked any statutory backing. Politicians in support of the Fed legislation consequently argued that the 'bill, for the most part, is merely putting into legal shape that which hitherto has been illegally done' (Timberlake Jr. 1984, 140).

The Bank of England exercised the LOLR function in 1797 for the first time. This occurred as part of the suspension of the requirement to redeem Bank of England notes in gold following specie outflows during the Napoleonic wars. It could fulfill this function due to its outstanding property position. It was, as already mentioned, the only note-issuing bank that held the privilege of incorporation as a joint stock bank and could have an unlimited number of shareholders, while other note-issuing banks were limited to the assets of their six partners.[97]

The Bank of England, founded in 1694, received this privilege in 1708 because it was created from the beginning to finance the debts of a particularly large debtor, the English government. Because of this set of special circumstances, English clearing houses were always able to utilize Bank of England notes, instead of their own loan certificates, to maintain the liquidity of numerous *country banks*.

For the Bank of England, Walter Bagehot therefore creates the term 'central bank' (Bagehot 1873, 88). Unlike the monetary theory literature of today, in no way does he view the central bank as a *monetary authority*. He conceives of a central note-issuing bank, the rationale of which is determined by the fact, that, in contrast to the competing private note-issuing banks, it can operate as the LOLR. Its essence, contrary to today's prevailing theory, is neither that the bank has the monopoly of note issue nor that it is owned by the state. During the time of the Reichsbank in Germany, private note-issuing banks continued to exist; and to this day numerous central banks remain joint stock companies – like the Swiss national bank – or even alliances of private banks. The Hong Kong dollar is issued by no less than three private commercial banks, which jointly employ part of their property to equip a LOLR (Jao 1992).

3.6 Money creation by the central note-issuing bank

In today's two-tier banking system, comprising a central note-issuing bank and commercial banks in their role as credit banks, the latter – unlike in Steuart's era with a one-tier system of private note-issuing banks with redeemable notes – can no longer create money, for which their debtors hypothecate property, by themselves.

How does fresh money come about in this system? For this, a commercial bank must approach the central bank. The latter is a bank – and not a monetary authority – and requires, like every other economic agent in an ownership-based society, capital. In this money-creating encounter – the same holds for the private note-issuing bank – both documents mentioned in Section 3.2 come into play. The central note-issuing bank lends (1) central bank notes, in the first instance secured by its own capital, to the commercial bank. At the same time it drafts (2) a credit contract, which is primarily secured by tradable debt securities held by the commercial bank, which represent claims against third-party property, sold to the commercial bank by private and government debtors.[98] The credit contract again specifies the repayment, interest, loan security and term of the loan. The difference from the system of private note-issuing banks is merely that the money-creating contract is not between a note-issuing bank as the creditor and a non-bank debtor, but between a central note-issuing bank and a commercial bank; whereby the non-bank with its loan security is only indirectly involved. In contrast to a private note-issuing bank, which is a creditor as note-issuing bank *and* commercial bank, the commercial bank now takes on the role of a debtor with respect to the central note-issuing bank. It remains a creditor, as a credit bank, only with respect to non-banks and other commercial banks.

What loan security is provided by the debtor commercial bank to the central note-issuing bank? In a system of private note-issuing banks, non-bank debtors provide the loan security required for the note issue. Now, loan security directly based on the property of commercial banks is not accepted for the note issue. Instead their claims on non-banks are the basis of the central bank note issue, for which the commercial bank becomes liable with its own capital.

Nevertheless, the contracts between commercial banks and their hypothecated non-bank debtors are not assigned or otherwise transferred to the central bank.[99] In the case of default, it is not the non-bank debtor of the commercial bank that is liable with respect to the central note-issuing bank, but the commercial bank itself. Claims are not transferred. Thus a central note-issuing bank does not have to chase the loan security of defaulting commercial bank debtors, unlike a private note-issuing bank that is a credit bank for non-banks at the same time. The central note-issuing bank recoups losses from the commercial banks as the creditors of non-banks, so that its own capital remains the last line of defense.

In order not to put its creditor's money at risk via the commercial banks, the central note-issuing bank typically only accepts titles from commercial banks that can be traded in markets without any problems, i.e., tradable securities.[100] Commercial banks must consequently transform direct claims against the property of their debtors into *new securities or debt titles*. These must be fully *liquid* titles that third parties are ready to buy at any time. An example are covered bonds (Pfandbriefe) that are issued by a mortgage bank and purchased by a commercial bank, representing an asset for the latter. Commercial banks remain directly liable with their property for the amount of their credit with respect to the central bank, and not just with the property of the mortgage bank. Of course, the liability of the securities issuer with respect to the holder (commercial bank) is maintained, but this is of no concern to the central bank.

Debt securities issued by a commercial bank against its own property, for example bank-issued bills, are not eligible collateral for central bank loans. The same holds for debt titles issued by companies that are closely related to the commercial bank.[101] In contrast, if these titles are purchased by another commercial bank, and therefore prove their tradability, they become eligible security for central bank loans for this bank. This is because they now represent, from the perspective of the acquiring commercial bank, a claim against an unrelated third party.

Accordingly, a central note-issuing bank does not create money against mere liabilities, nor against direct liabilities of commercial banks or liabilities of enterprises where the central bank holds a stake, but only against claims owned by a commercial bank against other un-related third parties. This distinction may appear confusing, as every title representing a claim (demand/asset) is at the same time a debt title (obligation/liability). As already shown in the discussion of Keynes in Section 2.3.1, a *debt* only turns into an *asset* when it does not remain with the issuing debtor but is acquired by someone else, i.e., assessed as sound enough to be added to the assets of an acquirer.[102] This buyer and new owner is then the creditor of the title that the debtor has issued.[103]

Central bank notes have a higher degree of backing – threefold, as we will soon see – than the notes of private banks with their mere double backing. Behind the notes of a private note-issuing bank[104] stands primarily its own capital and in addition the hypothecated property of its debtors, which secures the money-creating credit. The main stronghold behind the notes of the central bank is its own capital. However, it will only resort to its own capital if the capital of the defaulting commercial bank has proven to be insufficient. Moreover, in order to ensure that its counterparties are not defenseless against attacks, the central bank ensures that the titles submitted as loan security by commercial banks are underpinned by the property of non-banks, i.e., the commercial banks' debtors.

When a commercial bank knocks at the doors of a central bank, the notes to be issued by the central bank are for all intents and purposes already secured by the property of the commercial bank and the property of its debtors. The commercial bank is in the position of a creditor with respect to its non-bank debtor but an interest-paying debtor with respect to the central bank. The commercial bank loses ownership premium, because it needs to hypothecate[105] property. This premium, however, is not gained by its creditor, the central bank. The ownership premium of the commercial bank is lost. For this loss, the commercial bank receives central bank money as liquidity to be on-lent to earn interest from its non-bank debtors.[106] Like its non-bank debtor, the commercial bank retains any possessory rights over the hypothecated property. Thus, the commercial bank does not forego any material good that could be saved or consumed. The same holds for its non-bank debtor.

Where is the last line of defense for the central bank itself, and why can this defense not be supplied by the commercial banks or their non-bank debtors? The answer is that the central bank is subject to the same banking principles in relation to its note issue as any private note-issuing bank. This means that a central bank must back its notes in the first instance with its own capital and only in the second instance with the titles obtained as loan security in the note-creating credit from the commercial banks. The responsibility to back its notes with capital cannot be taken over by anyone else. Hence, the central note-issuing bank must have property that can be burdened as part of the note issue, thereby losing ownership premium. It is precisely this loss that the commercial bank must compensate for with interest. At the same time, the possessory aspect of the central bank property is unaffected, as is the possessory aspect of the hypothecated commercial bank property and that of the non-bank. In the money-creation process, central bank, commercial bank and non-bank continue to use the possessory aspect of their property.

The requirement for capital also limits the capacity of the central bank to create money. This[107] was demonstrated in the 2008 global financial crisis, when the Federal Reserve Bank of New York had to be furnished with an additional capital of $20 billion from the US Treasury when it set up the $200 billion Term Asset-Backed Securities Loan Facility (TALF), a vehicle created to provide loans secured by auto loans, student loans, credit card loans, small business loans and commercial mortgage-backed securities during the crisis.

However, even a central bank well endowed with capital cannot force its counterparties to become debtors and thereby deploy its capital fully. Accordingly, it can *never* determine the quantity of money *exogenously*. The *willingness* of commercial bank counterparties to *hypothecate property*, i.e., their supply of securities eligible as central bank collateral, and not the interest rate of the note-issuing bank, provides the crucial limit to money creation. The central bank interest rate, however, ensures that the sum of owed money is always greater than the sum of created money. As a consequence, for debtors in their aggregate, money is automatically scarce. The additional money needed for the service of interest payments can be created based on (1) newly produced

86 *The economic core of the ownership system*

property; (2) existing property freed up following the fulfillment of credit contracts; or (3) existing property not yet activated.[108]

Nonetheless, the quantity of money is *not set totally endogenously* either, as post-Keynesianism believes (Moore 1988, 112). The central bank is not obliged to fulfill all credit requests, even for first-class debtors. It has in this way a limited degree of freedom to decide over the volume of money that it wants to bring into circulation. It cannot issue more money than commercial banks demand, but it can offer less money than they desire (Steiger 2006b). The freedom to determine the interest rate is only available when the note-issuing bank as a central bank exercises the monopoly of money creation, i.e., it does not have to compete with other private note-issuing banks. Of course, the freedom of the monopoly central bank to determine the interest rate is not absolute. In competition with the notes of central banks of other currency areas it is at times forced to respond to their interest rate decisions.

The commercial banks as debtors for the newly created central bank money – central bank notes as well as central bank deposits[109] – pay interest and gain the potency of money, its liquidity premium. For ownership economics, as shown in Sections 2.3.1 and 3.2, this premium does not reside in money as such. Rather, the liquidity premium is linked to the nature of the money document as a claim against the property of its creator and *only for this reason* has the potency to transfer or redeem property in sales and credit contracts.

Hence money can only give rise to a liquidity premium because it is backed by property itself.[110] It should be noted that the distinction made between ownership premium and liquidity premium may suggest that both premiums have to be compensated for separately. However, this is not the case. When already existing money is subject to a loan, both ownership premium and liquidity premium are given up by the creditor. The payment of interest occurs because ownership premium (here embodied in the lent money itself – a property asset) is given up. This loss is compensated by interest. The interest-paying debtor receives money and has paid for all attributes of money including its liquidity premium. Therefore, compensating for the loss of liquidity premium by a separate money payment would lead to double-counting.

A similar situation is found for the original money-creating credit contract.[111] Here the creditor only loses ownership premium and not liquidity premium, because money (together with its liquidity premium) only materializes in the hands of the debtor. Again, interest is paid by the debtor for the loss of ownership premium suffered by the creditor and not for a loss of liquidity premium. In fact liquidity premium is lost by neither party but instead gained by the debtor.

The potency of money enables the commercial bank to conduct its typical bank business by deploying the central bank money through credit provision against interest,[112] the rate of which lies above the original money-creation rate. The interest charged by the commercial bank, however, does not originate from a sacrifice of liquidity premium that is inherent in the deployed central bank money, as one could assume in analogy to Keynes or monetary Keynesianism. In fact, the interest associated with the deployment of notes arises, like the interest associated with the original act of money creation, from the sacrifice of ownership premium by the commercial bank creditor.

Its interest is higher not because it requires an interest margin to make a profit, but because the commercial bank can only earn a profit through the burdening of its own capital, which results in a loss of ownership premium. Commercial banks lose ownership premium because they have to deploy bank capital (in addition to the assets used as central bank collateral) to underpin the refinancing operations with the central bank against unforeseen losses; this explains the interest margin over the central bank rate.[113]

It must be reiterated that the central note-issuing bank does not request interest because it sacrifices a 'money asset' (Riese), which it can even create for itself.[114] Rather, it must demand interest because it loses ownership premium as part of the money-creation process. This premium flows – as from commercial bank and non-bank – from its own capital, which it cannot create itself but has to earn or acquire by other means.

Only because the literature conceptualizes the central bank as an authority,[115] the capital of which in this view is of little importance, can the circulation of central bank notes between commercial banks, and commercial banks and the public, create the superficial impression that interest originates from the giving up of already existing money and not from money creation.

What situation shows whether a central bank has followed the banking rules for a creditor's money or not? It is the fall of the prices of central bank assets for which the central bank alone carries the price risk. This relates to assets that the central bank has purchased *outright*, for example, debt securities, foreign currencies and gold. For this price or market risk the central bank has to keep extra reserves, and thus must extend its capital.

The present chairman[116] of the Federal Reserve, Ben Bernanke, expressed the view that 'the balance sheet of the central bank should be of marginal relevance' as central bank losses arising from the large-scale purchase of government debt could be offset by corresponding gains of the debt-issuing Treasury department (remarks by Governor Ben S. Bernanke to the Japan Society of Monetary Economics, Tokyo, Japan, May 31, 2003). This philosophy, of course, is nothing but a view of central bank money as state money and the central bank as a note-issuing government authority.

Consistent with this view[117] are recent attempts by the Fed to lower long-term US interest rates and raise equity prices by large-scale government bonds purchases as part of the Fed's quantitative easing initiatives.[118] While government debt is still purchased in the secondary market, the capital requirements for outright purchases at this scale are not acknowledged. Should losses arise from these initiatives because the Fed is forced to sell government bonds in order to control the money supply (rather than holding the bonds until maturity) or is required to revalue its assets, losses exceeding the Fed's capital could result in technical bankruptcy. As per Bernanke's reasoning, losses on US government bonds could theoretically be offset by US Treasury gains if central bank government bond assets were bought back by the US Treasury and redeemed at face value (above the market price). However, money issued in this way is no longer a creditor's money but a debtor's money, equivalent to central bank notes that are issued directly in order to monetize a government debt. Hence central bank money is allocated by the government and not by the private sector.

Beyond the extension of reserves and capital, a central bank can mitigate price risks by accepting titles submitted by commercial banks through repurchase agreements (a sale and simultaneous repurchase commitment of the submitting commercial bank[119]), as discussed in Section 3.3. Here the risk of a fall in price or a total write-off, as in the case of the discounting of bills of exchange, remains with the commercial bank submitting the securities.[120]

In the case of gold and foreign currency assets, a central bank following sound banking principles should account for these assets *conservatively* at the lower of cost or market price,[121] hence typically at their *purchase cost*, as practiced in the past by the German Bundesbank and to this day by the Fed, and not at *current market prices*, which take price increases into account, as early on in the Eurosystem (see Heinsohn and Steiger 2002b and 2011).

If the price of its assets falls, even a central bank becomes exposed to the risk of insolvency. Because the assets acquired through the note issue have fallen in value, the bank can no longer withdraw its notes with its own assets from circulation. The central bank has suffered a loss that it needs to compensate for out of its own capital or that must be borne by a possible profit. In this case both the ownership and the possessory aspects of the involved property assets are lost. As Steuart recognized, the notion – in particular advocated by Riese – that a central bank can never become insolvent because it can always and without difficulty produce the means to liquidity – the missing notes – itself is misguided. Of course, a central bank can always produce notes; however, it cannot produce the property assets that allow its notes to circulate and that enable it to withdraw the notes from circulation.

The specialist literature has only recently recognized that many central banks – predominantly in developing countries – repeatedly suffered severe losses of a size that required recapitalization by their governments (Stella 1997; Fry 1997):

> For instance in Uruguay in the late 1980s, the central bank's losses were equal to 3% of GDP; in Paraguay the central bank's losses were 4% of GDP in 1995; in Nicaragua losses were a staggering 13.8% of GDP in 1989. By the end of 2000, the central bank of Costa Rica had negative capital equal to 6% of GDP.
>
> (Bindseil *et al.* 2004, 8)

A graphic example for the near insolvency of a central bank was provided by Bank Indonesia during the 1997 Asian crisis. The bank lent 50,000 billion rupiah (at the time seven billion US dollars) to domestic commercial banks to maintain their liquidity against loan security that had become worthless in the crisis. A large proportion of these rupiahs was immediately transferred abroad and converted into US dollars. When several commercial banks failed to make repayments to Bank Indonesia and no more assets could be recovered from these banks, the central bank had insufficient capital to clear the losses from its balance sheet. As a result, its capital became negative, which made the bank 'technically' insolvent. This position was averted by the Indonesian government – as the LOLR, to be discussed below – providing recapitalization funds, i.e., through the transfer of debt titles that were purchased with taxpayer's funds (see Leahy 2000).

Developing countries are not the only examples that reveal the deficiencies of the prevailing central bank theory. Besides monetary Keynesianism (see Section 2.3.3), the idea of the omnipotence and invincibility of central bank money creation also lives on in the much more prominent school of monetarism. For example, Milton Friedman and his longstanding co-author Anna Schwartz maintain the view that a central bank can create money without limit: 'The only institution that had the resources to provide ... loans in a [liquidity] crisis is the central bank, which could create high-powered money without limit, and hence was the lender of last resort' (Schwartz 2002, 450).

How could this school of thought come to such a grave misjudgement? A single look into the standard economics references shows that their authors have never asked themselves why a central bank – like a commercial bank or an enterprise – must have a position for capital (equity)[122] on the liability side of its balance sheet. Often enough its capital is not even mentioned, for example in Bofinger (2001, 41–43) or Blanchard (2003, 76). And where it is mentioned, it is dismissed as a negligible entity, for example in Krugman and Obstfeld (2003, 486); or, as in Mishkin (2000, 214 and 392–394), it is analyzed as only relevant for commercial banks (for more details see Steiger 2006b).

When it becomes clear that economic theorists of such eminence have overlooked the essential point – that a central bank can only create creditor's money when it not only has capital but also burdens this capital in the money-creation process – it is brought home that the entire body of economic theory has not recognized the ownership foundation of economic activity. It is only because the central bank has been misunderstood that it can so bitterly disappoint the unlimited optimism of scholars in relation to its LOLR potency. Every banking crisis quickly shows the limit of central banks because the permissible losses due to its note issue are limited by its own capital: 'While a central bank can extend emergency loans for unlimited amounts, its capacity to absorb losses is limited (up to the size of its capital)' (Schoenmaker 2000, 222; see also Folkerts-Landau and Garbert 1992, 99 for a similar argument). While the central bank has the special functions to enable the liquidity of commercial banks as LOLR, it has to perform this function as a business even when it is a body corporate of the public sector. This was highlighted repeatedly by Charles Goodhart, an important central bank theorist: 'A LOLR [lender of last resort] loan by a CB [central bank] is like any other loan, in that it may be repaid (plus interest) or alternatively will be subject to default and some potential loss', independent of whether the central bank is private or 'becomes explicitly a public sector body' (Goodhart 1999, 233).

Why are LOLR loans particularly risky? In any financial crisis, for example when stock exchanges closed after the 11 September 2001 attacks in New York, a central bank has only a few hours to calm the markets. The time-consuming verification of whether a certain commercial bank is insolvent or illiquid is impossible in such a circumstance. Therefore, loans may be provided not only to merely illiquid but also to already insolvent banks. The resulting possibility of extreme losses has long since led to the recognition of the LOLR function as a myth:

> The ... myth is that it is generally possible to distinguish between illiquidity and insolvency.... So, as a generality, whenever an individual commercial bank approaches the CB for direct bilateral loans (LOLR) ... , the CB must/ should suspect that the failure of the bank to adjust its liquidity on the open market means that there is at least a whiff of suspicion of insolvency. It is not, however, possible for the CB, at least within the relevant timescale, to ascertain whether such suspicions are valid or not; and if valid, what the extent of the solvency problem is.
>
> (Goodhart 1999, 229 and 232)

The principle that a central bank is limited in its capacity to create money by its own capital being burdened in the process continues to operate in a crisis. Therefore, a government interested in avoiding the deepening of the crisis must become the LOLR itself (Steiger 2002).

During the 2008 global financial crisis this was recognized only very late.[123] It was initially misdiagnosed as a liquidity crisis; even large-scale central bank interventions failed to restore confidence. Only once governments announced measures to directly recapitalize insolvent or near-insolvent banks did confidence begin to return. State interventions included the de facto nationalization or part-nationalization of banks and government bank guarantees in most countries. The state became the final LOLR or 'proprietor of last resort' on an unprecedented scale.

In the case of a central bank threatened by insolvency, new capital must come from outside and therefore, as a general rule, from the state: 'The deep pockets do therefore not lie with the central bank as sometimes is suggested, but with the government' (Schoenmaker 2000, 222); 'What stands behind the liabilities of the CB [central bank] is not the capital of the CB but the strength and taxing power of the State' (Goodhart 1999, 234). The government must, of course, deploy the assets of its taxpayers, and even this is not without limit. Moreover, financial markets would assess such state support to the central bank no differently from direct central bank financing of the state, a situation where government debt titles that are no longer sellable in the market are pushed per enactment into the portfolio of the central bank. In either case, the central bank will lose its reputation as an issuer of creditor's money. In the first case the state replaces the loan security, which has become worthless, of central bank debtors that can no longer fulfill their debt obligations; while in the second case the liability of a creditor as part of the money-creation process is dispensed with upfront.

The prevailing central bank theory – as previously mentioned – does not distinguish between creditor's money and debtor's money. The experts of the International Monetary Fund (IMF), who want to control inflation with their support programs, have primarily criticized the high government budget deficits of their clients. However, they have set no conditions for the transformation of the associated note-issuing banks into truly bank-like enterprises. The classic example was provided by Argentina with its Austral Plan – named after the new currency – in December 1983 under President Alfonsin, supported by the IMF. This plan particularly focused on fighting high inflation rates through reversing the budget deficit, which at the time was at five percent of GDP. Brief initial successes did not prevent the failure of the plan, under which inflation reached 400 percent per annum for the first time in 1988, and between March 1989 and March 1990 culminated in a hyperinflation of 20,000 percent (Jonas 2002, 6).

Were budget deficits really the cause of failure for the Austral Plan? In Japan, where since the mid 1990s yearly budget deficits have amounted to eight percent in order to stimulate total demand, and regardless of the fact that the state debt in 2005 reached 170 percent of GDP, there has been no inflation. Rather, the measures have contained the risk of deflation following the share and real estate crisis at the end of the 1980s without violating the rules for creditor's money.

How would it come to inflation? Besides direct financing by a note-issuing bank, this requires a monetization of state debt by a central bank conducted in a way where state debt titles sold to commercial banks are in turn immediately purchased from the market at a fixed price by the central bank. An example is the US during World War II:

> Budgetary ... deficits would indirectly ... lead to inflationary financing. This occurred as a means of war finance during World War II in the United States when the central bank purchased government securities from the market at a fixed ceiling price, thus in effect monetizing the debt; price controls were employed in an effort to suppress the inflation.
> (Axilrod and Wallich 1992, col. 76b)

Also inflationary was the legal obligation of commercial banks in Sweden until 1983 to hold a set proportion of their asset portfolio in government titles. Another opportunity to create inflation is the procedure established for the British Chancellor of the Exchequer where state titles are sold not directly in the open market but through the Bank of England. Because the Bank is not obliged to on-sell the titles, this opens up the opportunity to simply print money. Indeed, after the nationalization of the bank in 1948 this option was exercised and significantly contributed to the deterioration of the British pound (Stadermann and Steiger 2001b, 292).

If one considers – together with the IMF researchers – the financing of the Argentinean budget in more detail, it becomes immediately apparent that before, during and after the Alfonsin government (1983–1989) budget deficits were directly balanced by the central bank: 'During the period 1960–1988, 82.6

percent of consolidated government deficits were financed by central bank advances' (Jonas 2002, 7). However, this abuse is not identified by the IMF as resulting from the issuing of the Austral as debtor's money, as the previous issuing of pesos, but in the continuing budget deficit. The monetization of state debt by the note-issuing bank is down-played as an inappropriate dominance of fiscal policy over monetary policy, or demonized as fiscal abuse. Finally the IMF makes a completely misguided complaint that due to the Austral becoming worthless, any further state financing by the central bank had become impossible:

> No one wanted to hold the currency, which was rapidly losing value. The Argentinean economy was becoming demonetized. But demonetization was undermining the ability of the government to finance budget deficits by printing money.
>
> (Jonas 2002, 7)

Therefore, nothing could prove more helpful for the stability of the global financial system than an agreement between the leading countries (like the G20) to (1) outlaw zero interest, (2) homogenize the quality of securities employed as capital by central banks; and (3) homogenize the quality of collateral required for re-finance operations. This in itself will also contribute to a harmonization of exchange rates that international bodies (like IMF or the World Bank) time and again fail to achieve because these three conditions are not taken into consideration.

It was not the malpractice of the treasurer that led to the devaluation of the Austral but the inability of the central note-issuing bank to conduct its affairs like a bank. This in turn was caused by the fact that Argentinean banks were not able to offer first-class loan security to the note-issuing bank. The IMF only concedes this indirectly by supporting a *currency board* (CBA) in 1991 under the Menem government. Here, a new currency, again named peso, was pegged with a ratio of 1 : 1 to the US dollar (*convertibility plan*). While this can stop the printing of money and inflation, it cannot create a deep domestic capital market enabling an internal capacity to generate loans. Deep capital markets require the anchoring in a reliable property system, which is precisely what Argentina did not achieve, notwithstanding the privatizations carried out under Menem in the 1990s.[124] A property system alone would have established Argentina's economic viability and would have rendered superfluous the enormous foreign debts, which more than doubled from 64.7 billion dollars in 1991, the beginning of the CBA, to 144.8 billion dollars in 2000. Moreover, the lack of ability to create domestic credit, and not the CBA as such, resulted in the collapse of the *convertibility plan* at the end of 2001. To date, the IMF has insufficiently recognized the reasons for its failure in Argentina. The only insights produced have been cautioning remarks against an ongoing abuse of the central bank (Jonas 2002, 40). Instead of imposing conditions that mandate bank-like operations to the central bank, even in mid-2005, as in 1983 or 1991, the IMF merely cautioned: 'Further fiscal consolidation is needed to prevent a budgetary financing gap from arising in the second half of 2005' (International Monetary Fund 2005).

Based on the Argentinean experience, one must not draw the incorrect conclusion that state debt titles as such are a disadvantage for the creation of creditor's money. On the contrary, the Fed up to 2008[125] predominantly accepted Treasury bills through repurchase agreements as loan security from commercial banks. Similarly, debt titles of the German finance ministry (Bunds) are recognized as first-class security for the refinancing operations of commercial banks within the Eurosystem and provide the benchmark for assessing the quality of state debt from other EMU member states. The Bank of Japan accepts in the majority short-term debt titles issued by the Japanese government.[126] In an ownership-based society, a state debt instrument can indeed be the safest and most liquid title of all. However, this is not because it is separated from property assets and thereby from the core of the economy. While government-issued titles are nothing other than debt titles, they are not per se debt titles of property owners. They become first-class property assets when they are purchased voluntarily by the domestic and international public who trust the tax-raising power of the state against the property assets of the inhabitants within its territory. While state titles are not secured by specific state property, interest and repayment obligations can, per the state's authority to raise taxes, be serviced out of the income of the total population.

State titles can even beat the titles of the largest corporations, because they are underpinned, like securitized future tax revenues, by the property of all citizens. As long as the government creates them at a volume where the interest service only affects the tax revenue marginally, they are first-class because they can be serviced more securely than even those of the strongest enterprises, as only a subset of all property owners within a state territory is liable for the latter. In other words, the most important potency of the state in relation to ownership is its power to raise taxes, which is precisely the right to interfere with the property rights of its citizens.

When this power is in doubt, state titles are no longer purchased or are only purchased at a higher rate of interest. These variations in the willingness to buy reveal how closely the soundness of state titles is linked to the 'core' of the economy from which they are serviced. Doubts about the future debt service capacity quickly turn state titles into bad loan security, regardless of how powerful the associated governments[127] may be, for example, Nazi Germany in the Greece today or the United States in the future.

In contrast to the notes of private note-issuing banks and early central banks (in the US until 1971), today's central bank notes are *not redeemable*. This can create the impression, not only for the lay person, that central bank notes are decoupled from any backing – whether based on property like gold or on debt securities – and are therefore created out-of-nothing. For example, Rudolf Richter (2000, 320), the leading German-speaking representative of new institutional economics, believes that the central bank is a monetary authority or 'central authority'[128] and hence, unlike a private note-issuing bank, not part of the 'privately regulated sector of the economy'.[129] Therefore, 'with the issue of bank notes this authority does not enter into an exchange obligation. The holder of a bank note cannot force ... the central authority by way of debt recovery action to fulfill a payment obligation'.[130] Its 'performance promise'[131] is limited to 'executing payment system operations and securing the stability of the value of money'.[132]

This view fails to recognise that redeemability continues to be available and also must be available. Independent of whether a central bank is owned by the state or not, it is not an authority outside the reach of property law but is, in addition to its monetary policy objectives, a bank like any private bank. 'A purely inconvertible fiduciary money' (Friedman and Schwartz 1986, 45) does not exist unless it is debtor's money.

In the case of creditor's money, its redeemability is obviously limited to holders of central bank notes who are permitted to refinance themselves at the central bank. Nowadays these are exclusively commercial banks that have been authorized as central bank counterparties. These counterparties might very well 'force' the central bank 'by way of debt recovery action to fulfill a payment obligation' (Richter 1987, 320) should it refuse or be unable to return the commercial bank assets provided as loan security. This exclusivity enjoyed by commercial banks is only due to the fact that today's central banks – in contrast to their nineteenth-century predecessors – do not provide credit to non-banks, so the public cannot approach its counters.

Central bank notes are therefore *redeemable* because commercial banks, which have obtained the notes by way of credit from the central bank, must be able to repay the notes in order to have *their* loan security *released*. Moreover, the outright sale of central bank assets (gold, foreign currency, claims on commercial banks from market operations), in which only central bank counterparties are permitted as buyers, are a form of note redemption. The notes returned to the central bank are destroyed as money. This is in no way different from the redemption of bank notes by any holder in the age of private note-issuing banks. Here, all holders could redeem the notes at the – private or central – bank of issue in gold property. In this process notes were destroyed *as money* but not necessarily as forms.

The deceptive impression that central bank money is unbacked also partly results from the already discussed LOLR role of the central bank. The rationale of this function is to guarantee the liquidity of commercial banks at all times. This undisputed obligation is, however – as shown – limited by the amount of central bank capital. Even in situations where the capital is not over-extended, strict rules apply to commercial banks regarding liquidity, which even for a lay person makes it obvious that even new money created to avert a crisis is not created out-of-nothing. Walter Bagehot, the originator of the notion of a central bank as 'the last lending house' (Bagehot 1873, 53), formulates the following principles for the avoidance of liquidity crises:

> For this purpose there are two rules: – First. That these loans should only be made at a very high rate of interest. This will operate as a heavy fine on

unreasonable timidity, and will prevent the greatest number of application by persons who do not require it.... Secondly. That at this rate these advances should be made *on all good banking securities*, and as largely as the public ask for them. The reason is plain. The object is to stay alarm, and nothing therefore should be done to cause alarm. But the way to cause alarm is to refuse someone who has *good security* to offer.

(Bagehot 1873, 197; emphasis added)

Bagehot knows to distinguish between the inability to pay due to insolvency (over-indebtedness) and the inability to pay when due while solvent, i.e., between a solvency crisis and a liquidity crisis. In the latter case, a commercial bank has a sufficient volume of good loan security but cannot turn the security quickly enough into money in the interbank money market. It therefore becomes illiquid with respect to its depositors. The LOLR function is only intended for such cases.

Bagehot knows very well that the principle of creating creditor's money only against good loan security cannot be deviated from, even when there is the danger of a liquidity crisis. This means that under no circumstance can commercial banks be allowed to submit titles that would not be recognized as a sound loan security during regular credit operations. Ralph Hawtrey, after Bagehot the second and before Goodhart the last great theorist of central banking, articulated this insight as follows:

The essential duty of the central bank as a lender of last resort ... cannot mean that it should lend to *any* bank that needs cash, regardless of the borrowing bank's behavior or circumstances. Neither a commercial concern nor a public institution could undertake to supply cash to insolvent borrowers.

(Hawtrey 1932, 126; emphasis added)

He justifies this prohibition, like Steuart, with the necessity to protect the bank's own capital. This is equally applicable to a central bank: 'A commercial concern in particular cannot afford to take risks out of proportion to its own capital' (Hawtrey 1932, 126).

Bagehot does not formulate his reasons why a note issue against bad loan security must be prohibited as clearly as do Steuart and Hawtrey. His predominant concern is the protection of central bank reserves and the protection of sound borrowers:

No advances indeed need be made by which the Bank will ultimately lose. ... That in a panic the bank ... holding the ultimate reserve should refuse bad bills or bad securities will not make the panic really worse.... The 'unsound' people are a feeble minority.... The great majority, the majority to be protected are the 'sound' people, the people who have good security to offer.

(Bagehot 1873, 198)

96 *The economic core of the ownership system*

Here, the possible central bank loss does not imply, as in Steuart and Hawtrey, a loss of capital – which is not a topic of inquiry for Bagehot – but merely the loss of the bank note 'reserve'.

The holding of such a reserve at the Bank of England was in Bagehot's time solely due to the division of the bank into an *issue department* and a *banking department*. Without this special characteristic, a central bank can never hold its own notes as reserve but must book them out as soon as they flow back when the property backing their original issue is returned. In the case of the Bank of England, the note redemption occurred in the *issue department* and gold left the department on the return of notes. However, the *banking department*, which could not create notes, required a note reserve to the amount of the deposits maintained by the London banks. The banks themselves did not have a note reserve (Bagehot 1873, 163).[133] Bagehot does not realize that the note reserve of the *banking department* could have been expanded through the acceptance of good security. Instead, he views the reserve as a fixed variable that requires protection as such. This is, in the end, the reason for Bagehot's first rule regarding the very high rate of interest for loans provided to prevent a liquidity crisis.[134] Without this measure the banking department would be at the risk of insolvency: 'It may be said that the reserve in the *Banking Department* will *not be enough* for all such loans. If that be so, the *Banking Department must fail*' (Bagehot 1873, 198; emphasis added; for more detail see Steiger 2002, 58, and 2006b).

Nevertheless, Bagehot understands what central bank theorists typically overlook, namely that the readiness of the public to surrender good loan security for money must not be considered as a given but as an extremely sensitive and therefore changeable variable (compare also Stadermann 1994a, 200). He argues that if 'unsound people' could obtain money against bad loan security, 'sound people' would withhold their good loan security (Bagehot 1873, 198). Hence, a liquidity crisis can occur not only because the central bank does not carry out its LOLR function but also because 'sound' commercial banks do not let the central bank perform this function.

Bagehot's rule about the significance of good loan security, which at his time had to be presented in the form of sound commercial bills at the discount window of the central bank, is today considered as secondary because central bank money is predominantly brought into circulation through the purchase of state debt instruments. Hence, the literature on the theory of central banking makes a distinction between these two forms of central bank money creation: (1) the discounting of commercial bills through *discount loans* creating the *borrowed base* and the so called *inside money*, i.e., central bank money, which comes from the inside of the economy; (2) the purchase of state debt, the so called *non-borrowed base* creating *outside money* '*exogenous* to the economic process, but capable of strongly influencing that process' (Axilrod and Wallich 1992, col. 75a; emphasis added).

Because nowadays the purchase of state debt by central banks dominates, it is frequently believed that Bagehot's 'open discount window' (for *inside money*) has been replaced by an 'open market window' (for *outside money*). As a result, it is assumed that an unwillingness of property owners to offer good loan security can be compensated for by the issue of state debt at any time. This is not the case. State debt titles cannot, as has been shown, be offered by the government to the central bank directly, because this would simply be the monetization of state debt. Instead, state titles have to be purchased in auctions from commercial banks, i.e., from enterprises directly within the 'core' of the economy. These have to constantly assess whether the respective government has sufficient property owners within its territory whose taxation capacity can beyond any doubt service the state debt titles. The commercial banks assess constantly whether the performance potential within the economy, the basis on which the state titles are issued, really exists.[135] The term '*outside money*' consequently proves to be highly misleading. It would only be justified in the case of debtor's money that is thrown into circulation at a mandated price and not in secondary markets.

If it is advisable to nurture the willingness of Bagehot's 'sound people' to hold property titles denominated in the same money of account as central bank notes, then also the *holders* of these notes or demand deposits, convertible into notes at any time, must be protected against asset losses. Therefore, a central bank must be concerned about maintaining a stable price level as well as a stable foreign exchange rate.

Of course, the central bank can attempt to stabilize the exchange rate of its currency against foreign currencies by demanding a high rate of interest for its notes. However, this will deter domestic property owners who are ready to enter into credit contracts but whose expected returns are below such interest rates. In this case, the interest rates are too high in relation to the productive growth and innovation potential of the economy at the given set of rates and prices.[136]

As the credit-based nature of money[137] implies that the nominal amount of money created is always less than the amount to be repaid with interest, the requirement for a net addition to the money stock is the underlying reason for growth (see Section 4.3). The level of interest rates together with the loan amount thus defines the absolute net addition to the money stock that has to be created to fulfill the money-creating credit contracts.

A typical way of fulfilling this net addition[138] is to monetize the net increase in assets and commodities produced (other ways are the burdening of previously unburdened property and money creation on the basis of assets at inflated prices). Thus productive growth provides the underlying basis for the required net increase in the money stock, and entrepreneurs must compete in realizing the required nominal money amounts to repay their loans with interest. If unsuccessful they become exposed to debt recovery actions. This pressure creates the impetus for innovation and new investment (see Section 4.3).

Consequently, if interest rates are set way above the growth and innovation potential of an economy,[139] as reflected in interest rates much higher than the expected returns from investments, economic activity will be inhibited. On the other hand, very low interest rates require a lower net increase in the money stock and lessen the burden to produce a surplus. This may result in an economy performing below potential (see also Stadermann 2002, 125–126). Furthermore, low or zero interest rates are likely to create severe asset price bubbles, as evidenced, for example, in the context of the 2008 global financial crisis (see Heinsohn and Decker 2010 and Taylor 2010).

The method of choice against inflation and currency devaluation is a note issue against first-class loan security that enables the withdrawal of notes from circulation without loss at any time. If this cannot be achieved, the central bank has lost the most critical measure to fight inflation. In an extreme case this can lead to a flight of capital and an inconvertible currency.

Philipp Lehmbecker (2005, 38), in an empirical investigation of the relationship between eligible central bank collateral and inflation in 34 currency areas based on a regression analysis, concludes what the inflation theory of ownership economics would have predicted:

> In two samples of 17 and 33 countries for the periods 1980 to 1989 and 1998 to 2003, respectively, a robust negative and statistically sufficient correlation between quality of eligible collateral and inflation has been found. This result supports the hypothesis of Property [Ownership] economics. On the basis of the survey the collateralization of the issuance of money [and the abandonment of] financing of the public deficit directly via the central bank have to be seen as crucial factors for monetary stability.

Because money can only be created in and *uno actu* with a credit contract, and is destroyed on fulfillment of this contract, there is no basis for the widespread idea, also shared by Keynes, that money is *hoarded*. The popular imagination of *loanable funds*, as represented by the metaphor of the *treasure chest*, the precious content of which is lent out against interest on suitable occasions, is based on a misunderstanding of money and interest. If bank notes had precious metal as security attached to them, then they could indeed be hoarded for their commodity value and disappear from circulation. Bank notes that are mere claims to issuer property and, therefore, can be made from worthless material typically avoid this fate. An exception is the deflationary crisis where bank notes are withheld because the price of money, the reciprocal price level (1/P), increases and it is therefore expected that the notes will purchase more in the future than at present.

Like the notes of private note-issuing banks, central bank notes are also destroyed as soon as the credit, in which the notes were created, is repaid by the commercial bank. Because the central bank returns the loan security of its debtors on repayment, the incoming notes must be booked out.[140] For the renewed creation of bank notes, which always implies a new credit creation, the central bank can, of course, reuse the previously returned notes a second time. However, until this reuse the returned notes are *not* money. They must nevertheless be kept inside a safe, where they represent forms only. If these forms are stolen – thus circumventing a contract in which a debtor is committed to pay interest, repay the loan principal and provide loan security – and brought into circulation, they will not be distinguishable from correctly issued money.

Even if the forms have been subject to wear and tear to a degree that they require physical destruction, they have to be kept inside a safe to be able to be traced without gaps between the time of the booking out and their incineration. Even a reach into the flames – as occurred at the German Bundesbank in the 1990s – turns the forms in the hands of the thieving furnace operators into notes, which end up in circulation and are no longer distinguishable from correctly emitted money. When the central bank does not reuse the refunded documents but destroys them, the bank does not lose money, but only the value embodied in the material of the forms. The central bank does not take the reusable note material out of a box, in which a stock of ready money is kept, but instead brings the old material as bank notes into circulation through renewed burdening of its property together with the renewed hypothecation of commercial bank property. As money, the reused forms are as *new* as money on newly printed forms.

When note-issuing banks give out coins, they almost exclusively utilize returned pieces for a new issue. This was the case for private note-issuing banks and early central banks and is still the practice of the Swedish *Riksbank*. In contrast, the German Bundesbank, together with most other central banks, does not create coined money but purchases coins from the state, which receives bank notes corresponding to their nominal amount. The coins are booked at their nominal amount as an asset in the balance sheet of the central bank representing a claim against the state. Only the state has the right to strike coinage. The difference between the cost of coinage and the nominal amount is a profit to the state. This seigniorage brings in much more today than under a precious metal standard, in which the current coins had a significantly higher intrinsic metal value than today's token coins.

Even though it may appear that the state can practically create means of payment in the form of coins out-of-nothing, their transfer through purchase to the central bank ensures that from here on they enter the circulation in a bank-like fashion that can be controlled. Commercial banks have to pay for their coinage needs in central bank notes, which are booked out thereafter. As such, the seigniorage of the state does not lead to an increased supply of bank notes (see Enghofer and Knospe 2005, 27).

4 The market as the result of the ownership-based economy

Ownership economics shows that interest and money cannot be understood or exist without a property rights system and the associated ownership premium. Ownership premium, interest and money provide the foundation of economic activity and constitute it as a mesh of mutual nominal *monetary obligations* that have to be fulfilled not only by debtors but also by creditors. Money-creating creditors originate credit contracts, in the money of account on which all actors – creditors and debtors alike – in turn have to base their economic operations. However, the money issuers also have the responsibility to ensure that money for economic activity is continuously created and destroyed through the drafting and the fulfillment of credit contracts, in which property is constantly burdened and unburdened and interest obligations are entered into and discharged. This overarching responsibility can only be fulfilled by the issuer, because debtors receive money in a credit contract not only against interest but above all against good loan security, and because creditors themselves are liable for the created money with equally sound property assets. Therefore, the operations of an ownership-based economy are not directed by an 'invisible hand' (classical economics) or an auctioneer (neoclassical economics). What turns out to be invisible are hundreds of millions of credit contracts, denominated in the same money of account, and the implied threat of debt recovery action, which keeps all actors, from banker to wage laborer and social security beneficiary, moving. For example, the German SCHUFA[1] monitors more than 300 million credit contracts alone in a country with a population of just 80 million.

How do creditor-debtor contracts create the typical elements of an ownership-based society that are only encountered in this type of human association: financial markets, profit and capital, goods production and commodity markets, accumulation, free wage laborers and technical progress, as well as business cycle and crisis?

4.1 The entrepreneur as an economic agent in his own right and the establishment of markets

Property owners interact with each other as economic agents by entering into nominal contracts denominated in money, for which they are liable with their property and which they have to fulfill with interest. It is only as a consequence of these contracts that owners establish markets, which in all great schools of economics are placed at the very beginning of economic activity and its analysis.[2]

Because markets are alien to possession-based systems, the establishment of markets was anything but easy. Human beings as such are not exchangers of equivalents; hence, as indebted individuals they had to painstakingly learn about the rules of markets. An instructive example was provided by the introduction of land rights in Austria in 1848, when serfs could acquire their previously feudal possessions as freehold land based on a 40-year repayment schedule. 'The consequences of being freed [from feudal chains] were not all positive for the farmers.... The first generation did not know ... the economic prerequisites of markets' (*Österreich Lexikon* 2005).[3] The farmers now produced not for feudal lords but for themselves and first had to acquaint themselves with the process of selling for the express purpose of repaying their debts. For this, a market had first to be established. Until this had succeeded, many farmers became over-indebted and lost their farms. While this was polemically described by the catchphrase 'Bauernlegen' (peasant clearances), the underlying reasons were not understood. It was only after 1868 that the new landowning farmers created co-operatives for the marketing of their products and in this way stabilized the system.

Contracts between parties in which neither party is a property owner, including contracts between parties in which goods are actually bartered, have nothing to do with markets and do not bring about markets. This is why the classical notion of the market, as the place to realize the physical reproduction with surplus (profit), fails. Equally, the neoclassical idea of the market as the place that determines optimal resource allocation misses the point. Both schools have in common the belief that an eternal and universal inclination of human beings to barter goods and resources is the underlying reason for economic activity. This is as misguided as the notion that an aversion to barter (or its prohibition) could succeed in inhibiting economic activity.

Even Polanyi, the most insightful opponent of the classical and neoclassical idea of the market within economic ethnology, owes us an explanation of the market. Even though he knows that markets are absent in tribal societies and under feudalism, he does not distinguish himself in his description of markets from that of his opponents. For Polanyi the *homo economicus* remains embedded in the market, where 'barter is facilitated' through 'quantifiable objects' or 'physical units' (Polanyi 1977, 102; for more detail see Heinsohn 2005 and 2008a). This is the neoclassical *numéraire* money from the sphere of goods *par excellence*.

Monetary Keynesianism, which derives economic activity from the concept of scarce money, cannot grasp the essence of markets because its theory is unable to identify the preconditions for scarce money – namely the willingness to burden and to hypothecate property. The 'Keynesian macroeconomics' of Michael Heine and Hansjörg Herr (1999, 315–379) should serve as an example.

102 The market as a result of ownership

Here the starting point is a world of 'capital free' enterprises, banks and central banks,[4] because enterprises – the authors remain silent about capital for banks and central banks – can acquire equity capital directly from 'households'.[5] In this context an actor appears who makes 'his money',[6] a part of his net worth, available to an enterprise. Where 'his money' and 'his net worth' come from, what they are and how they are created remains entirely unexplained. It is therefore consistent that Heine and Herr know exactly only one thing, namely that 'a linkage of money creation and property, in whatever way implemented, would be dysfunctional' (Heine and Herr 1999, 377),[7] a remark directly targeted against ownership economics. Indeed, in this view the absence of property makes any concern about its functionality unnecessary. Unfortunately, their total neglect of ownership makes the basis of money, whose origin they try to disclose, disappear too.[8]

Monetary Keynesianism simply does not know that at *all* levels of economic activity, economic agents are dealing in their capacity as property owners and not merely at the top of an alleged hierarchy. There are no special people, misleadingly referred to as 'asset owners' (Riese), who sit at the top of a hierarchy of markets and dominate the agents in all other markets. In fact, the idea of market hierarchies is a revival of the ideas of classical economics. While classical economics does not position the rulers over money at the top of its hierarchy, it sees in their place the rulers over the means of production. The latter can be decoded in all their details – as shown in Section 2.1 – as mere possessors, whom, however, classical economics incorrectly labels as 'private property owners' – an incorrect choice of terminology that resembles monetary Keynesianism.

Let us begin with the property owner as commodity producer or entrepreneur, who as debtor inevitably stands at the center of an ownership-based economy. He is neither the neoclassical curate[9] of a resource-endowed household, who transforms these resources through production into goods that he markets, nor is he a monetary Keynesian curate of the 'asset owner', who can generate assets. The entrepreneur is nobody's curate but a property owner who is *ready* and has the *capacity* to take on debt. He starts the production by sacrificing his ownership premium, and keeps the economy in motion by constantly switching between giving up and regaining this premium.

The ability of an entrepreneur to take on debt is reflected in his command over ownership premium, and his capacity and willingness to deploy property in economic activity by giving up this ownership premium. Only through this activation of property can the entrepreneur obtain money in a credit contract from a commercial bank, in the lending operation of which he is an essential counterparty. This credit for production purposes is governed by the same rules as the credit between commercial bank and central bank. An artificial division of credit *à la* Riese (1999, 152) into 'money creation' on the one hand and 'resource credit' on the other is unknown in an ownership-based economy.

It is obvious that an entrepreneur who has inherited money, stolen money or won money in a lottery must behave equally like a debtor, who has to extract more than he put in due to the interest burden. Any investment of the money obtained in this way has to compete with the alternative of on-lending it against interest. Entrepreneurs thus have to consider interest as an opportunity cost whenever they evaluate an investment. Of course thieves and heirs differ from the entrepreneur-debtor because they have not hypothecated or burdened any property.

Someone can engage in economic activity only when even as a debtor he remains a net creditor. He always requires a surplus of *assets* over *liabilities*. This surplus or net worth is the manifestation of his *capital*.[10] A balance sheet is not a simple dual of *assets* and *liabilities* but a trinity of *assets*, *liabilities* and *capital*. The essence of capital is therefore not that of an ordinary liability that in analogy to external capital simply reflects an obligation against the entity itself, and therefore does not require an analysis as a separate entity. Quite the contrary! Capital as the surplus of assets over liabilities is, as unburdened property, essential for the capacity to take on debt. It is only booked on the liabilities side of the property owner's balance sheet to ensure that both sides have the same total. However, this procedure does not turn capital into a liability. It remains property that is free of any claims. Conversely, in the case of a negative balance, the negative amount of capital is not turned into an asset just because accounting rules[11] require it to be booked as a positive amount on the asset side of the balance sheet.

Within monetary Keynesianism, which – as shown in Section 2.3.3 – lives in a capital-free world, at least Heine and Herr observe that 'most enterprises also have capital'[12] (Heine and Herr 1999, 334; on commercial banks see Hausknecht 2001, 51–54). Nevertheless, according to Heine and Herr, capital can be neglected in economic analysis because it represents, like other liabilities, simply a book entry that offsets entries on the asset side of the balance sheet, thus merely indicating the right to demand a yield on the invested capital:

> because the capital of an enterprise can be interpreted as a direct loan of the owner-household to the enterprise. This implies the assumption that capital is a liability of the enterprise towards the owner-household and that the utilization of external and own capital is equal in a state of equilibrium.
> (Heine and Herr 1999, 334)[13]

Of course this statement is not wrong, but it is trivial: who would argue that the capital (equity) listed on the liabilities and shareholders' equity side[14] of a balance sheet is anything other than the offsetting book entry from asset acquisitions representing the entitlements of equity owners (internal and external) over these assets and their returns? However, a theory of capital has to show that capital is more than evidence for the origin of the funds provided. Capital is first and foremost an indicator of the capacity to *secure assets in order to avoid insolvency* beyond what is provided through sound loan security.[15] This attribute of capital never appears in monetary Keynesianism. More insightful theorists of central banking therefore identify the liabilities and shareholders' equity side[16] of the central bank balance sheet not simply as 'liability side' but as 'liabilities *and capital side*' (Blenck et al. 2002, 39–43); emphasis added).

With the money advance or external capital resulting from the economic activation of property, the entrepreneur acquires the means of production or *physical capital*.[17] This deployment of money thus transforms means of production into physical assets and through this step brings about a production of *commodities*, which is assessed in monetary terms and results in employment and income. This acquiring or *purchasing* is already the *market*, in this case the market for the production factor, physical capital. Like money, the market is not simply always in existence, waiting for someone to be active in it. On the contrary, it is only established by purchases and ceases to exist when no purchases are taking place.

In order to take on debt, the entrepreneur requires property, or someone who as property owner can act as a guarantor. Yet his readiness to take on debt is not only determined by himself and also not solely by his profit expectations. He will only activate his readiness to take on debt repeatedly, if he can rely on the money obtained via credit contracts being accepted by other property owners, i.e., created as creditor's money according to sound banking principles. If this is not the case, he cannot establish a market with his money, i.e., he cannot get other entrepreneurs to sell him commodities for intrinsically valueless notes. He is then stuck with poorly-backed money, i.e., debtor's money, and cannot execute the operations that would follow debt-raising – investment, production, selling and loan repayment – even though he remains obliged as a debtor to carry these out. Due to these circumstances, any undermining of creditor's money must undermine economic activity, i.e., tear apart the mesh of mutual obligations (see the example of the German empire in Section 4.3).

An entrepreneur as an economic actor is therefore first and foremost an actor who needs to fulfill a credit contract in order not to lose his hypothecated property. This contract is denominated in a money of account, in the units of which the entrepreneur agrees to interest payments and repayment and in which the price of his property is set. The property is hypothecated at least to the amount of the credit sum. Contrary to popular belief, if the entrepreneur raises money through the issue of shares, these by no means represent additional 'money of entrepreneurs' (see Heinsohn and Steiger 2000c and 2000d). Even money obtained through share issues is not, as in the monetary Keynesian 'net worth',[18] already miraculously in existence, but has to have been previously created in a credit contract. Only the willingness to take on loans, the willingness to issue debt securities, and the acceptance of additional shareholders when raising new shares can establish *financial markets*.[19] Like the money-creating credit contract that can only exist when a note-issuing bank finds a debtor for its business who is ready to hypothecate his property, providers of funds (money) can only enter into transactions in financial markets so long as others are willing to take on debt, or, in the case of shares, are willing to accept new profit-sharing shareholders. Financial markets have nothing to do with a mono-polar world of 'asset owners' (Riese 2000b, §3, col. 546a), whose decisions alone set the economy in motion.

Only money, in whatever way obtained, supplies the entrepreneur with the liquidity premium that arises from creditor's money. The specific attribute of money, as emphasized by Keynes, is the ability to finally settle credit and sales contracts at any time. That mere (money) documents can transfer or redeem property, however, is based on the fact that these documents themselves imply claims against the issuer's property. This foundation of the liquidity premium has been overlooked by both Keynes and monetary Keynesianism. For Keynes, the sacrifice of liquidity premium is meant to result in interest, where the sacrificed money is either presupposed or even conceptualized as a debtor's money. In the case of monetary Keynesianism, the act of sacrificing liquidity premium is alleged to be the trigger of economic activity, whereby the sacrificed money is created out-of-nothing and is within the control of the 'asset owner'.

In contrast, ownership economics has to insist on a different logical sequence: the deployment of ownership premium creates money as creditor's money, while the deployment of liquidity premium takes place through the temporary *sacrifice* or the *spending* of creditor's money that has already been created.[20] The spending of money always implies the final fulfillment, i.e., the extinguishing of contractual obligations denominated in money of account, of credit contracts as well as sales contracts. Fulfillment thus means that potential claims to property as part of note redemptions or debt enforcement actions are cancelled.

From the perspective of the debtor, the liquidity premium is nothing but the compensation for his ownership premium, lost in the process of hypothecation.[21] Once the liquidity premium comes with creditor's money into the world, it is applied to all asset types including financial and physical assets. These assets are not money because they cannot finally discharge contracts or – like commercial bank deposits in particular – cannot be used to substitute an actual money payment. The ease of transformability of different types of assets into money determines the level of their liquidity premium or their degree of liquidity.

As means of production are always acquired by an entrepreneur with a money advance against interest, they are not themselves *capital* but are transformed into manufactured commodities and physical capital by the money advance in the first place. Commodities and physical capital are interpreted in neoclassical economics as a stock of capital *goods*. However, the capital is always a money advance. Consequently, the availability of pre-existing goods and resources, made available by saving (i.e., someone abstaining from consumption), is not required to bring about the creation of physical assets. The money of the capital advance does not correspond to a physical stock of goods. On the contrary, it is based on immaterial ownership rights that the creditor burdens when providing capital to the entrepreneur-debtor in a loan. The creditor's physical goods are never lent or temporarily transferred. Hence, the creation of physical assets is not limited by purely physical goods and resources but by the willingness to burden existing property, i.e., to give up ownership premium.

The money obtained by the entrepreneur in the credit contract enforces – through the risk of property losses – a mechanism by which products are offered as *commodities*, i.e., offered for sale against money and not for exchange against other goods. The *commodity market* establishes itself for the recovery of the money advance as well as for the acquisition of the interest debt, representing a surplus over the money advance, i.e., the *profit*. The entrepreneur has to engage in the acquisition of money because only money can finally extinguish his debt obligations and release the property he hypothecated. Only then is his property free and able to yield an ownership premium all over again.

The market is therefore not a place for the exchange of goods, where these move from one owner to another to their respective mutual advantage, either based on the preferences of consumers and determined by a subjective assessment of utility (neoclassical economics) or based on – objective – production costs (classical economics). Moreover, the market cannot be assumed, as in the monetary Keynesian model, to have long been in existence as a place for the exchange of goods before it eventually became dominated by the financial market, assumed to be positioned at a higher level within a supposed hierarchy of markets, via the emergence of interest yielded by money (as the price for lent assets). Rather, the market is an entity that becomes necessary *uno actu* with the money-creating credit contract, as it allows for the acquisition of sales contracts over commodities that provide the means to refund debts.

By entering into a *sales contract*, the entrepreneur, who as the result of a credit contract – his external capital – is a debtor who owes a claim to money, becomes, as the owner of a commodity, a creditor who holds a claim to money. Hence, any firm is not simply reduced to the position of a debtor but necessarily strives to be in the position of a creditor. Only by realizing a creditor position through sales can the entrepreneur clear his debtor position and in turn release the primary creditor of the enterprise from his position as a demander of funds. Only thereafter are both quantities of property assets able to be activated again, i.e., property premiums are able to be given up, in order to continue the flow of economic activity.

The counterparty of the entrepreneur-debtor turned seller is, in analogy to the credit contract, a buyer representing a debtor of a money claim. The debtor commits to provide the money sum demanded for the sale. Within the period prior to the fulfillment of the money claim, the purchaser-debtor is merely a possessor of the goods, because the full transfer of title to the property, something which can only be achieved with money, has not taken place. In contrast to a credit contract, a sales contract typically does not allow for the hypothecation of debtor property. For this reason, prior to the full payment in money, the creditor's (seller's) property is typically protected by a retention of title clause,[22] ensuring that the title to the property is not finally transferred, i.e., not already on payment by check or credit card.

Where the role of the entrepreneur as a creditor becomes a topic of investigation in the prevailing theories (Stiglitz and Greenwald 2003, 137–145), contractual provisions such as the retention of title clause for the protection of seller property in sales transactions never come into view. It is merely noted that the situation of the entrepreneur as a creditor is like that of a bank, and that the entrepreneur cannot mitigate the risk of non-payment by demanding an additional interest margin, because higher interest would further increase the risk of insolvency. The fact that hypothecation of property, as a mechanism to secure loan contracts exercised by banks, has its equivalent in the retention of title clause in sales contracts, is not recognized. For this reason, the prevailing theories have to refer back to the problem of obtaining information about the creditworthiness of debtors, in the context of which banks conceived the method of demanding collateral. However, it remains unclear what method is to replace the lack of complete credit information in the case of the entrepreneur: 'Each firm will presumably earn rents on its informational advantage; and it is these rents that make it attractive for firms to enter the lending business' (Stiglitz and Greenwald 2003, 143).

4.2 Monetary price setting versus adjustment to relative prices

As soon as the entrepreneur-debtor purchases means of production or factors of production with the money advance, he enters into *nominal* contracts denominated in money of account. Contracts thus unavoidably exist as monetary quantities. This means that the quantity of means of production has to be valued in terms of *prices* – so-called factor prices or *costs* – which must be denominated in the same money of account as the contracted money advance, i.e., in absolute *money prices*.

The same holds for the prices of the products that are created by the means of production, the so-called goods prices. The products have to be valued at a price that at least corresponds to the sum of capital and interest as well as the sum of factor quantities times their unit cost. It is this special *monetary production* that leads to *commodities* and not simply physical goods. It ensures that an entrepreneur is not interested in the production of goods per se, i.e., mere quantities, but in product *values* measured in money prices, hence realizable sums of money.

These prices have nothing to do with the relative prices referred to in the theories of value based on the barter exchange of goods. Nor do prices result from barter exchange relations between goods, however determined, which can be determined as absolute prices via a given quantity of money. Prices are also not determined by the relations between the quantities of labor embedded in goods and *predefined* through a reproductive wage *a là* classical economics. Finally, prices do not result from the – equally *predefined* – relations between goods or factor quantities, which adjust themselves to marginal utility relations of households and marginal productivity relations of producers respectively, *a là* neoclassical economics.

The founders of neoclassical economics, Carl Menger, William Stanley Jevons and Léon Walras, have always asserted but never explained the price formation mechanism (Stadermann and Steiger 2001b, 221–251):

> The 'utilities' therefore do not *explain* prices but merely serve as a scholarly but empty phrase to assert the given price relations as 'correct'.... Walras could only determine the maximum exchange utility by assuming the prices as a *given*. However, he forgets this assumption in the following and now, in reverse order, derives prices based on a theorem that was obtained with the help of assumed prices.[23]
>
> (Hofmann 1964, 167/178, emphasis added)

108 The market as a result of ownership

In modern microeconomics the circular nature of the argument has not changed. This can be demonstrated based on the two fundamental models underlying the microeconomic partial-equilibrium analysis: the utility maximization of the consumer and the cost minimization of the producer. Both optimization problems assume actors that have a predefined budget to acquire consumption goods and means of production, the respective quantities of which are unknown. It is merely their relative prices, i.e., the ratio in which the quantities are exchanged, that are known and predefined. This means that the actors chose those quantities from their predetermined budgets so as to result in the maximum utility and minimal cost respectively.

In the simplest model – the case of two goods (two factors) – actors can exchange the quantities contained in their budgets based on the predefined relative prices of the goods (factors) in any possible way, i.e., to spend the budget for one good (one factor) at a time or subsets thereof. The actors continue to exchange the respective quantities as long as the total utility (in the model for the customer) and the total quantity produced (in the model of the producer) respectively are greater than those resulting from any random initial combination. The total utility (the total quantity produced) is characterized by the fact that an exchange of goods (exchange of factors) leaves the sum of the marginal utilities (marginal products) of the corresponding goods (factors) multiplied by the exchanged quantities unchanged. This means that the ratio of possible quantities, the so-called marginal rate of substitution, equals the inverse ratio of their marginal utilities (marginal products). Because the marginal rate of substitution also equals the inverse ratio of relative prices, maximization of utility (minimization of cost) is achieved when marginal utility ratios (margin product ratios) adjust themselves to the predefined ratios of prices. Because marginal utilities and marginal products merely adjust to assumed prices, they cannot explain these at the same time. Marginal utilities and marginal products thus do not lead to relative prices. Instead, marginal utilities and marginal products are brought in line with predefined exchange relations through adjustments of goods and factor quantities.

In general equilibrium theory, the prices for all goods of a market system are expressed in terms of an arbitrary standard good, the price of which is set to one (1), and all prices are dependent on each other. In contrast to the partial-equilibrium analysis, relative prices are termed *current prices*, which can create the incorrect impression that we are dealing with true money prices. In reality, for general equilibrium analysis current prices are unavoidably *prices for accounting purposes* expressed in the number of units of a given standard commodity serving as the *unit of account*.[24] This unit must not be confused with the *money of account* used in ownership economics, which[25] is an abstract unit with no physical existence and no associated good.

A view of money as a commodity itself, of course, immediately raises the question of how the price of money would be determined in this case:

> If money is a commodity, what is its price? Can a commodity be, simultaneously, the numerical expression of prices and a real good whose price must

be expressed in terms of money? Consider the relative exchange between commodity money *m* and a real good *a*. If, for example, 10 units of *m* are exchanged against one unit of *a*, it can equally be said that 10 units of *m* are the price of one unit of *a*, or that one unit of *a* is the price of 10 units of *m*. Yet, in order for money prices to be univocally determined, it is necessary to have one unit of measure. The problem can be solved neither by choosing one of the two commodities as a reference nor by arbitrarily assuming that it can be taken to be equal to a mere number. Relative exchange can only occur between real terms, a necessary condition which allows neither for the determination of a unique unit of measure nor for the association of numbers with real goods and services.

(Cencini 2001, 30; emphasis added)

The attempt to determine prices via real barter exchanges inevitably fails due to the fact that money is indeed not a physical good. Then again, the determination of relative prices must consider money as a good. There is no escape from this paradox.

The model of general equilibrium theory assumes that the budgets of all actors and the prices of the goods (factors) to be exchanged with these budgets are a given. Here, the attention is not targeted at the maximization of utility and the minimization of cost respectively, whereby relative prices are brought into equilibrium through marginal utilities and marginal products. This optimization carried out by actors is assumed as a given. Instead the focus is on the mechanism by which markets as a whole are brought into a state of equilibrium. This happens by changing the predefined prices through variations, as in an auction, until the so-called amounts of excess demand[26] and excess supply respectively have been removed. Markets thus clear in the state of equilibrium. However, what specific entity is varied remains unexplained. It is merely asked whether certain prices create amounts of excess demand or not. Prices are therefore not determined by given amounts of excess demand. What is considered is merely the functional relationship of how increases or decreases in prices eliminate amounts of excess demand. Why there is a positive price at all, i.e., why auctions do not give away goods at the price of zero, but always require a reserve or minimum price, remains unexplained.

It should come as no surprise that the microeconomic theory of the market of profit-maximizing producers also fails to explain prices, but sets them as market prices. As in general equilibrium theory, these are defined as 'current prices' valid for transactions involving goods and services within a particular market period. Here, prices are considered as absolute prices and no longer as exchange relations, even though this difference is never highlighted. This is explained by the fact that money does not play a role in microeconomics. Absolute prices, however, always represent money prices that are being hidden by the seemingly harmless terminology of 'current prices'.

In the model of the so-called polypolistic or perfect competition, i.e., with an unlimited number of producers, the individual producer has no influence on the market price, so that it becomes a fixed quantity for him. The producer has only the choice of adjusting his production quantity to the market price until his marginal revenue, i.e., the market price, equals his marginal costs.

In the model of the monopoly, i.e., with a market-dominating producer, the market price is equally set externally but is not fixed. The producer can vary the price, while considering the elasticity of demand, in order to maximize his profit to the point of equal marginal revenue and marginal cost. The preconditions for this price, however, are beyond his price-setting power. The same holds for the model of monopolistic competition, in which the number of producers is unlimited, as in the model of perfect competition, but where the individual producer can vary the predefined price like a monopolist due to strong customer dependence. Finally, in the model of oligopolistic competition, in which one large producer can respond to the price strategy of another large producer, one producer can undercut the market price to stem the competition. However, he needs to know this lower limit. It is not determined by the pricing game of giant monopolists.

The authors of these models, of course, see that money has a role to play in relation to their prices. Money, however, is not understood, and its origin is not reconstructed by the authors. It is simply conceptualized as a neutral standard good to facilitate barter and as a *numéraire*, respectively. A noteworthy fact is merely that changes in the quantity of money cannot change relative prices. However, because simultaneous increases in absolute prices or market prices cannot be denied and must remain unexplainable within a *numéraire* concept, one is for the time being clueless about the difference between relative and absolute prices. How is the difference to be overcome? The first step uses Fisher's equation of exchange, $MV = PT$, where M stands for the quantity of money, V for the velocity of circulation, P for the price level and T for the sum of excess demand transactions for goods. Under the assumption that V and T are constant, absolute prices are determined by the quantity of money, while the relative prices are unchanged because they are determined by the excess amounts of demand and supply for goods respectively. This creates the so-called classical dichotomy: real factors determine relative prices, while monetary factors determine absolute or money prices.

In order to overcome this dichotomy, Don Patinkin (1965) introduced the concept of the real balance[27] (M/P) to general equilibrium theory. In this model, the demand for goods is considered as a demand for the holding of goods in which the demand for holding of real balances is integrated.[28] This means that relative prices are deflated in the same way as the quantity of money along with the price level. Moreover, the excess demand for real balances can be conceptualized as the difference between demand and supply that is dependent on relative prices and the real balance. In Patinkin's model, current prices, which still represent relative prices of goods markets, turn themselves quietly into money prices in order to be able to determine the price level as the weighted average of current prices.

In the fundamental model of neoclassical economics, absolute prices cannot be determined at all. The Fisher model can determine absolute prices but ends up in a dichotomy with relative prices. Finally, in the Patinkin model both absolute and relative prices are determined in the same way by excess demand. Hence, the demand for money is considered analogous to the demand for goods. The dichotomy between the goods market and the money market can only be avoided because the money market is considered as an additional goods market. In this model, the price level is nothing but the relative price for the good money. The quantity of money and the price level operate in no way differently from the standard good, money, with the price set to one. In both types of prices, price level and price equal to one, relative prices can be expressed.

The monetary theory of ownership economics does not base its argument on relative prices, on a standard good money with the price set to one, or on the weighted average of current prices as price level with the mere label 'money price'. Ownership economics also discards the attempts by Keynes and the post-Keynesians to overcome the barter paradigm of classical and neoclassical economics, by considering money as an asset rather than a standard commodity: the asset, money, is held as a means against the uncertainty arising between the present and an uncertain future. While money can play this role, it cannot be explained on this basis. Uncertainty is a constant feature of human systems. Genuine money and money prices, however, are only encountered in an ownership-based society.

Where do money prices come from and how are they determined? This questions leads back to the genesis of the indebted entrepreneur (Section 3.2). He is a producer who got into difficulties with respect to the possessory aspect of his property assets, but who can still refer back to the ownership aspect of his property that underpins his creditworthiness. An example[29] is assets that do not generate enough income but that have not yet been fully burdened by mortgage or otherwise. The maintenance and expansion of their credit standing by enlarging the amount of their property assets must become the central motive for all property owners. Because they cannot rely on rations provided in systems based on reciprocity or command, the protection of income must be achieved through the deployment of property. This pressure is also imposed on someone who is confronted with the possibility of not being able to generate enough income from the possessory (i.e., physical) aspect of his asset in the future.

By entering into credit obligations, the property owner gains, in addition to the possessory aspect of his property, money. This imposes a claim, which is denominated in money of account and not in the accounting unit of a standard commodity. These credit contracts in turn force sales contracts to be denominated in precisely the same money of account. Therefore, quantities must be valued in prices that are never simply units of account but are always priced in money of account or money prices.

The producers, and in their train all other economic agents, are therefore not endowed with an initial goods budget that they optimize. Rather they are forced, due to the hypothecation of their property (affecting only the ownership aspect), to invest the borrowed money in relation to the possessory aspect of their property in a way that allows them to defend their property assets and to have the hypothecated property released at the end. In this sense, the defense of the property position could indeed be viewed as 'optimization'. If this is not successful, not only will agents encounter even more severe difficulties in relation to the possessory aspect of the property, but they will also lose the ownership aspect of their property and with it their credit standing.

How then are money prices set? The entrepreneur can neither influence the amount of the ownership premium, and therefore the amount of interest on the money advanced to him, nor the sum of this capital to be repaid. The interest is – like the money advance to which it is applied – a variable denominated in money of account and therefore an *absolute* price. However, interest, as Fisher's formula $i = r/R$ shows, is not only the price of a cost, but also the price that determines the value of financial and physical assets.[30] This is of relevance when the indebted producer sets prices as a reduction of his asset values due to an increase in the rate of interest that lowers his credit standing. Moreover, he has to factor in an additional risk margin on top of the increased interest. This fact is a very uncomfortable truth for neoclassical economics, which is oriented towards the exchange of goods, and deals a severe blow to its theory of interest as a relative intertemporal price – the ratio of the sacrifice of a quantity of present consumption in favor of a larger quantity of future consumption. Neoclassical economics does not even recognize that changes in the rate of interest do not primarily concern the allocation of consumption between two points in time, but change the valuation of property assets and with it the creditworthiness of a debtor.

When setting prices the entrepreneur can influence, in contrast to interest, the prices in factor markets. The cost components of wages and product inputs can be varied by pursuing alternative options in production technology. However, it is most importantly in the setting of new prices in product markets that, from the perspective of the entrepreneur, nothing is predetermined. Here, he has the opportunity to advance the creation of new products, innovative technologies and new offers to fulfill needs not previously commercially explored. An example is the introduction of smart phones. In 2011, Apple – the inventor of the iPhone – with a market share of barely four percent, pulled in more than half of the total of global mobile-phone makers' profits.[31]

The actual price formation process is therefore very different from the monopolistic price setting of neoclassical economics in which the entrepreneur is guided by prices that are already predetermined by the existing *preferences* of consumers. In reality, the relative prices reflected in consumer preferences are unknown to the entrepreneur when setting prices and are also not relevant. Solely an *ex-post* investigation can establish price relations, which can indeed be of interest for the better understanding of the interaction of markets. Relative prices are – as has been shown – never the *reason* for the formation of prices and therefore have nothing to do with a theory of prices.

> The relative 'exchange ratios' are not the reason for absolute prices, which are set without any knowledge of exchange ratios. On the contrary, only the equilibrium price settings of suppliers lead in their result to a system of relative prices and to the allocation of goods in an economic area. This process,

however, can never create more than a temporary constellation as new price settings continually overcome the relative stability of the system.[32]

(Stadermann and Steiger 2001b, 373)

Why can a system of relative prices only be a temporary constellation? Any innovation, which other producers need to implement too, includes an element of price-setting power, because innovation is precisely defined as something that others do not have and that they, in the short term, cannot offer more cheaply. One may complain about this pricing power, but it is the factor to which demand must adjust. Demand does not only respond by a variation in the demanded quantity of the commodity or by the abandonment of other commodities. As mentioned, customers may even be forced to take on new debt, i.e., hypothecate property, in order to be able to acquire the funds required to pay the price for the new product because it is essential to maintain their own competitiveness.

Mere consumers cannot force producers to orient themselves according to their preferences. In situations where a producer conducts seductive marketing or takes consumers by storm with an irresistible product, it is revealed that consumers' needs and preference are never something given. Consumer needs do not have to be 'artificially' created, but need only be awakened, as the so-called market revolutions in dormant markets show (Ballin 2005).

As a very simple example, one should recall Steuart's remarks on the demand for seasonal clothing. While the unfree serf of Europe wore the same type of clothing in fewer layers in summer and in additional layers in winter, producers succeeded in awakening the need in free laborers, who now had wage money, for light summer clothing and heavy winter coats. Very similar was the transition from the footcloth to shoes for everyone. More recent examples are optometrists offering fashionable glasses at government-funded health care rates,[33] or the home furnishing industry with easy-to-assemble designer products (IKEA revolution; see Ballin 2005 for more details).

Neoclassical economics subscribes to a fiction by assuming predefined preferences. Moreover, the consumer is not constrained by a predefined budget out of which he creates the demand for goods according to his preferences to maximize his utility. He can, as creditworthy property owner, take on debt and expand his budget by hypothecating property at once. This operation is entirely neutral with respect to goods. This potential for taking on more debt, which only becomes visible when considering individual property positions, increases the price-setting power of the producer.

4.3 Accumulation, business cycle and crisis

The interest demand implies that the value of the production output – quantity times money price – of the entrepreneur-debtor must result in a larger sum than the money advance obtained as capital. Hence, in a credit contract, it is always the case that less money is lent than owed. For the economy in aggregate, money must therefore be inherently scarce, because the sums owed are larger than the sums

114 *The market as a result of ownership*

lent. Consequently, it is the interest claim resulting from the ownership premium that extorts a value surplus with reference to the value of production, the *rate* of profit. This profit is, like interest, denominated in money of account. It goes without saying that this does not mean that the 'rate of profit turns into a form of interest via production processes that are kept scarce'[34] and that interest becomes 'the price for the temporary sacrifice of money'[35] (Riese 2000b, §3, col. 546a).

Keynes (1936, 213) could see that profit does not arise because the deployment of capital equipment is in a physical sense *productive*, as neoclassical economics assumes:

> It is much preferable to speak of capital as having a yield over the course of its life in excess of its original cost, than as being *productive*. For the only reason why an asset offers ... [such a yield] is because it is scarce; and it is scarce because of the competition of the rate of interest on money. If capital becomes less *scarce*, the excess yield will diminish, without its having become less productive – at least in the physical sense.
>
> (Keynes 1936, 213; emphasis in original)

However, Keynes fails to recognize that this scarcity does not simply result from the fact that fixed-income securities exist as an alternative to the holding of money. Only interest demanded after the burdening of property can play this role.

The sacrifice of ownership premium must be compensated by interest, which in turn mandates a profit. It is this profit that enables the *accumulation* so typical in the ownership-based economy. This gets its dynamics neither through the so-called *original* or *primitive* accumulation of capital goods (classical economics) nor through *previous* savings of consumption goods that are subsequently transformed into capital goods (neoclassical economics). Therefore, it is not thrift, originated somewhere in relation to a predefined income of goods (Keynes 1936, 179–181), through which the means for investments are created. On the contrary, it is the interest burden of a debt that creates the tendency to save, which is typical for the ownership-based economy alone. This dynamic also does not result from the availability of money *beforehand* – either in the form of exogenously created central bank money (Keynes) or of 'money assets' that are first created by a central bank for itself and then given up (Riese).

Accumulation always relates to stocks of property assets measured in money. Its precondition is the ability and willingness to burden the ownership aspect of these assets, i.e., the giving up of the ownership premium p. This happens when the (expected) rate of profit r is larger than the rate of interest i, whereby i always equals p and also equals the liquidity premium l. Hence, in a state of equilibrium, the condition:

$$p=i=l=r \tag{1}$$

holds. This is unlike the equilibrium condition in monetary Keynesianism:

$$l=i=r \tag{2}$$

On the surface, the two equilibrium conditions only appear to differ because monetary Keynesianism is not aware of the ownership premium. For monetary Keynesians, the giving up of money, i.e., l, is the economically crucial step that results in i and in turn enforces r. In contrast, for ownership economics the burdening of creditor property, i.e., the sacrifice of p, is the fundamental step for economic activity in the first place, which enables i and money. In a second step this supplies a debtor with l, the giving up of which, taking place in the form of purchases with money, results in the acquisition of physical capital and in the accumulation of physical assets respectively. In turn, physical assets enable the debtor to engage in a monetary production with r. The fact that l also allows the on-lending of money in order to obtain a higher i is obviously undisputed. This only needs to take into account that instead of a uniform rate of interest (i), there are now different central bank (i_{cb}) and commercial bank (i_b) rates, and in place of a uniform liquidity premium (l) the different premiums of commercial bank (l_b) and entrepreneur (l_e) respectively. In a state of equilibrium, nothing will be changed because the different interest rates and liquidity premiums must be the same:

$$p = i_{cb} = l_b = i_b = l_e = r. \qquad (3)$$

Based on this simple formula, it becomes clear that it is only the party who has borrowed money or acquired money, through sales or in some other way, that has liquidity premium, and not the party who created the money in the first place.[36]

A special characteristic of the modern ownership-based economy, in contrast to its predecessor in antiquity, is the existence of the free *wage laborer*. Human beings are no longer property. It is not power but contract law that regulates the capacity of free persons to enter into agreements. In contrast to a slave, who could be mortgaged and sold by his owner, the wage laborer enters into an employment contract and retains the 'ownership' in himself, which cannot be lost, be hypothecated or be subject to a debt recovery action.[37] Like all contracts in an ownership-based society, the employment contract, which resembles a creditor-debtor contract, must be denominated in money of account. The wage laborer in the role of the 'creditor' temporarily transfers use rights over the possessory aspect of his 'property', i.e., his manpower and work outputs, to the entrepreneur, who performs the role of the 'debtor'. The entrepreneur as the debtor in relation to the employment contract must in return fulfill the demand of the wage laborer to money, which takes the form of a *money wage* measured in money wage units based on time or outputs.

The money payable as wages is not in *existence* to begin with. Hence, the entrepreneur has to *raise* the money *beforehand* as a money advance in a credit contract in which he is again the debtor. Repayment and interest must be generated through the deployment of wage labor. The wage laborer is hence the only economic agent who can obtain money without interest and loan security. However, he can only obtain money without interest and loan security because his employer has hypothecated property and has entered into interest payment obligations. In return, the wage laborer allows the entrepreneur to produce with the labor force transferred to him. It is only this that enables the producer to generate commodities with a total sum of values that realize at least the amount to be repaid *plus* interest in the commodities market.[38] Karl Marx's famous 'surplus-value' therefore does not arise from a power relation within the production process – owners of means of production *versus* property-deprived wage laborers. Rather, the surplus-value is a compensation for the effort to supply someone with money, i.e., wages, who neither pays interest nor provides loan security. Economically – albeit not socially – it is of no consequence whether someone is looking for employment contracts because he does not have property that can be hypothecated or because the individual does not want to put his property at risk.[39]

In an ownership-based economy, the entrepreneur is therefore subject to three contracts that he cannot avoid and that he can fulfill only if he can acquire an additional fourth contract, the sales contract, without any use of force:

1. the *credit contract*, a nominal and binding contract specified in money of account, stipulating the repayment of loan principal and interest and the surrender of the hypothecated property in the case of default;
2. the *supplier contract*, an equally nominal contract for the delivery of means of production by third-party suppliers, which are at least physical assets that in an emergency can be sold to regain some of the money borrowed from the bank; moreover,[40] production inputs can often also be used as loan security and therefore directly assist in the raising of money (this is not possible with labor inputs, unless these are, as in ancient Greece, Rome or some former British Colonies, provided by slaves);
3. the *employment contract*, also a nominal and binding contract, where the money outlay is always lost because the wage laborer, unlike the slave, does not become part of the entrepreneur's property; and
4. the *sales contract*, also nominal and binding but, in contrast with the above three contracts, without a predetermined contractual counterparty. The sales contract is never a certainty as counterparties have first to be attracted. It allows the entrepreneur to obtain money for his commodities, which is used to fulfill his credit contract with the bank, to release the hypothecated property and, in the case of surplus, for accumulation or income.

Because the entrepreneur has to meet the money obligation agreed in the employment contract regardless of whether or not a third party purchases his commodities for money in a sales contract, he is constantly forced to improve his prospects of realizing sales contracts in the market. This is achieved not least by underbidding the money demands (prices) of other *competing* sellers of commodities in relation to potential customers. This reduction of the money demanded in turn requires a reduction of levels of debt for wage money. This he achieves by replacing labor, which he can only obtain for money, by *technical progress*. This state of constant innovation is hence, next to the free wage laborer, the second unique characteristic of the modern ownership-based economy.

Why does technical progress in the first instance target the substitution of labor and only in the second instance the improvement of physical capital? This is because money that is spent on wages is irrecoverably lost, while money spent on physical capital can be recovered to a certain extent, because the latter – unlike wage laborers – becomes the collateralizable property of the entrepreneur.

Because wage money is lost, an entrepreneur must attempt to replace as much labor as possible by investing in labor-saving technical progress.[41] While the suppliers of innovative production equipment must also be paid, they at least provide commodities that can be salvaged in an emergency. Technical progress therefore responds to the double pressure of reducing the money wage and simultaneously and repeatedly creating a surplus for the payment of interest within the period of the loan. Therefore, constant technological upheavals occur only in systems that create money by burdening property assets, whereby interest must be demand for the act of burdening, and in addition economic activity is conducted with free wage laborers rather than slaves.[42]

Any producers in a monetary economy who no longer took part in the reduction of wage money through technical progress would worsen their prospects to gain sales contrasts from the outset, because they would produce more expensively and/or would have to offer less attractive products. They would be at risk of not being able to fulfill even their current contracts with banks and would have to transfer hypothecated property to them. Their creditworthiness would decline accordingly.

Because all property owners must strive to stay away from a state of excessive indebtedness, the whole *industry sector* is forced to participate in process or product innovations initiated by the most innovative competitor. This step is even inevitable from a microeconomic perspective, when entrepreneurs can clearly see from a macroeconomic perspective that after a general implementation of the innovation, all producers in aggregate produce faster and more than before without a matching increase in the number of customers. While increased production may create higher incomes, these do not necessarily flow to wage recipients, whose numbers will initially fall due to the technical progress. Even if this number does not decrease, higher incomes are not automatically used for the consumption of the new commodities.

For the individual and indebted entrepreneur, the information that there is a possibility that no additional customers for the commodities may be found may, however, not result in any problem-solving insights. He has the choice between (1) not taking part in the technical progress, which would result in an immediate loss of competitiveness and the fall of his property's price; or (b) the chance to be among those who can gain enough money from their customers to release their hypothecated property after implementing the technical progress. In reality, the entrepreneur has no choice but to take part, with open eyes, in the potential 'overproduction' of tomorrow, or suffer an immediate property loss today.

In the process of implementing technical progress, which is necessary for tomorrow's survival, individual industry sectors move into and out of boom phases and asset price inflations. The sellers of innovative technology products hypothecate property in order to obtain credit for their investments. The same is done by the purchasers of the modernization technologies. The borrowed money creates new demand, because in order to be able to purchase one has to take on debt or leave a net creditor position, i.e., either accept further claims against one's own property assets, or turn claims against the property of others into money.

In particular the manufacturers of modernization technologies, from which all potential users – including companies that later fail – must buy, experience an increase in the value of their company assets, for example reflected in the appreciation of their share price, because initially all indicators suggest increased earnings and therefore asset prices. Both groups, suppliers and producers, however, activate more property via loans for investments than before the innovation.

An expansion of credit alongside this innovation process is inevitable. Innovators and their customers must – and can – be supplied with credit because at the beginning of a boom the debtors' collateral and in addition the capital of banks and companies increase in value. Even money that, in particular, booming innovators could often obtain more easily than their customers through debt or share issues, i.e., without hypothecation of property, is most commonly obtained by the purchasers of these securities through bank credit with hypothecation of property.

Out of the aggregate of all firms forced to modernize, several must go near their credit and hypothecation limits when acquiring money, despite the fact that the physically unchanged but more valuable collateral has allowed increased debt positions and loans virtually overnight. Even in the case that all loans provided by a bank are secured to the nominal amount of the loan principal, the overexposure of banks in aggregate – incorrectly maligned as negligent behavior or greed – cannot be avoided. Banks, like entrepreneurs, cannot simply exit the business of defending their property assets in advance. In this race, banks can at best guess which debtors will fail and thereby will be unable to top up their devalued collateral and leave the bank with impaired loans.

Hence, the simultaneous participation of all industry sector firms in creating a possible 'overproduction' is not originated by a periodic infection of economic actors with greed. 'Overinvestment', as identified by Friedrich Hayek and the Austrian school as the cause of overproduction and crisis, is not due to a collective madness[43] but follows from the inescapable law of property defense. This law must also be followed by the investor. While not defending his own firm, he takes on debt to acquire additional assets in the boom precisely in order to improve his net property position and to stay away from a state of overindebtedness.

A 'speculator' does not act in any way different from an entrepreneur, who in general bases his expectations on so-called 'fundamentals'. However, these are no different from speculative expectations, with the exception that [fundamentals] are the result of expectations in the past while 'speculative' valuations are formed based on expectations formed in the present. The phenomena of the economic world cannot be divided into *actual values* and *expected values*, but are based on valuations coagulated in contracts that have been set on the basis of past expectations as well as valuation from the present. It is ridiculous to term the former as *real* and the latter as *speculative* just because the expectations of yesterday have not *yet* been shown to be outside the equilibrium.[44]

(Stadermann and Steiger 2001b, 377)

An 'overproduction', which is only identifiable *ex post*, manifests itself as soon as sufficient sales contracts for the collection of the owed money can no longer be found. The inflated valuations of publicly traded companies, reflected in an ever-increasing price-earnings ratio, bring with it the danger of a reversal, leading to the devaluation of collateral and as a consequence the insufficient backing of many loans. The drop in the value of loan collateral can in this situation no longer be compensated for by a rise in share prices. Downturn and asset price deflation set in.

At any given point in time, in an ownership-based economy, single or multiple industry sectors will have to implement innovations at the same time, the costs of which not all industry participants will be able to recover. This is the real essence of the statement that 'overinvestment' soon afterwards leads to 'overproduction'. Modernization phases hence result in periodic upturns and downturns contained within a sector. While noticeable, these fluctuations typically do not have a drastic economic impact.

The situation is different when many or all industry sectors suddenly engage in major investments because an innovation is far-reaching, not limited to a specific sector, and must be implemented across industries. This is mainly related to revolutions in transport, energy (steam, fuels or electricity) and information technology because all property owners are impacted. New materials with a broad range of applications also fall into this category. These nevertheless do not always occur with the same cycle time akin to a law of nature. Rather, the occurrence of several simultaneous innovations predates the beginning of great recessions. This is illustrated by a number of historical examples (see Heinsohn and Steiger 2003):

- During the start of the boom of 1789 (recession 1815) transport on canals began and at the same time production was moved to large factory halls;
- Around 1849 (recession 1873) a new steel metallurgy for railway track construction and steam engines impacted not only locomotives but also shipping and with them the whole industry, requiring a rapid growth of coal mining;
- From 1896 (recession 1920) not only the integration of combustion engine and oil exploration on a large scale, leading to the automobile, but also the general use of electricity;

- From 1922 (recession 1929) radio, telephone and mass-produced cars delivered innovations which were acquired in all industry sectors and also private households;
- From 1951 (recession 1966) the same was true for the transistor, plastics (nylon) and television for the masses; and
- From 1989 (recession 2000) computerization coincided with the interconnection of billions of people through mobile phones and the internet.

In booms across industry sectors, the illusion that 'this time it is different', together with the belief that there will never be a downturn, are fed precisely by the fact that the boom phase must take longer – in comparison to cycles affecting single industry sectors – because innovations have to be implemented everywhere. Under the general impression that business cycles are a thing of the past, a lot more members of an ownership-based society start to hypothecate property, previously not activated, to obtain credit and risk their property in order to take part in the boom as entrepreneurs or shareholders. Increasing the exposure and moving closer to the credit limit is not wrong in principle. After all, economic activity is based on the activation of property for credit, which in turn is deployed for investment in physical capital or the creation of loans to earn interest.

The seed of destruction for any boom is that asset prices move faster than profits. For example, where the share price doubles from 100 to 200 while an exceptionally high rate of profit – which is always limited by the growth rate in GDP – increases from five percent to ten percent, no harm is done. However, where the share price moves from 100 to 500 while the rate of profit 'only' doubles from five percent to ten percent, or this doubling is merely expected in the future, miracle capital gains have been achieved but the value of the firm's collateral as assessed by the banks will have already shown a tendency to be reduced. This is because the value of a property title held as collateral is determined in the long term – according to Fisher's formula – at constant interest rate by expected earnings and not the current share price.

While during a boom collateral can be temporarily forgotten, because profits are made from capital gains and not earnings, the importance of collateral becomes paramount during the downturn. When the share price has peaked at 100 while profits have dropped to two percent, during a rapid fall in share prices, share purchases will only resume once the price earnings ratio is attractive again, i.e., at least equal to fixed-income government securities. Assuming their yield is four percent, a halving of share prices is easily achieved.

After a period of industry-wide and unavoidable 'overinvestment', which indeed had to turn into a period of overproduction, all entrepreneurs that have failed to sell their products would love to outperform their competitors during the resulting downturn by initiating a new wave of investments for modernization. At the very least they will hope for bridging loans and support in settling their debts. This, however, can only succeed in a limited way. As a consequence of the downturn, their property assets will have already been largely hypothecated and in addition will have lost some of their value. These entrepreneurs will no longer have sufficient loan collateral and will no longer be able to take part in the new creation of money and demand, of which debtor collateral, when following the correct procedure, is always a key part.

Credit contracts for the temporary transfer of claims over creditor property – i.e., creditor's money – only come into existence when property assets are hypothecated as loan security. The value of the loan security, like the associated loan obligation, is expressed in *fixed* nominal money prices. Loan security, in the form of physical assets and nominal (fixed-income) securities, is subject to *fluctuating* valuations in financial markets. Nominal fixed-income securities are in addition exposed to the deterioration of the value of money, i.e., inflation. This creditor risk, not to be able to receive a repayment to the full value of the original claim, is responded to by increasing the interest demand. However, rising interest rates not only reduce the profit expectations of the entrepreneur-debtors but also have a negative impact on the value of their hypothecated property assets and all other asset holdings.

What happens when the hypothecated property is no longer sufficient to secure the loan? The commercial banks will immediately be overexposed, i.e., the book value of their loans will exceed the price of the underlying collateral. In order not to break out of the network of obligations themselves they will have to demand additional contributions from the very debtors that have just experienced a deterioration of their net property position. Thereupon the willingness to provide credit and the capacity to take on debt will be further reduced. As an unavoidable consequence, output and employment will be at risk of contracting and the chains of debtor-creditor relations will be at risk of breaking. In particular, this will be the case when inflation turns towards deflation.

Why is this happening? When the money borrowed from the banks and spent by the firms on physical capital and wages appears irretrievable, firms will start with the aggressive acquisition of sales contracts by lowering prices. Over-indebted firms will offer to customers, who will most likely be equally over-indebted, the sweet poison of deflation, which is sweet only for the customer. Deflation increases the nominally fixed obligations of firms in real terms in the same way that these obligations decrease in the case of inflation. However, the apparent symmetry between inflation and deflation, in the sense that one counterparty always wins what the other counterparty loses, in fact only holds in the case of inflation. Here the debtor gains what the creditor loses. In the case of deflation, *both* parties lose. The debtor loses because he is exposed to higher obligations in real terms. However, the creditor is not benefiting from this increase in the end. While his claims will be higher in real terms, this will also increase the bankruptcy risk of his debtor, and on default he will lose capital and move closer to the edge of bankruptcy himself.

Debt recovery actions and associated property losses are much more likely in a period of deflation. This will be anticipated, and existing debtor positions will be reduced more quickly than usual, or new positions will not be built up in the first place. The consequence will be a reduced level of money creation. These factors bring about the *crisis* and are the explanation for the rising ownership premium in this situation.

The rising liquidity premium merely reflects this aggravation, as the increase of the ownership premium precedes that of the liquidity premium. Obviously, when new money is no longer created the premium on existing money will rise. An interest offer for the transfer of money, however high, may nevertheless be unable to compensate for the premium on property that is neither burdened nor hypothecated.

A downturn also rapidly shows the limited effectiveness of interest reductions, whether achieved by the lowering of the central bank discount rate or by government interest support payments. Even at interest rates close to zero, debtors still require first-class loan security to obtain loans, as only the sale of the underlying assets allows the lenders to indemnify themselves for outstanding repayments in the event of their customers' default. Cheap central bank loans are therefore primarily used by banks to reduce their own liabilities or even to invest in higher-yielding titles.[45] Hence they typically do not reach the entrepreneur, as could be well observed in the Great Depression of 1929–1934.

A different rationale for the need to reduce interest rates in a crisis is provided by Stiglitz and Greenwald (2003, 126–127) in their critique of Hicks's IS/LM model. They realize that due to deteriorating expectations in relation to the profitability of investments, not only does the IS curve (the equilibrium curve for capital markets) shift to the left but also the LM curve (the equilibrium curve for the money market), which in the standard model is incorrectly assumed to be stable. The reason for this shift is that not only future expectations, z, are deteriorating but also the capital of banks, K, and firms, K_f: 'The $L*M*$ curve shifts because $\{K, K_f, z\}$ all vary with the business cycle'. Hence, in a downturn not only do expectations about the future become more pessimistic, but also both 'firm and bank capital may well decrease.... [A]s K decreases, banks' willingness (and ability) to lend decreases, while when K_f decreases, firms' desire to borrow may increase or decrease'. In either case the LM curve shifts to the left. Banks therefore demand a reduction in the central bank refinancing rate in order to regain their capacity to lend. Stiglitz's explanation thus differs from the neoclassical analysis. Neoclassical theory assumes that a reduction of the refinancing rate will lead to an equal reduction in the interest rate offered to firms. In contrast, Stiglitz and Greenwald (2003, 128) suggest that the refinancing rate must be lowered '*just to keep the lending rate from rising*' (emphasis in original). While neoclassical economics does not even consider a bankruptcy risk for banks, Stiglitz and Greenwald attempt to reduce this risk by providing banks with an alternative compensation mechanism to charging an increased interest margin. Higher commercial bank interest rates would increase the risk for the entrepreneur and prevent investments. Stiglitz and Greenwald hence argue that it is more appropriate to reduce the higher-risk position of banks by increasing their earnings through a low refinancing rate and the associated increase in margin between refinancing and lending rates respectively. While this approach clearly goes beyond the neoclassical blindness towards risk, Stiglitz relapses into a state of blindness towards the economic role of collateralizable property during a crisis. That the shortage of loan security remains beyond the reach of any interest rate policy is yet again not recognized.

The lack of loans to entrepreneurs despite the lowering of bank refinancing rates has been demonstrated by the period of stagnation in Japan since the beginning of the 1990s. While the Bank of Japan increased the money supply available to commercial banks in 2002 by 28.6 percent, the quantity of money reaching entrepreneurs increased by a mere 3.2 percent. This symptom of stagnation had been worked on since 1990 with the refinancing rate for commercial banks at less than one percent since the mid 1990s (September 1995: 0.5 percent). In September 2001 the rate approached zero at 0.1 percent. As further support, the government implemented billion-dollar financial stimulus packages and accepted debts of 170 percent of GDP (2005). Firms that were willing to take on debt at this low interest rate, however, could not find credit providers, with the exception of unofficial capital markets at rates up to 20 percent. This was for two main reasons. (1) Firms lacked good loan security suitable for hypothecation by banks. For example, on 9 May 2001 the Bank of Japan could only accommodate 243 billion yen out of a liquidity offer of over 600 billion yen because at the time only few firms in need of additional loans were considered 'sound' (Tett 2001). (2) Commercial banks were at the time 'not willing to provide credit due to their huge positions of bad loans. Never had such a persistent reluctance in the provision of credit been observed in Japan'[46] (Odrich 2001). Hence, only a fraction of the increased money supply, achieved through a lowering of interest rates, is received as investment loans by firms. The majority remains in the financial sector, through which it can not only recapitalize itself but also make significant profits.

Banks with bad loans resemble firms with a lack of loan security. The Bank of Japan cannot provide the missing loan security or compensate banks for bad loans. Popular suggestions with no clue about a central bank's capital position, in particular by Paul Krugman (1998), that the bank should aggressively purchase long-term government debt and in this way induce an inflation to overcome what in the meantime had become a deflationary crisis, were rejected by the Bank of Japan with the insightful comment that this would have implied a likely devaluation of its assets: 'If the Bank held only ten percent of the long-term government bonds outstanding and interest rates rose by two percentage points, the resulting losses would wipe out the institution's entire capital and reserves' (Lerrick 2001, 13; see also Section 3.6).

A central bank can fight inflation by increasing the ownership premium through an increase of its interest rate. In contrast, it can influence the lowering of the ownership premium, required to overcome a crisis, only in a very limited way. This is due to the fact that in a crisis a central bank – or any other institution in an ownership-based society – cannot produce the missing collateral, which is indispensible for the creation of creditor's money, by itself.[47]

What governments have repeatedly attempted can be characterized as no less than the fabrication of phantom property. Here loan security is created out-of-nothing and becomes the basis of money creation. The history of paper money shows, not least for the German empire, several cases where governments have circumvented the troublesome provision of genuine property by fabricating the missing titles in collaboration with central and commercial banks. The result has always been debtor's money:

> Instead of removing the root cause for the lack of commercial bills, the [German] imperial government together with the [German] Reichsbank decided to create the missing material for commercial bank refinancing operations in collaboration with the commercial banks itself ... without realizing that the economy [became paved with a] dysfunctional arbitrary money.[48]
>
> (Stadermann 1994a, 191 and 193)[49]

The phantom property from German imperial agencies included 'Darlehenskassenscheine' (state treasury warrants) during World War I, 'Finanzwechsel' (accommodation bills) under the government of Brüning (1930–1932) and, from 1934, the 'Mefo-Wechsel' (bills drawn on the Metallurgische Forschungsgesellschaft) under Hitler against which the German Reichsbank was forced to issue notes (see for more details Stadermann 1994a, 119–122, 191–194 and 201–205). In all these cases the destruction of the German monetary system was no different from that of the present-day developing country Argentina – discussed in Section 3.6 – which prior to the Great Depression (1929–1933) was among the 10 wealthiest countries in the world, ranking at the time above Sweden, France, Japan or Italy (Rojas 2002, 43).

Similar concerns began to emerge[50] when the European Central Bank (ECB) in May 2010 intervened in debt markets (see, for example, Blackstone 2011) with the purchase of predominantly Greek, Portuguese and Irish government bonds under the Securities Markets Programme (SMP). As a result of the sovereign debt crisis initially affecting Greece (bailed out at near bankruptcy), the ECB had become the only purchaser of these government bonds. While these interventions were officially justified as measures to stabilize dysfunctional markets (European Central Bank 2011a, 128) they were effectively reallocating central bank money from the private sector to governments with imprudent fiscal policies. Similar ECB interventions resumed in August 2011 to reduce yields of Spanish and Italian government bonds (see, for example, Barley 2011), further undermining the position of the ECB, holding €143 billion of such assets as at 9 September 2011[51] compared to the ECB's subscribed capital of €10.7 billion (European Central Bank 2011b, 231). Consequently, when Greece defaulted in March 2012, the biggest sovereign default in history, the ECB had to sidestep the coercive debt write-down (the exchange of bonds for longer-dated bonds at less than half their face value). Special legislation ensured that the ECB was treated as a preferred creditor and could obtain bonds with new registration numbers at their full face value.[52]

Therefore, in a crisis, commercial banks can only seemingly be provided with property on their way to the central bank counter. Moreover, this only appears to be painless because the price is the destruction of creditor's money. Entrepreneurs who approach commercial banks willing to invest cannot be furnished by them or by anyone else with sound loan security. Commercial banks can create asset-backed securities eligible for central bank discounting by transforming debtor property into those titles. However, banks cannot transfer property to potential debtors in order to receive the same property from these debtors as collateral in return. The transfer of new property to potential debtors therefore requires a new distribution or redistribution of property, the radicalism of which would parallel the great historic moments that saw the creation of full-blown ownership rights in the first place.[53]

When a state is not able to reinstate the capacity of its citizens and its entrepreneurs to take on debt, it can take on debt in place of its citizens to make investments and generate income with the created money. Nowhere – before the global financial crisis of 2008 – was this practiced more radically than in Japan between 1992 and 2005 in the aftermath of the financial crisis at the end of the 1980s. Yearly budget surpluses of 2 percent were followed by deficits of up to 8 percent. This policy of *Keynesian deficit investment spending* tripled the percentage of state debt from 60 to 170 percent.[54] While state spending was conducted at a rate of twice that of the US (7 percent compared with 3.3 percent in 2000) the focus on investment spending (Shiraishi 2003, 5) meant that the policy so far has not resulted in an inflation fiasco. The latter was expected by European Economic Community (EEC) policymakers at a budget deficit of over 3 percent and a ratio of state debt to GDP of above 60 percent, as is reflected in the targets of the 1992 Maastricht stability and growth pact set up for this purpose. However, Japan has never been subject to an inflation risk since that year.

Rather, *deficit spending* – together with the low interest rate policy of the Bank of Japan – prevented an impending deflation and with it a deep depression with bank failures and mass unemployment. In contrast, the EEC, which did not experience a financial crisis comparable to that of Japan at the end of the 1980s, has today[55] an unemployment rate that is twice as high as Japan's (4.7 percent). Attempts to comply with the conditions of the Maastricht stability pact have proven to be counterproductive. Efforts were made – in particular in the three large nations of Germany, France and Spain – to keep within the deficit limits by saving on state investment expenditure.[56] As a consequence, growth stimuli have not materialized and tax receipts have decreased.

Hence, as the end result, budget deficits have increased instead of decreasing, and accordingly public debt has risen further. On the other hand, the long period of stagnation in the Japanese economy has shown that the state can at best replace private investment but cannot stimulate it. There have been no *pump-priming* effects worth mentioning. Only since mid-2005 have there been some signs of an upturn. Whether this growth can be maintained long enough to reduce the high public debt (as in the US and the UK after World War II at over 130 percent) given a shrinking and aging population (highest average age in the world at 43 years) remains to be seen.[57]

5 Issues associated with ownership in developing and transformation countries

The process of overturning a tribal or command system and replacing it with an ownership-based society always struggles with the issue of social safety. Relations based on solidarity provide support in a tribal community. Similarly, the rulers of a command/feudal system have an obligation to look after their due- and service-providing serfs. An ownership-based society does not develop a similar social safety network from within itself. While the traditional safety networks operate at the same low levels as the associated systems of production, this protection against the uncertainties of a much more dynamic ownership-based economy is often vehemently defended.

Even where it is understood today that simultaneously with the establishment of property rights collective insurance systems need to be established, the new system can still be rejected, for example when the newly-created property titles are immediately removed by purchase. This can occur when individuals within or connected with the still-ruling political party rapidly acquire enormous amounts of property assets as part of their initial privatizations by using debtor's money forced onto the population by the state. The same can happen with the aid of foreigners from systems with well-established property rights, when the new and now free owners sell their correctly acquired assets for the foreigner's creditor's money, which is in high demand. The end result is the same. It leaves a high proportion of 'freed' individuals without property and hence without the capacity to take on debt. They can neither become entrepreneurs nor ease their hardship. When others fail to take on debt in their place by using the money obtained in credit contracts for their employment as wage laborers, they are, without a social safety network, left with nothing, or even where such a network exists they are confronted with poverty and a lack of future prospects.

John Stuart Mill (1848, 324–328) observed for the case of British India that property rights did not automatically lead to economic development. The British colonial administration confused the so-called zemindars, dues-collectors in a local feudal system without formal ownership rights, with English-style aristocrats who held ownership rights and whose peasants were free farmers producing a money rent. The zemindars, who had previously collected dues for their governments, were now to serve the new masters of the colonial administration. Because the zemindars could not fulfill the demands of the colonial administration, it confiscated the feudal land holdings and transformed them per sale into property. As a result, not only did the zemindars lose their part of the feudal dues but also the serfs lost the previous protective arrangements. While the purchasers turned into property owners – predominantly officials paid by the British or local money dealers – they did not behave like owners but rather like new feudal rulers, though without honoring the traditional protection. They overextended the exploitation of farmers and were reported to 'live as useless drones on the soil which has been given up to them' (Mill 1848, 327; see also Steppacher 2008 for more detail).

5.1 The unabating poverty of developing countries[1]

After more than two trillion US dollars in development aid between 1970 and 2004 (Siddiqi 2005), out of which 570 billion went to Africa alone, and yet with poverty prevailing (less than US$825 gross income per capita per year) in 77 out of 191 UN member countries, the reasons that trigger economic development continue to be mysterious. The September 2005 issue of the IMF journal *Finance and Development* finally gave its authors, after 45 years of development aid, the hopeful topic of 'Making Aid Work'. Even though the economic growth rate is a largely undisputed yardstick for the success of development programs, all that was produced were vague statements about the positive influence of civil rights and in particular the need of 'good policies and institutions' (Radelet *et al.* 2005, 17). Authors were reluctant to embellish these statements with specific details.

One has thus hardly advanced beyond Jan Tinbergen and Ragnar Frisch, the first Nobel laureates in economics (1969). These two originators of econometrics and founders of economic development planning hoped that economics would create decisive breakthroughs by orienting itself methodologically closer and closer to the natural sciences. Frisch (1970, 31) refers his audience to the Nobel laureate for physics of 1968, Luis W. Alvarez, who in his acceptance lecture regards the developmental problems of a country such as India as much more complex than the questions of his discipline, in which, for example, the increased temperature of an object when adding heat can be precisely predicted. Frisch noted:

> I quite agree that such problems as that of India are not yet solved. But to help solving them is precisely the high ambition of the econometric planner. The *difficulty* of such problems is our excuse for not having reached the same level of precision as the physical sciences have. *But we are on our way.*

Tinbergen (1969, 3) shares this optimism. It is merely the lack of data that presents an obstacle for development planning: 'This also implies that for the choice of the best investment projects of some developing country much preciser information is needed than ordinary statistics can give us'. He expects progress from a model considering several social and political variables and refers to the impressive attempt made by Irma Adelman ... using factor analysis and discriminant functions in order to discover which of some thirty odd factors, measured in a heroic way, seem to play a preponderant part in the process of development.

Unfortunately, nothing useful has ever come from this 'heroic' attempt.

What is the status today of the 'good policies and institutions' demanded? 'Good policies' refer mainly to macroeconomic *stabilization programs* through which fiscal deficits and excessive money supply growth are to be prevented. 'Good institutions' refer predominantly to the liberalization of markets and privatization. However, any concept that in developing countries de facto possessory rights prevail, with formal property rights the exception, does not exist. That markets can only develop when property rights have already been created was the bitter experience of Austrian farmers as early as 1848 (see Section 4.1). However, this appears no longer to be current knowledge for today's scholars specializing in the theories of economic development.

The same holds true for stabilization programs, which in reality can only be effective when the foundations of an ownership-based society have been laid and hence when the preconditions for a banking system with creditor's money are met.

The Millennium Project designed by Jeffrey Sachs (2005a), which aims to achieve a boost in wealth creation through *infrastructure projects* (see also Sachs 2005b, 2005c), is an example of this helplessness. Every poor village in Africa, Asia and Latin America is to be supplied with a school, hospital ward, well, diesel generator, truck and seeds, at a cost of US$350,000, within 20 years to achieve a constant improvement of living conditions. Even though it is almost touching that the proposal modestly omits to mention motorways, seaports and airports, the estimated costs of the total package is still US$70 billion per annum or a total of 1.4 trillion dollars up to the year 2025. The proposal hence seeks to double the current public development aid. It is hoped that future aid proceeds of US$2.8 trillion will become effective via the indirect route of improved infrastructure. Nothing was further from the mind of Ferdinand I of Austria when he created new property rights in 1848. Despite its desperate poverty at the time, Austria caught up with the wealthiest countries in the world within a few generations.

Sachs defends his numbers by pointing to the fact that the current development aid at 0.3 percent of GDP of donor countries falls significantly short of the self-imposed target of one percent of GDP, and even at double the current amount would remain below target. However, if one considers the GDP of countries receiving aid, up to 20 percent of their GDP is already provided from outside without any reduction in poverty. Many countries are worse off than a quarter century ago, for example, sub-Saharan Africa with a yearly per capita income of US$514 (Dreher 2005).[2]

Sachs' infrastructure would be taken care of if supply contracts and due dates were setting the pace in these economies. In an ownership-based society, the failure to meet due dates ultimately results in defaulting credit contracts and the loss of hypothecated property. Therefore, anyone who sees infrastructure as the initial step without ensuring its sustainability through a contract-driven property system wastes creditor's money, which had to be earned under the strict discipline of contracts in the donor countries.

However, the Peruvian Hernando de Soto (2000) realized during his studies at the University of Geneva that a land of mountain farmers, not unlike his own, could advance to the top based on a strict property rights system. Eugen Huber's Swiss civil code of 1907 became the most modern civil code in the world. De Soto takes up Huber's reform and shows that developing countries are poor not because they suffer from a lack of real estate assets but because the majority of the population has no access to property rights and as a consequence is not able to obtain credit.

In developing countries only 10 percent of real estate is held under formal ownership rights, while at least 70 percent of loans in the developed world are secured by real estate. Therefore it does not come as a surprise that the OECD countries, together with a group of similar number – in total 59 countries with 1.3 billion people – create within their property rights systems 96 percent of world GDP, while the 140 developing countries with their population of 5.2 billion only account for the remaining 4 percent. Measured in terms of the world market capitalization, which measures the value of listed companies, the former group even accounts for 98 percent while the latter only accounts for 2 percent (Merrill Lynch et al. 2002, 17).

De Soto founded the Instituto Libertad y Democracia (ILD) in 1980 to design property reform programs – initially for Peru – based on seven principles for the institutional transformation of extralegal 'informal' into legal 'formal property rights' (ILD 2003): (1) implementable institutional change; (2) the creation of the cultural and technical capability to identify, localize and classify rights to extralegal assets; (3) reforms to the legal system so that property rights can be enforced; (4) the engagement of the poor so that they voluntarily accept the rule of law; (5) the removal of obstacles related to the legalization of informal possession of the poor; (6) the legal documentation of property titles and transformation of 'dead' resources into 'living' assets; and (7) the state acceptance of this documentation of the property of the poor so that they can obtain credit through the hypothecation of this property.

The ability to hypothecate property is indeed the be-all and end-all of economic activity. In this respect, de Soto and the property rights program of the ILD are on the right track, although the differentiation between informal and formal property is a little clumsy from a theoretical point of view. 'Informal property', i.e., informal ownership of property, does not exist. What exists is de facto possession. In turn, a formal property rights framework can transform de facto possession into *de jure* possession, a full property right, which cannot exist without the associated right of ownership in the property asset (see Section 1.3).

The reasons for the resistance against property reform programs, encountered not only from the great feudal landholders but also from the poor, in whose interest the reforms are introduced, remain unexplained by de Soto. The poor fear the loss of their social support networks no less than the former serfs of India who were conquered by the British. They cannot be sure that they will be able to survive the competition in national markets, nor that they will be able to rely on an initial protection from international competition and markets (see also Brockmeier 1996).

The ILO (International Labour Office) comes very close to identifying the property rights issues of developing countries when it makes the distinction between possession and ownership and wants to be active in areas where small and medium producers cannot obtain credit due to a lack of collateral. The ILO discards the idea of de Soto's ILD to transform de facto possessors into legal owners and in this way to endow them with loan security. With explicit reference to Stiglitz, the ILO considers collateral merely as a means requested by banks due to the asymmetry of information, i.e., required due to lack of information about the debtors. The endangering of bank capital when collateral requirements are waived is, as in Stiglitz, not a topic (see Section 2.3.1). For this reason the ILO wants to improve the credit capacity in so-called *social finance programs* through *collateral substitutes* (ILO 2001), which are designed to remove problems associated with informational asymmetries. Hence *microfinance* is to be provided not to individual producers – for example, the home-based needleworker – but to producers associated in small factories, who can incentivize and control each other, and in this way, become more manageable for banks. However, no specific pressure is to be exerted. Hence any form of debt recovery action in the case of non-payment – for example, against yarns and sewing machines – is precluded. The only form of sanction is the refusal of additional credit.

The ILO's enthusiasm about microfinance has in the meantime been shared by the World Bank and many development economists: 'There is arguably more widespread support for microfinance today than any other single tool for fighting world poverty' (McIntosh and Wydick 2005, 272). Triggered by a resolution at the so-called Microfinance Summit of 1997 to grant such credits to 100 million of the poorest households in the world, estimated at a sum of US$50 billion (C.W. 2005, 8), a worldwide industry with 1,600 microfinance institutions has sprung up.

The most important country for this industry has become Bangladesh, with the Grameen Bank as the flagship institution.[3] Initially the bank appeared, with a loan default rate of only 5 percent, to be quite successful. However, in 2001, when the rate increased to 19 percent, the bank nearly faced insolvency. As a consequence, interest rates for microfinance in Bangladesh have now reached up to 30 percent, once again excluding the poorest debtors from access to loans. The development economists Craig McIntosh and Bruce Wydich believe, in agreement with the World Bank, that the reasons for this development are imitators, who 'have brought on more competition, making it harder for Grameen to control their borrowers' (McIntosh and Wydick 2005, 274). As a result, the asymmetry of information *à la* Stiglitz between banks and debtors has increased. This can only be mitigated by a centralization of competition and risk management:

More 'centrally managed' competition between lenders in Bangladesh will both help to foster healthy competition between MFIs while bringing down arrears rates in MFI portfolios.... Another clear implication of our research is the need for ... central risk-management systems, which identify outstanding debt *in addition* to cases of default.

(McIntosh and Wydick 2005, 274 and 292)

These are all touching ideas about the functioning of banks under competition and in a situation where there is a lack of loan security. However, the above authors fail to recognize, like Stiglitz, that for the equalization of risk between creditor and debtor, even in the case of perfect information, the provision of loan security cannot be dispensed with. It remains to be seen if one day factories in the developed world would also make a stand against their closure with reference to the past accessibility of their premises to bank inspectors. Why not also waive the 'unproductive' rate of interest, which could also be held to arise from informational asymmetries? Besides, the general abandonment of property creation will neither result in spending power nor markets in which the, certainly industrious, textile collectives can sell their goods. And to the extent that markets do emerge, the competition with high-technology textile companies from countries with cheap and skilled labor such as India and China needs to be taken into consideration.

Social problems associated with missing collateral are also encountered in the developed world. An example is the 'young and innovative entrepreneur', who is prevented by a lack of collateral from setting up his own business. Hence, in some countries the state with its access to the taxes of all property owners provides venture capital and guarantees, with which entrepreneurs can secure bank loans.[4] The rules of an ownership-based economy, which provide that loans can never be created out-of-nothing but must always be based on property titles, are in every respect fulfilled.

Which programs are offered to the poor by the World Bank, the most important institution for developing countries? Programs are administered by the International Development Association (IDA), the World Bank organization for the poorest developing countries. Until recently, the World Bank has not taken notice of the importance of legal ownership for economic development. The last official statement in relation to property rights is found in a Land Reform policy paper of 1975. In the context of such a land reform, rights to land were analyzed with a focus on the physical, i.e., mere possessory use of the land but without regard to the capacities of legal ownership. Consequently, the analysis targeted the distribution of land. The access to property titles over land that can be hypothecated did not play a role.

Finally in 2003, Klaus Deininger, in a research report for the World Bank, takes a new look at property rights, which he believes can lead IDA development programs in a different direction. Many insights of ownership economics are applied in this work. Deininger's focus is on land rights. In his view land is the crucial asset in developing countries and provides the ideal collateral, based on its immobility and near indestructibility. However, land is also the only basis for a social safety net. Deininger thus views the collateralization of land only as a secondary option. Debt recovery actions in the land of the poor that are unable to repay their debts would destroy the basis of their subsistence and benefit only the already wealthy. This closeness to the ILO position, however, does not tempt Deininger to adopt their social finance programs with collateral substitutes. He favors leasehold tenures and marketing support. Because leasehold only requires minimal upfront capital, the missing collateral becomes a secondary problem and does not adversely impact the incentives of the leaseholder to invest in his leasehold, an impact which would reduce growth.

That Deininger's proposal is appropriate in principle can be confirmed by looking at the historical example of the creation of land ownership in England. After enduring social conflicts, the former aristocrats became a landed bourgeoisie, while in the sixteenth century the leaseholders became the first capitalists of modern times (Heinsohn and Steiger 1981a,b). However, Deininger's recourse to Stiglitz's theory of credit rationing, with the associated explanation of collateral as a means against asymmetric information and moral hazard, leads him, like the ILO, onto the wrong track. Deininger does not appear to realize that the asymmetric distribution of risk between bank and debtor must always be balanced by sound loan security. This holds equally in developing countries. Even if a lender had perfect information about the *current* state of the most respected debtor, the requirements for loan security could never be waived because this would create an unacceptable risk to the capital of the bank should the debtor become insolvent for whatever reasons in the *future*.

Developing countries can learn more from the study of history than from current development programs. We have already referred to the Netherlands, Austria and Switzerland and their race to catch up with the English ownership economy.[5] Other territories in Western Europe gained their property rights through the *code civile* implanted by their conqueror Napoleon. The showpiece for the inducement of economic development, however, was provided by Stein and Hardenberg's reforms of ownership rights in Prussia in 1807, which are often misinterpreted as mere emancipation policies. These reformers only got the chance to implement their policies because Prussia had suffered a devastating defeat against Napoleon in the battle of Jena (1806) and could not generate enough proceeds under the existing feudal system to repay the imposed war debt. Stein and Hardenberg knew that feudal 'land ownership'[6] was different from land ownership that was freed from feudal dues and restrictions. Nevertheless, they alternate in their terminology between the terms 'possession' and 'ownership'. As as result of the reforms, the former feudal lords became full property owners. Previously they could hypothecate their harvest but not the land, which was considered to belong ultimately and by divine right to the King. Similarly, the former serfs were permitted to purchase their previously feudal allotments. By 1914 the per capita income of the German empire founded by Prussia had overtaken the then developed world, at the time broadly identical with England. Similar developments were induced in the second half of the nineteenth century, with varying degrees of success, in Russia under Tsar Alexander II, and in Japan under the Emperor Meiji.

After World War II, South Korea was one of the first countries to take a path towards the introduction of ownership. Through the 1949 land reform, President Syngman Rhee increased the proportion of land able to be hypothecated from 14 percent to 93 percent in 1959 (Lankov 2003). Not even held back by a devastating civil war (1950–1953), what was at the time one of the poorest countries in the world accomplished arguably the most impressive economic development in history. There are only a handful of countries left today that can compete with Korea's advanced technological innovations. Only comparable is the once-backward Chinese province of Taiwan. Chiang Khai-shek, who fled from the communists of Mao Zedong to Taiwan, in 1953 created with his property development program, 'Land to the Tillers', the second 'tiger' economy of East Asia.

The above examples represent radical reforms generally in exceptional historical circumstances in which social transformations can occur that in normal times would be suppressed in their earliest stages. If reforms are to succeed, undisputable documentation of property rights and the rule of law must be guaranteed for all. While such measures can be recommended from the outside, they require a genuine revolution for the affected countries, and not just the stroke of a pen.

For instance, someone who wants to register property requires just a single procedure in Norway but 16 in Algeria. In the case of property transfers through sale, the administrators in Nigeria and Senegal take 30 percent of the property value, while a maximum of 5 percent is common in the developed world. The safeguarding of creditors is so difficult because they are the most likely group to be compared with the masters of (de facto) possessions in the old system, and in consequence are resented. However, if creditors cannot be protected from their own demise when their debtors default or from the loss of property for non-economic reasons, the whole system stagnates or comes to a complete standstill. For these reasons, the differences between developing countries and the developed world are the most dramatic in this sensitive area. For example, while in Mumbai, India's leading financial center, a creditor on average can only recover 13 percent of the loan sum from an insolvent debtor, the recovery rate is 90 percent in Tokyo. Creditors who want to enforce their contracts need 13 procedures in Denmark and 53 in Laos (see World Bank 2005, 2; see also de Soto 2000).

5.2 Successes and mistakes of countries transforming from state socialism

State socialism, from 1917 to 1990 referred to as the 'second world', is even more distanced from the ownership-based society than the developing world. Its program, however, sought to outperform the ownership-based society, misunderstood as 'capitalism', in per capita income, social safety and level of technology. In this transformation, the socialist revolutionaries misunderstood the de facto possessions of the state, created after the abolition of private ownership, as 'ownership by the people'. This misunderstanding was perpetuated by western transformation consultants in the 1990s. Their principle of privatization sought to privatize the assets held in 'state ownership' without realizing that they merely turned these into private de facto *possessions* without the underlying property rights framework.

Fantasies of attaining technological world leadership by unleashing productive forces (Marx) would have simply provoked Homeric laughter in an ordinary developing country. For the Marxist-Leninist politicians, however, these ambitions were deadly serious, and in the end the number of people worked to death in state socialist territories numbered more than 100 million.

A large group of victims were, not surprisingly, the former property owners themselves. The second major group were formed by those who demanded the promised wealth. They were tormented to the last day and worked to death in gigantic numbers. 'Where are the "fountains of wealth" opened up through the abolition of private ownership?' remained the stated or unstated question of the trained Marxists. Pressured by this question, the nomenclatura had principally four responses:

1 One could admit that one had followed the wrong economic theory and that the cursed 'private ownership' is linked to collateral, interest and money, the risking and deployment of which ensures the superior dynamic of the ownership-based economy. However, as a consequence one would have also had to admit that the abolition of ownership has a similar effect on wealth as the removal of the motor on the speed of a motor car or the removal of the lung on the progress of the treatment for tuberculosis. Admissions of this nature were in particular difficult because the challengers did not have an alternative economic theory which could have done justice to the economic potency of ownership. From classical economics to Keynesianism, the same cluelessness ruled, including in the classical economist Marx.

2 One could also speedily kill the people who had asked for the fountains of wealth. This indeed explains a significant proportion of the deaths. The cleansing of parties, the removal of factions (those oriented towards the West) were on the whole actions against people within their own ranks, who, when the wealth failed to materialize, began to doubt the doctrine of the abolition of ownership. They were denounced as 'poisoned' by ownership. This included at times Lenin, who in 1921, with his New Economic Policy (NEP), after all returned to ownership, interest and money. This betrayal of the Marxist doctrine was corrected by Stalin, who between 1928 and 1938 took radical steps to eliminate ownership by forcing farmers into collectives, killing the resisters along the way.

3 Questions about the fountains of wealth could also be put to rest by references to saboteurs: had not so many hostile forces sabotaged the genial economic doctrine of the creation of wealth by the abolition of ownership, socialism would have much further advanced in overtaking the West. The

corresponding extermination of alleged saboteurs and allegedly sloppy workers became a further segment of the incredible wastage of human life under socialist rule.
4   Finally, it was possible to deploy the person demanding the promised wealth in its creation in a very special way. This became the most important way of killing – in Russia the termination through the Chief Administration of Corrective Labor Camps and Colonies (GULAG) and in China by 'reform through labor' (laogai): 'You, poisoned by ownership, will not experience the wealth yourself, but we will allow you to take part in bloodstained socialist wonders like White Sea canals or cathedral-like metro systems that in a flash will illuminate our superiority before the world'.

But now to the recreation of economic activity in Eastern Europe: during the transformation of state socialism, beginning in Poland in 1990, Jeffrey Sachs did a dry run for his UN Millennium Project of 2005. Here he also failed to recognize ownership creation as the foundation of economic development and declared that 'transforming the state's property into private property' was to be only the 'the *final step*' (Sachs 1993, 80; emphasis added).

The resulting delay in the establishment of ownership rights in turn impacted on the banking system that emerged at the same time. Until 1989, commercial banks had not existed. After their creation they had to experience how customers looking for credit, and active in the markets recommended by Sachs, believed that the drawer with the cash would simply be opened as long as they committed to repayment and interest. Moreover, the freshly-inducted bank employees did not know what steps were involved in approving a loan. Sachs and the other Western advisors remained silent on this issue, and Poland's central bank did not offer any assistance. It continued with the real-socialist practice of printing and distributing debtor's money, in the old system referred to as 'state money token'[7] or 'reckoning token'[8] (Payandeh 2004, 150). The central bank believed that everything was in order as long as it would request repayment and interest from the commercial banks. Sound titles for the backing of its notes, which it could have demanded from the commercial banks, were of course not available due to the rarity of property-rich owner-debtors. Not surprisingly, the realization of the existence of such a thing as a bad loan came as a shock. What neoclassical economics, which was adopted in these countries with great admiration and excitement, is not aware of became rapidly the priority issue through a panic over bad loans. Only now were academic advisors left aside and Western banking practitioners engaged. In hastily-set-up crash courses they taught Polish bankers the most important banking rule in an ownership-based economy: 'Lesson 1: In the new economy, ask the borrowers for collateral' (Stevenson 1993, 17).

Despite these instructions, property rights in Poland have remained constrained and well-intentioned measures to prevent social hardship have undermined their economic potential. For example, legislation in Poland, and similarly in the Czech Republic, prevented until the end of 2003 foreclosure on owner-occupied residential property. This avoided forced evictions, but as a consequence banks no longer accepted residential property as collateral. In order to protect 3 to 4 percent of the population from social hardship, 100 percent no longer had the opportunity to obtain credit based on their residential property.

The extent of this strangulation of credit creation is evidenced by the fact that until today, outstanding mortgage loans in Poland and the Czech Republic are merely 3–5 percent of GDP, while they are at 50 percent in the European Union. Only in the latter are mortgages unfolding their significant force in the support of economic growth (Immobilia 2004).[9]

Policies regulating property rights are always an integral part of economic policy and must not be watered down by other objectives. Social consequences of lending must be addressed by social policies and never by putting a halt on hypothecation, which reduces the right of ownership to mere possession. Nations that are experienced in ownership therefore provide simple housing in which evicted individuals are accommodated at the expense of the taxpayer, rather than 'protecting' these individuals through a general inhibition of lending.

Highly advanced nations with a somewhat better understanding of ownership even use taxpayers' funds allocated to social emergencies to directly create property assets for the affected individuals. Instead of paying for the housing of such families, enriching landlords already endowed with property, the rental support payments are used as down payments for state-financed apartments. This form of forced saving allows the individuals to acquire the apartment when the period of hardship has passed. The affected individuals are not just receiving temporary support but are equipped with a permanent capacity to take on credit. This generally increases their motivation to perform within their society. The prime example for such a path is the city-state of Singapore. Here almost every citizen, including the lowest 20 percent of income earners, owns residential property – on average valued at S$138,000 or about €68,000 (Loong 2005).

The difficulties associated with creating ownership in transformation countries also have dramatic consequences for foreign investors. For these, the taking up of credit in the domestic currency is difficult as long as only a limited number of property titles are fully enforceable. For this reason they fund the majority of their investments with imported creditor's money (foreign currency). This capital import creates a demand for the domestic currency, which stabilizes or even pushes up their exchange rate. Hence the lack of a domestic property basis for the granting of credit can remain hidden or be downplayed.[10] Because the resulting profits of foreign companies can again only be turned into secure domestic property titles in a limited way, the accumulation that could be enabled with these moves back into the country of origin. When such a capital flight is no longer offset by capital imports, the exchange-rate-stabilizing demand for the domestic currency disappears. Only now does it become obvious that the central bank, with its relatively valueless assets, cannot compensate for the falling external demand for its currency.[11] The depreciation runs its course (see Heinsohn and Steiger 2001, 218).

The prime example demonstrating the consequences of a currency system not based on domestic property is the Russian financial crash of August 1998. Here an IMF stabilization credit, provided in July 1998, of over 10 billion US dollars led to a reduction of the central bank foreign currency reserves to an equal amount: 'In the end, defense of the currency turned out to be fruitless and expensive, costing around ten billion dollars in reserves' (Bracho and López 2005, 61).

It cannot come as a surprise that in all transformation countries the mistakes made in the creation of property, or even its absence, are mirrored by inadequate legal systems, which prevent effective debt recovery actions and hence do not protect the property position of creditors, critical for sustainable economic development. Hence, in 2002 it was noted with some frustration:

> Virtually no transition country succeeded in rapidly developing a legal system and institutions that would be highly conducive to the preservation of private property and the functioning of a market economy.... This lack of market-oriented legal structure appears to have been the Achilles' heel of the first dozen years of transition.
>
> (Svejnar 2002, 7)[12]

An exception, as Ulrich Aldenborg (2005) has shown, was Slovenia (population two million). Immediately after 1990, about 100,000 houses and apartments, formerly in state possession and not economically activated, were transformed into hypothecatable property.[13] This generated seemingly out-of-nothing loan collateral to the value of €4.5 billion available for the financing of investments. Even ambiguities related to the registration of property titles, still a problem to this day (Kaps 2005, 18), were dealt with by the Slovenians in a flexible way through the establishment of legal protection even for suspected owners (Aldenborg 2005, 52–53). With these steps the country enabled itself to generate creditor's money. Hence, Slovenia demonstrates to other transforming countries that capital imports, typically viewed as critical, become secondary when money advances can be created domestically by emancipating citizens as property owners. This small south Slavic state advanced so rapidly in comparison to other transformation countries because it, contrary to the recommendation of its advisors, made the acquisition of property very difficult for foreigners and instead supported the acquisition of property by its own citizens in a significant way.

The People's Republic of China followed the despised 1953 reforms of the defeated Chiang Kai-shek, at least in selected territories, but only after 1990. Shanghai, with a population of 15 million, became the richest city on the mainland because between 1992 and 2002 it increased, like Slovenia, the proportion of real estate held with ownership titles, including houses and apartments, from 0 to 90 percent (McGregor 2002, 13). This required the establishment of a new registration system for hypothecated property. Only in August 2002 was legislation passed for the whole of China, which set in motion the same revolution towards money-creating property in the rural districts. On 8 November 2001, the then President Jiang Zemin invited 'industrialists, entrepreneurs, employees of foreign companies and self-employed individuals' to join the communist party.

The ultimate goal of communism was no longer mentioned. Instead he requested a withdrawal from the old maxim 'the more property the less developed'.

Under communism – as in feudalism – peasants were tied to the soil without the right to change their place of residence. On 5 January 2003 these peasants obtained the constitutional guarantee to be allowed to work anywhere. Only now did they become the owners of themselves (Hutzler and Lawrence 2003, 2) and become able to enter into employment contracts in order to obtain money without loan security and interest obligations. In turn, their wage labor generated the interest proceeds firms owed the banks for the credit provision of wage money.

However, many of the 145 million migrant workers – a number equalling the USA's total labor force – who, by October 2011, were exercising the right to enter work contracts all over China are still somewhat dependant on the *hukou* system that forces them to return home if they want to collect social benefits and take advantage of publicly funded education for their offspring. Thus, the right of choosing one's residence is not yet fully liberated from feudal shackles.

At the National People's Congress on 5–14 March 2004, the right of Chinese citizens to property was lifted to a constitutional right. Finally, on 1 October 2007, the 'Property Law of the People's Republic of China' went into effect. It regulates not only the transfer and ownership of property but also the creation of the rights of ownership. More than six centuries after the first establishment of property rights and the abolishing of serfdom in England in the wake of the Lollard revolt (1381), the country with the world's largest population followed a development model that in the nineteenth century and the early twentieth had transformed one of the most backward territories in Europe into the leading empire of the world.

Editor's glossary of ownership economic terms and concepts

Table B

Burdening	A burden is placed on property assets when a note issuer reserves or sets aside part of his property to back a money note issue.
Capital	Money advance.
Claim against assets	A legal right for the payment of a nominal money sum with respect to a property owner. Claims can be secured and unsecured. Examples for unsecured claims are promissory notes (promises to pay) including money notes. If not fulfilled these can be enforced in debt recovery actions, where on non-payment the debtor's assets are sold and the proceeds distributed to the creditors. Hence these rights represent claims against the debtor's general assets. Secured claims are created in secured loan contracts and provide the creditor with a direct recourse against the debtor's asset over which the security has been taken.
Coin	Not money, but a nominal asset (with defined face value); resembles a debt instrument 'printed' on non-precious metal (nominal coins) or debt instrument with attached collateral in the form of precious metal (specie).
Command system	Economic system governing reproduction (production, distribution, consumption) through coercive mechanisms. For example, a ruling class extracts dues and services from serfs or serf-like workers as in a feudal/socialist seigneurie.
Creditor's money	Money notes created according to sound banking principles on the basis of good collateral or short-term repurchase operations of market-valued assets and backed by the issuer's capital.
Debtor's money	Money created by the direct monetization of debt, typically government debt. For example, a central bank purchasing debt instruments directly from the government (and not in secondary markets), the granting of direct government loans or significant purchases of government debt in secondary markets that influence the prices and are not matched by corresponding government debt sales transactions within an appropriate period of time.

continued

Economic activity	Economic activity in a genuine sense results from the activation of property titles through burdening and hypothecation for the creation of money. The resulting creditor-debtor contracts create a specific form of monetary production. Producers engage in economic activity and deploy the money advance as physical capital and labor. Products must be sold at an aggregate price (volume × unit price) that must at least generate the money advance with interest.
Enforcement	The enforcement of secured or unsecured claims over assets in debt recovery actions, leading to a sale of the debtor's assets.
Firm (company)	Entities that must defend themselves against a decline in the price of their assets and the risk of foreclosure. They do this by implementing continuous innovations in their physical possession (plant and equipment) where goods are modified, manufacturing processes are revolutionized or new consumer needs are created. Firms invest money in plant, equipment and wages and must enter into credit arrangements with commercial banks. The money sum owed to the banks (loan principal and interest) is always greater than the money advance creating the need to realise a profit.
Hypothecation	Security rights over assets where the possession stays with the debtor.
Interest	Compensation for the loss of ownership premium. In a money-creating creditor-debtor contract the rate of interest compensates the loss of ownership premium experienced by the creditor (typically a note-issuing bank), who has to reserve or set aside property assets to back the note issue.
Liquidity premium	Premium arising on money balances because money can settle obligations at any time. In a money-creating creditor-debtor contract the liquidity premium compensates the loss of ownership premium experienced by the debtor, who has to hypothecate or set aside property assets in the process.
Market	The market is an entity that becomes necessary *uno actu* with the money-creating credit contract and allows for the acquisition of sales contracts over commodities that provide the means to refund debts. Like money, the market is not simply always in existence, waiting for someone to be active in it. On the contrary, it is only established by purchases and ceases to exist when no purchases are taking place. The market is not found in possession-based command and tribal systems that do not have the property-based credit contracts from which markets are derived.
Money	Abstract claim over a property asset created in a creditor-debtor contract. Examples are bank notes and deposits created by private note-issuing banks or central bank notes and deposits. Deposits created by commercial banks are not money but claims to central bank money.
Money of account	Abstract unit for measuring debts.

Editor's glossary

Ownership	Residue of legal rights in an asset held by a person after other rights – such as possession – have been granted to others. An example is a title to land created through entry in a land titles register.
Ownership-based society	A society of free individuals based on property rights that has replaced rules based on reciprocity, custom or coercive orders with *enforceable contracts* denominated in money of account.
Ownership premium	Premium on property that is neither burdened nor hypothecated, i.e. that is unencumbered and free.
Possession	Factual occupation, control or physical use of property.
Property	Object subject to property rights, for example, land, buildings, livestock, goods, machines, cars, financial assets.
Tribal community	Possession-based economic system governing reproduction (production, distribution, consumption) based on mutually binding *customary* rules (following the principles of reciprocity) imposed on its dependent members collectively.
Wage labor	Labor provided under a contract where a laborer provides his manpower and work outputs to an entrepreneur for the payment of money wages. The laborer – unlike the slave – retains the 'ownership' in himself, which cannot be lost, be hypothecated or be the subject of a debt recovery action. The money payable as wages is not in *existence* to begin with. Hence, the entrepreneur has to *raise* the money *beforehand* as a money advance in a credit contract in which he is the debtor. Repayment and interest must be generated through the deployment of wage labor. Wage labor is the dominant way to gain access to money without the obligation to pay interest and to burden or hypothecate property.

Editor's summary of the role of property rights in the modern ownership-based economic system

Table C

Aspect	Note-issuing central bank	Commercial bank	Enterprise/entrepreneur	Wage laborer
	bank capital	bank capital, bank assets	production assets	human 'assets'
Ownership aspect (activated through burdening and hypothecation)	• non-physical title • ownership premium lost when capital is set aside (burdened) to back the creation of money • lost ownership premium is offset by interest received from commercial banks • capital and assets can be sold and are subject to debt enforcement actions	• non-physical title • ownership premium is lost when assets are hypothecated (or transferred in repurchase agreements) and capital is set aside to obtain central bank notes • lost ownership premium is offset by interest received from loans to non-bank enterprises • ongoing income stream from assets used as collateral for central bank loans • capital and assets can be sold and are subject to debt enforcement actions	• non-physical title • ownership premium lost when hypothecated to obtain bank loans for investment in production assets and wage labor • assets can be sold and are subject to debt enforcement actions	• freedom (humans no longer property chattels/slaves) is non-physical too but cannot be burdened, sold or subject to debt enforcement actions • right to hire out labor to gain interest-free wage money
Possessory aspect (activated through physical use and control)	• if tangible property, can be used simultaneously with activation of ownership aspect	• if tangible property, can be used simultaneously with activation of ownership aspect	• physically deployed in income-generating production activities (to refund debt and interest) • defends competitive position by technical progress and innovative investments	• wage labor deployed in production to generate income to repay loan with interest • defends competitive position through qualification and training

Notes
Editor's addition based on Heinsohn 2010.

Notes

Ownership economics: An introduction – by Frank Decker

1 For example, Heinsohn and Steiger (1981b, 1983, 1989, 1997, 2000a, 2006a, 2006b) and Steiger (2006a).
2 Hence the sequence ownership, interest and money.
3 For example, as noted by Keynes in 1934: 'There is, I am convinced, a fatal flaw in ... the orthodox reasoning ...; the flaw being largely due to the failure of the classical doctrine to develop a satisfactory theory of the rate of interest' (Keynes 1934, 489). Similar statements can still be found 70 years later: 'The question why there is a rate of interest was never answered by the discipline of economics. This burdens the economist with a moral problem which he cannot escape' (Binswanger 2003). (Original: 'Die Frage, warum es Zinsen gibt, hat die Ökonomie bis heute nicht gelöst. Dies ist eine moralische Frage, die der Ökonom nicht los wird'.)
4 Heinsohn 2011, private communication.
5 Original: Das Patriarchat.
6 Original: Ursprung und Zerfall des Patriarchats?.
7 Original: Theorie für die Entstehung der Hochpatriarchate, der deduktiven Logik und der Notwendigkeit des Geldes.
8 Steiger in a private discussion saw this as one of the key insights that helped to develop the ownership-based explanation of interest.
9 Decker (2010, 169–181) further investigated the role played by physical assets commonly identified as 'money' and concluded that these were in fact not money but 'settlement assets', a missing category in the theory of money.
10 Original: Das Geheimnis des Zinses.
11 Original: Zins: Grundlegung der Wirtschaftstheorie.
12 Original: Eigentum, Zins und Geld: Grundlegung der Wirtschaftstheorie.
13 A late change introduced only in March 1996, two months prior to the completion deadline of the manuscript.
14 Original: Schulökonomie.
15 See, for example, the insightful comments by Childs (1914, 1–2) who notes '[t]he word "property", in law, has two significations, meaning, first, "something owned"; and, second, "ownership". ... Property in its first sense – that of "something owned", is classified into Real Property, or Realty, and Personal Property, or Personalty'. Blackstone uses the term 'property' in the sense of dominium (ownership right over a thing): see Blackstone (1893 [1753]), for example Chapter II. In contrast, Pollock in his seminal work on possession uses the term 'ownership', while the term 'property' mostly identifies the thing owned; see for example Pollock (1888, 8–12; also Pollock and Maitland 1898, Chapter IV).

Preface to the first German edition of *Ownership Economics* – by Gunnar Heinsohn and Otto Steiger

1 The editor's footnotes are in braces {}.
2 {Original: Eigentumsökonomik; Heinsohn and Steiger 2006b.}
3 {Original: Eigentumstheorie des Wirtschaftens versus Wirtschaftstheorie ohne Eigentum: Ergänzungsband zur Neuauflage von 'Eigentum, Zins und Geld'; Heinsohn and Steiger 2002a.}
4 {Original: Eigentum, Zins und Geld; Heinsohn and Steiger 1996.}
5 {Only included in the German edition.}
6 {I.e., which has become this English edition.}
7 {Original:

> Mit ihrem 1996 veröffentlichten Buch 'Eigentum, Zins und Geld' ist den Autoren etwas gelungen, was man gemeinhin als einen 'großen Wurf' bezeichnet, möglicherweise sogar ein 'Jahrhundertbuch'. Inzwischen liegt die zweite Auflage vor, wie bei 'Klassikern' üblich, mit umfänglichen Vorworten und Vorreden versehen, einem Register sowie einer sorgfältig ausgearbeiteten Seitenkonkordanz ... Die Lektüre des Buches ist nicht einfach. Sie setzt nicht nur umfassende Kenntnisse der Geschichte der ökonomischen Theorie voraus, was noch angeht, nein, sie verlangt auch die genaue Kenntnis der Auseinandersetzungen der letzten zwei Jahrzehnte zu diesen Fragen ... Aber das Buch ist, im Unterschied zu vielen anderen wirtschaftstheoretischen Abhandlungen, auch ein Lesevergnügen und Bildungsakt, denn die Autoren verstehen es ganz hervorragend, mit den Quellen umzugehen, Beispiele zu formulieren und überraschende Schlußfolgerungen zu präsentieren.}

1 Possession and ownership: Use of goods versus economic activity

1 {Original: Eigentumsökonomik.}
2 Already for John Maynard Keynes '[t]he essential question for enquiry is ... why the rate of interest exceeds zero' (Keynes 1934, 455). He answered the question two years later in his *General Theory*, courageously but unsuccessfully, by arguing that interest compensates a loss of liquidity premium (see Section 2.3.1). In Heinsohn and Steiger (1996), the interest rate question was for the first time made the topic of a broader enquiry.
3 {Original: 'Belastung'. I have avoided the legal term 'encumbrance' because this term commonly refers to easements.}
4 {For example, by reserving or setting aside property as capital to back a money note issue. The best example for Heinsohn and Steiger's money-creation process is that of a private note-issuing bank. Here, promissory notes payable to bearer on demand (bank notes or 'money notes') are issued when credit is provided to a debtor. This creates a loan asset and a matching note liability in the bank's books. The notes are backed by bank capital and the debtor's loan security; see Decker (2010, 27–31) for a discussion of promissory notes and bank notes and the significance of the bearer clause.}
5 {In the following, departing from the original text, I have introduced a distinction between *de jure* and de facto possession in order to clarify the use of the term possession (factual control, occupation or use) in systems with and without property law, respectively.}
6 {Original: Eigentumsprämie.}
7 {Original: Bewirtschaften.}
8 {Original: Besitzseite.}
9 {Original: Eigentumsseite.}
10 {Original: Unternehmerkapitalisten. The term entrepreneur is used here and in the

remainder of the text for the German term 'Unternehmer'. It is used in the general sense of 'business owner', including already established businesses and not just risky start-ups as suggested by the contemporary use of the term.}
11 {Original: Güterzins.}
12 {Original: Geldzins. Geldzins is usually translated simply as 'interest' or 'interest on money'. However, such a translation does not sufficiently emphasize the implied source of interest. Our term 'yielded by money' is inspired by Jevons's usages of the term 'interest yielded by capital' (Jevons 1957, Chapter VII, 245).}
13 {For example, by reserving capital for note redemptions or unforeseen loan losses.}
14 {Together with the associated security rights.}
15 In Heinsohn and Steiger (1996) we referred, following Polanyi (1944a), to three different types of society. However, we now reserve the term 'society', which is a system constituted by contracts, for ownership-based systems alone; see Niemitz (2008), who also points out that only ownership-based societies are based on a system of law.
16 {Manor in England.}
17 {Assuming property rights in other territories exist and are respected.}
18 {An interesting study by Cronon provides a very careful analysis of English common-law property rights and tribal customary rights for the Southern New England Indians:

> When lands were traded and sold [by indigenous people]..., what were exchanged were usufruct rights, acknowledgements by one group that another might use an area for planting or hunting or gathering. Such rights were limited to the period of use, and they did not include many of the privileges Europeans commonly associated with ownership: a user could not (and saw no need to) prevent other village members from trespassing or gathering non-agricultural food on such lands, and had no conception of deriving rent from them ... different groups could have different claims on the same tract of land depending on how they used it.
> (Cronon 1983, 62–63)

As a consequence, land purchases from Indians under English law constituted a fuller transfer of rights than Indian communities ever intended (Cronon 1983, 68).}
19 {Original: Bemerkenswert ist, daß hier wie dort weniger Gewicht auf Zins und Zinshöhe gelegt wird. Das Interesse konzentriert sich auf das geliehene [Vieh-] Kapital.}
20 During contact *between* ownership-based societies and tribal communities, tribespeople can certainly adjust to a pattern where in one year they receive glass beads and steel blades and in the following year they deliver fur or rubber. One could argue that they understand creditor/debtor relationships when these opportunities are presented. However, this is not the same as creditor/debtor relationships within tribal communities, as Alain Parguez and Mario Seccareccia (2000, 101–103) have assumed in response to some of our earlier work, taking the post-Keynesian 'money circuit' approach. In particular, de facto possession-based systems do not treat fur or rubber as 'collective property', as Parguez and Seccareccia have argued. In such a case, both commodities would have a possessory and an ownership aspect, a distinction which the post-Keynesian authors do not even attempt to make. See Heinsohn and Steiger (2000a) as antithesis to Parguez and Seccareccia in the same volume, and Graziani's (1997) critique of the post-Keynesian 'money circuit' approach from an ownership economics point of view; see also Graziani (2008) in support of ownership economics.
21 {Original:

> Die herrschende Schicht ist der Stamm der Inkas. Die Masse des Volkes ist verpflichtet, neun Monate für den Staat zu arbeiten, drei Monate ist sie frei, um den eigenen Lebensunterhalt zu schaffen. Es gibt keinen Individualbesitz [hier als Eigentum zu lesen] an Grund und Boden, daher weder Reichtum noch Armut.

Notes 147

  Alles Land ist entweder Tempel-, Staats- oder Gemeindeland. Für Kranke und Schwache sorgt die Gemeinde. Es gibt ... keine individuelle Freiheit oder Freizügigkeit.}

22 {Original: reich an Gold und Silberschmuck ist.}
23 {Original: Staats- oder Volkseigentum.}
24 {Original: Volkseigentumsfonds.}
25 {Original: Bodenreformfonds.}
26 {Original: 5–8 ha.}
27 {Original: über 100 ha.}
28 {Original: Die auf Grund dieser Verordnung geschaffenen Wirtschaften [sic] können weder ganz noch teilweise geteilt, verkauft, verpachtet oder verpfändet werden.}
29 {Original:

  Durch die Verfügungsverbote [der Verpfändung, der Teilung und des Verkaufs], das Verbot der Verpachtung und das Gebot zur Bewirtschaftung [sic] war das Eigentum an den Grundstücken aus der Bodenreform seiner Bedeutung als Eigentum im Sinne des Bürgerlichen Rechts im wesentlichen entkleidet.}

30 {More accurately referred to as state-run factories and plants.}
31 {Original: Willkürgeld.}
32 This includes means of production, which also becomes a monetary variable, and which now dominates the economic process as physical capital that generates the means to fulfill the loan repayment and interest commitments that were entered into when the money advances needed for the capital outlay were obtained.
33 Even an ownership-based society has operations that are not part of economic activity but that are nevertheless subject to optimization. An example is the ergonomic design of home kitchens, the labor savings of which will not be reflected in the calculation of the national product. This may disappoint supporters of the 'wages for housework' movement but makes sense from an economic point of view.
34 See John Locke (1690a; 1690b), referring to property as 'life, liberty and estate'. Interpretations of ownership economics from a civil law perspective have been provided by Wolfgang Theil (2000; 2001), Hans-Ulrich Niemitz (2000; 2008) and Steiger (2005a). See also Heribert Illig (1996), Rolf Steppacher (1999) and Jean Beaufort (2001).
35 This point is argued not only by us, but also, with different focuses, by Tom Bethell (1998 and 2008), Richard Pipes (1999 and 2008) and Hernando de Soto. De Soto makes explicit references to our ownership economics approach: see de Soto (2000, 54–58 and 218); see also de Soto (2008), Betz (2008), U. Heinsohn (2001 and 2008) and Steiger (2006c–e, g).
36 An introduction to the principles of ownership economics is provided in Grünewald (2001).

2 The blindness of the great schools of economics towards ownership

1 For a detailed discussion of Steuart (who had not yet been considered in Heinsohn and Steiger 1996), see Stadermann and Steiger (1999, 19–49; 2001a; 2001b, 45–86; and 2006).
2 {Original: aus Nichts}.
3 Ralph Hawtrey (1932, 131) uses the phrase 'create currency ... out of nothing', because the stock of gold, used as backing, is not unlimited. However, he does not forget that commercial banks, even in crisis situations, can only obtain Bank of England notes (which don't suffer from the same limitation as gold) against good security.

4 {Original: Vielmehr ist es da völlig klar, daß Kaufkraft geschaffen wird, der zunächst keine neuen Güter entsprechen. ... Nicht nur über die vorhandene Geldbasis, sondern auch über die vorhandene Güterbasis ladet das Kreditgebäude aus.}

5 The use of the term 'own' contributes to Debreu's confusion. Based on the economic context, 'own the resources' would have been better formulated as 'possess the resources', as for Debreu the use of resources is the most important attribute.

6 'The most serious challenge that the existence of money poses to the theorist is this: the best developed model of the economy cannot find room for it' (Hahn 1982, 1).

7 {Original: Kapitalzins}.

8 {This sentence added by editor.}

9 Jürgen Backhaus (2000), in his review of *Eigentum, Zins und Geld* (Heinsohn and Steiger 1996), assesses our core conclusion as 'correct'. However, he limits his endorsement by noting that our theory simply 'reinvented the theory of property rights and applied it in an effort to understand the role of money' (a similar critique can already be found in Malte Krüger, 1996) and that

> [s]everal sources on the economics of property rights make the same point as Heinsohn and Steiger. In the *New Palgrave Dictionary of Economics and the Law* (1998), for instance, in the entry on property rights written by Harold Demsetz, property rights are said to be exclusive, alienable and presumptive.

However, Backhaus remains silent on the fact that Demsetz himself emphasizes that he found it difficult to determine the core economic attribute of property rights (see the discussion above). Consequently, in Backhaus' discussion, à la Demsetz, hypothecation is yet again missing and the essential role of ownership for economic activity remains obscured. The important distinction between ownership and possession is also not covered by Backhaus. The three attributes of property rights named by Backhaus exclude the critical attributes of burdening and hypothecation. Alienability alone partly captures an element of ownership that is absent in possession: the power to sell. In possession-based systems, free alienability by sale does not exist. There are only transfers, which are generally limited to gift, inheritance and the allocation of rations. The power to sell is absent, and it is telling that the property-rights school cannot even identify this critical distinction within its own property law of sales transactions.

10 {The ownership of a right is defined by Demsetz as a three-element bundle: 1) to use a scarce resource; 2) to exclude others from the right of use; 3) to transfer control (Demsetz 1998, 145). Again Demsetz's focus is entirely on the use of resources, consistent with his statement at the beginning of his article that 'the use of scarce resources [is] the functional objective of property rights. This serves here to limit the scope of our inquiry' (Demsetz 1998, 145).}

11 {For example, ownership as evidenced in a registered title deed.}

12 Had economic historians also considered legal history, they would have easily discovered that a belief in the separate nature of common and private property reveals that the essence of property rights has not been understood. For example, the post-Napoleonic constitution of France, dated 4 June 1814, states in Section 9: 'All property is inviolable, without any exception for that which is called national, the law making no distinction between them' (Heidelmeyer 1997, 68) {Original: Alles Eigentum ist unverletzlich, ohne Ausnahme dessen, was man Nationaleigentum nennt, da das Gesetz zwischen beiden keinen Unterschied macht.}.

13 {Original: Eigenkapital ('own capital'). While every enterprise requires capital (net equity), it is a crucial requirement for banks. Bank capital is a buffer against unforeseen and even improbable losses and is indispensible for the operation of a bank; see, for example, Matten (2000, 17).}

14 {Resulting in a 'duplication of a proportion of the entrepreneur's risk, which is added *twice* to the pure rate of interest' (Keynes 1936, 145).}

15 {For example, money notes that are created when mere debt titles (notes and bills) are discounted.}
16 {See also the discussion in Stadermann and Steiger (2001b, 290).}
17 {Keynes's statements suggest that he believed that state debt was equivalent to money and always easily convertible into money. This belief may have been based on his experience when working in the British finance ministry during World War I. During this time, legal-tender treasury notes were issued as war finance; see Stadermann and Steiger (2001b, 290–293).}
18 {The first case describes a creditor who owns an existing debt security from an unrelated third party obtained in a secondary market. The second case describes the issue of new securities by a debtor in what is in fact a primary market.}
19 {See also Stadermann and Steiger (2001b, 293–294).}
20 {Original: Güterzins.}
21 {Original: Geldzins.}
22 Stiglitz's belief that he was the first to theoretically derive the necessity of loan security in credit contracts is due to his lack of knowledge of Steuart's (1767) work; for details see Section 3.5 below.
23 {Original: ihre eigenen Eigentumstitel, ihr Eigenkapital}. Stiglitz does not characterize capital as the necessary surplus of assets over liabilities, or net equity. Instead, Stiglitz discusses the raising of additional equity capital by joint stock companies. Here, additional equity issues can have a negative effect on firms' net worth, so firms ration equity. This is again due to informational problems. Firms often hesitate to increase their capital through additional share issues because the 'willingness to sell shares conveys a negative signal to the market', in particular that 'the market has overpriced their shares'. Thus companies avoid an uncertain market response by financing investments with bank credit, or if that is refused, by credit rationing through their retained earnings (Stiglitz and Greenwald 2003, 34–36). Stiglitz and Greenwald's information-based argument overlooks that even with full information about the reaction of markets a share issue may be withheld. In contrast to bank credit, the raising of capital through new share issues can introduce new ownership structures that threaten the position of the old owners.
24 {Original: Eigenkapital.}
25 {Original: Kreditrisiko als einen unerwünschten Output der Bankenproduktion (*Abfall*).}
26 {Original: *Vermögensmarkt.*}
27 {Original: da 'Geld aus dem *Nichts* entsteht'.}
28 {Original: Zahlungsfähigkeit.}
29 {Original: eine Übertragung der Verfügung über Güter und Dienstleistungen vom Gläubiger [auf den] Schuldner.}
30 {Original: Individualkalkül.}
31 {Original: Zahlungsmöglichkeit.}
32 {Original: Elastizität der Geldversorgung und der Vermeidung von Liquiditätakrisen.}
33 {Original: Zahlungsschwierigkeiten der Zentralbank.}
34 {Original: daß *jede* aus einem Kreditverhältnis resultierende Nachfrage nach Geld befriedigt wird, es nunmehr die Frage bleibt, zu welchem *Preis* sie befriedigt wird.}
35 {Original: *Sicherung der Funktionsfähigkeit der Ökonomie.*}
36 {Original: strikt konservativen Kurs ... neben einem hohen Zinssatz als Marktbarriere des Drangs in die Liquidität die Dominoeffekte einer Liquiditätskrise zu vermeiden.}
37 {Original: *Entkopplung von Geldnachfrage und Kreditnachfrage.*}
38 {Original: Geldhaltung.}
39 {Original: *Gefahr von Vermögensverlusten.*}
40 {Original: der *sicheren* Vermögenswerte, die sie gegen ihre Noten ankauft.}

41 {The currency foundation is represented by all assets eligible for discount or rediscount. These back the note issue and provide the underlying property basis of a currency system; see Stadermann (2002, 28; 2008, 225–226). The currency foundation for nineteenth-century private note-issuing banks included not only gold but more importantly promissory notes and commercial bills; see, for example, Gibbons (1870 [1858]).}

42 {Original: sieht nicht, daß mit der Entscheidung darüber, *was* die Währungsgrundlage sein soll, eine Festlegung getroffen wird, *wer* in einem Währungsgebiet Produktion und Einkommen veranlassen und beschränken kann.}

43 {From here to end of paragraph added by editor.}

44 {From here to end of paragraph added by editor.}

45 In these models, all three sectors have asset holdings that exactly match their debt liabilities. Thus their net equity is zero. Only the wealth-owning households are shown as net creditors. As households are assumed to be without debt liabilities, their net equity position is represented by their asset portfolio. This portfolio is assumed to be a mixture of money and capital assets. The net equity position of households could be interpreted as a capital buffer for losses. However, the risk of loss is only considered in the context of portfolio selection, which is held to be the key strategy for risk reduction. Thus the portfolio theory of optional asset allocation replaces the theory of the requirement for (bank) capital (for more details see Heine and Herr 1999, 334 and 346).

46 {Original: Die Zentralbank ist die einzige ökonomische Einheit, die (in inländischem Geld) *nicht zahlungsunfähig* werden kann. ... Eine wie auch immer geartete Bindung der Geldschöpfung an Eigentum ware dysfunktional.}

47 {Original: die Zentralbank in ihrer Geldschöpfung quantitative begrenzt ware und unter Umständen ihre Funktion als *lender of last resort* nicht ausüben kann.}

48 {Original: 'Daß nicht sein kann, was nicht sein darf'. This is a popular German saying from a poem by Christian Morgenstern (1910).}

49 {Original: Nichts wäre falscher als eine solche Auffassung. Denn eine Zentralbank hat nur unter der speziellen Bedingung, als Garant von Konvertibilität zu fungieren, ein Liquiditätsproblem, wobei ihre Kunden selbst dann den Wechselkurs gegen sich gelten lassen müssen. Demgegenüber haben Geschäftsbanken ein prinzipielles Liquiditätsproblem, da ihre Verpflichtungen, so oder so, in Zentralbankgeld [das sie selbst nicht schaffen können] transformierbar sein müssen.}

50 {Original: Liquiditätsproduktion ... eine Vermögensbildung der Zentralbank aus.}

51 {Original: Der Geldumlauf stellt eben nicht, wie bisweilen immer noch unterstellt wird, eine irgendwie geartete Verpflichtung dar. Zu was sollte die Zentralbank verpflichtet sein? Ironischerweise formuliert, kann sie, da sie als Liquiditätsproduzent *ex definitione* selbst kein Liquiditätsproblem hat, immer nur selbst fabrizierte Liquidität in selbst fabrizierte Liquidität transformieren.}

52 {Original: unterliegt als universeller Liquiditätsproduzent *keinem Gläubigerrisiko* und kann somit nicht aufgrund eines Forderungsausfalls in Zahlungsschwierigkeiten geraten. Die Risikolosigkeit ihres Geschäfts zwingt sie zwar zu besonderer Sorgfalt bei der Kreditgewährung. ... *Entscheidend aber ist, daß die Geldhaltung zur Vermögensproduktion wird* – was sich buchungstechnisch darin äußert, daß eine Zentralbank die Geldemission als Passivum verbucht. Darin drückt sich in Analogie zum Reinvermögen der *Verzicht über das Vermögen 'Geld'* aus.}

53 {A central bank can, however, hold government debt instruments as assets; for example, legal tender notes issued by the government, such as United States Greenbacks.}

54 {For example, on termination of a central bank loan and return of the central bank notes (or deposits), both the central bank's assets (loan with commercial bank) and liabilities (note issue) are reduced by the corresponding amount. The liability created by the loan ceases to exist.}

Notes 151

55 {Original: 'knappgehaltenes Nichts', Riese's definition of money; see, for example, Riese (2000a, §38, col. 493a).}
56 {See Section 3.3 for more details on how banks set prices.}
57 {Referring to the tall tales of the adventures of Baron Münchhausen.}
58 {Original: beliebig vermehrbare, weil nicht marktmäßige Schulddokumente.}
59 {An open market subjects these instruments to an independent market valuation and thus will reflect an over-issue in the price of these instruments. For this reason, the law governing the German Bundesbank prohibited the bank from taking on debt instruments directly from an issuer. Only open market purchases of debt securities were permitted; see Bundesbank (1995, 111).}
60 {Original: 'theoriegeschichtlich herausragende Leistung' weil 'sie die markttheoretische Aporie einer Verknüpfung des Kredits mit dem Geld vermeidet'.}
61 {Original: Dichotomisierung von Geldmarkt and Gütermarkt.}
62 {Original: Medium der Kontrakterfüllung.}
63 {Original: wenn es 'ein *knappgehaltenes* Nichts ist'.}
64 {Original: Knapphaltungszins.}
65 {Original: Güterleihe.}
66 {Original: Apokryphen.}
67 {Original: Er hat daher ... zu einem fürwahr kühnen Befreiungsschlag ausgeholt.}
68 {Original: Verfügung über das Vermögen 'Geld'.}
69 {Original: im Individualexperiment der Preis für den temporären Verzicht auf die Verfügung über Geld ... durch Vermögensbesitzer.}
70 {Original: im Marktexperiment den Preis für knapp gehaltenes Geld.}
71 {Original: Die Eigentumsökonomik hätte ihm – 'völlig sinnlos' – die Ansicht vorgehalten, 'die Zentralbank' und nicht der Vermögensbesitzer sei 'bereit', 'einen Preis für eine knapp gehaltene Verfügung über Geld zu zahlen'.}
72 {Original: 'Entgeld für die Nichthortung eines exogen fixierten Geldangebotes' also 'als Entgeld für die Aufgabe von Liquidität interpretiert'.}
73 {Original: als (zu zahlender) Preis für die Verfügung über Geld.}
74 {Original: der Preis für den temporären Verzicht auf die Verfügung über Geld.}
75 {Original: Mit Hans-Joachim Stadermann bin ich (bis auf wenige interpretationsbedürftige Details) einer Meinung.}
76 {Original: die bisherige Ökonomie als Wissenschaft die *Neigung zum Tausch* als Beweggrund der Ökonomie hypostasiert (emphasis in original).}
77 {Original: Nicht ... Tauschakte zwischen Individuen haben eine Marktpreisbildung begründet. Das zeigt den Tausch als eine ahistorische und, aus der Sicht einer angemessenen Theoriebildung, zugleich als eine atheoretische Konstruktion. Es hat *niemals* (niemals!) in der gesamten Wirtschaftsgeschichte, zu keiner Zeit und bei keiner Gelegenheit, einen Güterverkehr gegeben, der den tauschtheoretischen Bedingungen einer Preisbildung entsprochen hätte.}
78 {Original: der Zinssatz diejenige Preiskategorie [ist], die die Welt im innersten zusammenhält.}
79 {Original in English.}
80 Nikolaus Läufer (1998, 1) has assured us that such investigations are available in significant number. However, he does not name a single specific reference.

3 The economic core of the ownership system: Interest, money and property assets

1 {For example, between a debtor and a note-issuing bank or a central bank and a commercial bank.}
2 {For example, between a commercial bank and a non-bank.}
3 {For example, when an enterprise invests the borrowed money in production resources and capital goods and, in turn, sells the resulting output.}

4 {A sales contract is an agreement to transfer the property in goods for a money consideration; see, for example, Goode (2004, 194–195). The purchaser appears as a debtor when the purchase is made on credit terms.}
5 Claims against burdened property can also be enforced: for example, the right to redeem money notes in the property of the note issuer.
6 {The original German text includes a passage where Heinsohn and Steiger have extended the use of the term 'burdening' to include the hypothecated property of the debtor. Thus the property of the debtor is hypothecated and at the same time burdened (as the hypothecation imposes a burden), while the property of the creditor is only burdened. We have modified the original text and kept the meanings of the terms 'burdening' (creditor property) and 'hypothecation' (debtor property) separate, which is in line with Heinsohn and Steiger's practice in earlier chapters. In some cases, for example unsecured credit, no formal security is taken. In this case the debtor's property will be described as 'blocked' rather than hypothecated.}
7 If the loan security provided is insufficient, the creditor may often have an additional claim against the remaining general property of the debtor.
8 {The importance of enforcement is nicely illustrated by the early history of the colony of New South Wales. Here almost all civil law cases dealt with debts and actions related to promissory notes, which made private notes the backbone of the early economic system; see Decker (2010, 71–77).}
9 Carsten Köllmann (1999a, 270–272; 1999b, 351) has tried to show that ownership economics incorrectly equates the immaterial concept of 'utility', from neoclassical economics, with the everyday-language concept of physical 'use'. In this way ownership economics kept silent on the fact that neoclassical economics deals not only with goods but also with immaterial variables. Indeed, neoclassical economics clearly distinguishes between the terms 'utility' and 'use'. The term 'use' is understood as a specific right, which, however, is incorrectly interpreted as *property or ownership right*. Moreover, neoclassical economics has no concept or notion of immaterial ownership rights. Utility, conceptualized as a subjective variable, is an attempt to derive relative prices, but cannot contribute anything to the understanding of money and interest; for more details see Heinsohn and Steiger (1999a, 312; 1999b, 356).
10 {Of course, debtors can take out a second mortgage, but the loan proceeds can be expected to be significantly lower than those arising from the first mortgage.}
11 {For example, theft and expropriation.}
12 In the German language these rental payment are often incorrectly referred to as rental interest {Pacht- und Mietzins}. However, interest as compensation for the loss of ownership premium is something completely different.
13 {Original: 'Güter'-Seite.}
14 {Because the subject of a credit contract is money.}
15 {Original: Güterleihe.}
16 {Original: kann 'man sie nicht auf Zinsen leihen'.}
17 {Original: Die Bereitwilligkeit, arm gewordenen Hirten Tiere herzugeben, war bisweilen so groß, daß der reiche Entleiher durch Verschenken und Ausleihen seine große Herde bis auf eine geringe Zahl verminderte und gelegentlich sogar völlig verlor.}
18 {According to Varro, *De re rustica*, I:10, Romulus is reported to have allotted a fixed amount of land referred to as the *heredium* to each citizen, representing the amount that could be transmitted to their heirs by will. Hence, the emphasis of the first land division to create private ownership (dominium) in land was the fact that the land was inheritable. Based on this evidence, Heinsohn (2011, and private communication 16 June 2012) has argued that distributing land as inheritable titles made land division attractive to former serfs, representing a privilege that they understood from the feudal system predating the Roman *civitas* and that they were previously

not entitled to. This also suggests that the founders of the new society would have not foreseen the special dynamics unleashed by an ownership-based society composed of individual property owners.}
19 {Original: Urkredit.}
20 {Original: Weizenkörner sind ihrer ungleichmäßigen Schwere wegen für Gewichtszwecke kaum geeignet. Ich habe eine Partie von 60 Körnern gewogen und ein Gewicht von 3,08g ermittelt, eine andere Partie wog dagegen nur 2,99g. 60 Gerstenkörner wogen dagegen 2,81g und andere 60 wiederum genau 2,81g. Danach ergäben 180 Gerstenkörner ein Gewicht von 8,43g. Der Siklu [Schekel] der sogenannten leichten babylonischen Mine von 504g wiegt nun aber 8,4g und diese hat ohne Zweifel der babylonischen Silberwährung zugrundegelegen.}
21 {See Decker (2010, 19–20) on this choice of legal terminology.}
22 {This would typically refer to promissory notes issued by a bank.}
23 {This is strictly speaking only correct for the most common and important types of loan security. For example, the common-law pledge transfers possession; see, for example, Goode (2004, 617).}
24 {From here to end of paragraph added by editor.}
25 {Unsecured credit.}
26 For example, Riese's student Walter Heering (1999b, 337) believes that 'it appears daring to base a general theory [on the taking of loan security]' {original: 'ziemlich kühn erscheint, darauf [auf Sicherheiten] eine allgemeine Theorie gründen zu wollen'}. Heering follows his fellow student Hansjörg Herr (1999, 193), who after consulting Schumpeter firmly believes that 'hypothecation "is not part of the essential nature" of granting credit' {original: 'daβ die Verpfändung bei der Kreditvergabe "nicht zum Wesen der Sache" gehört'}. This view of the unsecured nature of credit is repeated by Herr in his work with Michael Heine: 'Banks also accept convincing business plans or special qualifications of the debtor as sufficient security. Thus the analytical linkage between the granting of credit and property is unnecessarily limiting' (Heine and Herr 1999, 376) {original: 'Als hinreichende Sicherheiten warden bei Banken durchaus auch überzeugende Unternehmenskonzepte oder besondere Qualifikationen der Kreditnachfrager akzeptiert. Insofern ist die analytische Bindung der Kreditvergabe an die Eigentumskategorie unnötig einschränkend'}. Following on, both authors reveal their happy ignorance of lending practices: 'in addition, a creditor can demand a pledge over the productive capital that is purchased with the borrowed money. In this case the option of a pledge arises together with the granting of the loan' (Heine and Herr 1999, 376) {original: 'Zudem kann ein Gläubiger ein Pfand an dem Produktivkapital verlangen, das mit seinem verliehenden Geld gekauft wird. In diesem Fall gibt es die Möglichkeit eines Pfandes, das erst im Akt der Kreditvergabe realisierbar wird'}. This can indeed happen in this way, and typically the loan security demanded will exceed the borrowed sum. But it would be nice to have an explanation of why loan security is demanded in Herr and Heine's 'principal model of an enterprise without capital ... that obtains credit without loan security' {original: 'Grundmodell [des] kapitallosen Unternehmer[s] ... , der ohne Pfandrechte Kredit erhält'}. See our reply to Herr in Heinsohn and Steiger (1999a, 322), and to Herring in Heinsohn and Steiger (1999b, 355).
27 {Alternatively, loan covenants are often used to ensure access to sufficient assets in the case of default. Similarly, guarantees and negative pledge clauses are used as an alternative to taking security over specific assets.}
28 {Modern banking and lending practice suggests that loan security, while not the only criterion for determining the approval of a loan (for example, cash flow is another important factor) 'is an *extremely important part* of the lending process' (Weaver and Kingsley 2001, 127; emphasis added). That the taking of security is the underlying principle of banking becomes particularly clear when small businesses or entrepreneurs face difficulties in obtaining bank funding: '*Banks operate as lenders*

on security rather than as providers of venture capital' (Weaver and Kingsley 2001, 240; emphasis added).}

29 {Technically, however, the ownership of assets may be transferred. In English common law, for example, the legal mortgage transfers ownership. However, the mortgagor is left with an entitlement to redeem the security, the equity of redemption; see, for example, Bridge (2002, 179, 181).}

30 {In the common-law context chattels cannot be recovered by action. Damages are payable instead; see, for example, Goode (2004, 29).}

31 {Historically, this note-redemption process followed two stages. In the first stage, money notes typically had to be redeemed in a specified asset, for example specie in the case of private nineteenth-century banks. In colonial economies, notes could at times be redeemed in commodities and government debt. As argued in Decker (2010, 169–181; 2011), these property assets form a special class of 'settlement assets' that can finally discharge obligations. In the second stage, if the settlement asset is not produced, debt recovery action can commence and the notes are redeemed from the execution proceeds against the general assets of the note issuer. Settlement assets thus perform the role of an 'enforcement trigger'.}

32 {Original: monetärer Zins.}

33 {Original: Güterzins.}

34 {This paragraph added by editor. See also the discussion in Decker (2010, 173).}

35 {Or block his property, in the case of an unsecured credit contract.}

36 {Even if ownership is transferred, the debtor retains an equity of redemption in a (common-law) legal mortgage. Another reason why debtor property cannot compensate the creditor's loss of ownership premium is the requirement for the creditor to hold capital to cover the event of unforeseen loan losses. The amount of property burdened thus must always exceed the money sum advanced and always involves additional creditor property.}

37 {One could argue that this principle could even be extended to the case where full property rights are received for the period of the loan, as is the case in a money-creating repurchase agreement. The latter resembles a secured loan contract but fully transfers the ownership and possession of the assets in question through a sale and repurchase by the debtor. However, repurchase agreements carry the obligation for the creditor to sell the acquired property at a defined time for a defined price to the debtor (i.e., the corresponding repurchase by the debtor). As with a mortgage, the disposition over the acquired debtor property is constrained by the obligation to return the transferred property at the end of the loan.}

38 Spahn (1998, 388) has interpreted our interest explanation so as to suggest that the two parties to the credit contract exchange property rights, so that in addition to interest the creditor obtains the (smaller) ownership premium of the debtor. Interest then represents the difference between the two ownership premiums. Roy (1999, 169–170) has added creatively to Spahn's misinterpretation by suggesting that the creditor has already been compensated by receiving the debtor's ownership premium, and as a result could not demand interest. Hence, we were not delivering a theory of interest at all (see our reply in Heinsohn and Steiger 1999a, 315).

Roy has turned Spahn's interpretation of our theory, as a theory based on the differential of ownership premiums, into an interpretation based on Keynes's liquidity preference theory. The creditor has property in the form of money. The ownership premium on money is higher than the ownership premium arising from the debtor's – non-monetary – property. The interest then measures this difference. Therefore the creditor receives, as suggested by Keynes, 'interest because he temporarily gives up liquidity' (Roy 1999, 170) {original: 'darum einen Zinssatz, weil er temporär auf Liquidität verzichtet'}. Roy, like all monetary Keynesians, simply presupposes the existence of money so that he does not have to deal with the emergence of interest in the creation of money. The money-creating creditor, however, does not have a rich bag full of money that he can open and close for lending purposes. In reality, he never gets access to his money when it is created, because it is created for the debtor; see Heinsohn and Steiger (1999a, 316).

39 Roy (1999, 169) in this sense cunningly tries to interpret our theory as being not only monetary Keynesian but also neoclassical. He argues that the creditor, who does not receive anything from the debtor, receives interest because he suffers an 'intertemporal deferment of his ability to act and consume' {original: 'intertemporalen Aufschub seiner Handlungs- und Konsummöglichkeiten'} when he loses ownership premium in the money-creation process. Roy overlooks the fact that no limitation of the creditor's ability to consume (the basis for the neoclassical theory of interest) takes place: the creditor gives up opportunities to burden, but not consumption. The first option relates to ownership, the second option to possession; see Heinsohn and Steiger (1999a, 315) for more details.

40 {See, for example, Kaser (1981, 128).}

41 {From here to end of paragraph added by editor.}

42 {Section 2.3.1.}

43 In the mid-1990s 'mezzanine debt' was created for strongly growing enterprises that, based on the extensive hypothecation of their assets, could no longer obtain bank credit. The debt paid interest like fixed-income securities or loans, but in the priority of creditor claims it ranked behind unsecured credit and just before shareholders' claims. As a result, the risk premiums were very high – 16–23 percent – as compared to 5 percent for secured credit with first-class loan security (Da. 2005, 20). Essentially, these instruments show that a lower ranking of a creditor is always compensated by a risk premium.

The practice of UK banks of providing credit beyond the value of the underlying real estate, in contrast to Germany where loans are limited to 60–80 percent of the real-estate value, must be judged in a similar way. Banks have to compensate for the increased risk by charging an additional interest premium, without being able to remove the risk in this way. This practice has been one of the contributing factors to an increase in British household debt levels to 140 percent of income and a reduction in savings to 4.6 percent of income. Consequently, the Bank of England noted 'its concerns about the stability of the British financial system' (Zehnder 2005, 49) {original: 'ihre Besorgnis über die Stabilität des britischen Finanzmarktes geäußert'}.

44 {Original: Das Geschäft wird dann durchaus nicht ohne Sicherheiten realisiert, sondern mit den Haftungsmitteln des Gläubigers abgesichert, der im Fall einer nicht korrekten Vertragserfüllung dann den Schaden tragen und unter Umständen sogar Dritten gegenüber mit seinem Vermögen haften muß.}

45 Läufer (1998, 5) believes that the ownership premium is the same as the risk premium. He has not perceived the fundamental difference between the two.

In contrast, Bernd Striegel (2005a and 2005b, 30) would like to give up the ownership premium of the creditor altogether and replace the logical sequence of ownership economics – ownership → interest → money – with the sequence ownership → money → interest. He challenges the requirement to back the creditor side in the money-creation process. In his view, only the hypothecation of debtor property is required to create money; interest emerges after money is created as a compensation for the 'aging of the collateral' {original: 'Alterung des Kollaterals'}; for more details see Betz (2005, 43).

Of course, a loss of collateral value is possible, but it is by no means the only possible outcome. The value of collateral can decrease, remain constant or even increase. Following Striegel's logic, the creditor would in the latter two cases waive interest or demand a negative interest. In reality, when the value of collateral falls, for example in the case of marginal loans involving shares, the price of the shares used as collateral falls and margin calls are made. Hence, creditors do not demand an interest increase but demand additional collateral. The creditor's risk of property losses, however, will not be removed altogether. He cannot waive his demand for interest. {As even additional collateral will not completely remove the risk of loan losses, a part of the creditor's own capital remains burdened. As he forgoes ownership premium he must demand interest.} Stiegel's interest explanation from the deterioration of collateral resembles Hicks's curious derivation of the level of interest rates from the level of bad loans; see Section 2.3.1.

46 Being the ratio of interest (on the loan principal) to the loan principal.
47 {The original text (Heinsohn and Steiger (2006b, 110) has been edited to clarify that the interest rate *and* the loan principal are inputs to this price-setting process. Both variables (R and i) are set *together* when the notes are issued and the loan terms are documented in the contract. Similarly, in a secondary market purchase, the act of purchasing defines the price of the purchased asset in terms of the bank notes provided. The issued notes specify the money of account and represent the total money sum. Furthermore, once the loan principal/asset price (R) and the interest rate (i) are set through the note issue, the price of the asset earnings (r) (expressed in terms of the issued notes) is implied through the perpetuity formula and simultaneously set. This treatment is also consistent with Stadermann's (2006, 63) description of the price-setting process. Here, in a scenario where a bank purchases a plot of land and pays in its own notes, the value of the plot of land is set through the purchase and together with the interest rate provides the inputs that determine the demanded prices for the products of the land. In this way, creditor property, debtor property and asset earnings, for example the fruits of land, are set by the note issue. Once one asset price is set, the price of other assets follows by comparison.}
48 {This is a special case of the corporate finance principle that the value of an asset is given by the net present value of its discounted cash flows; see, for example, Copeland and Weston (1992, 25).}
49 {Edited to clarify that the interest rate and the loan principal are set by the note issuer and are the inputs to the price-setting process.}
50 Läufer (1998, 10) imagines that proper money cannot be based on property, because the value of property cannot be determined before its value is known through the choice of a standard good. In that case, our theory would present a theory of commodity money. Läufer overlooks the idea that the interest rate determination {together with the determination of the loan principal} as materialization of the ownership premium provides the variable from which the valuation occurs.
51 The term was first used by James Steuart (1761, 151; and 1767, vol. I, 526).
52 {Original: Besitz-Güter.}
53 {Original: Güterseite.}
54 {It follows from this statement (originally formulated in Heinsohn and Steiger 2002a, 67) that note issues and redemptions are the underlying reason that a monetary standard exists and can be maintained. The chosen unit is of course arbitrary, and, as Stadermann has pointed out with reference to Riese (2000a, 491), is in fact the economic category that is created 'out-of-nothing' (Stadermann 2002, 28; and Stadermann 2006, 63). However, only the decision about the unit is made 'out-of-nothing'; the money notes themselves must be backed by property (Stadermann 2006, 63).

The early history of the colony of New South Wales provides an interesting example for this. Here, contrary to the intentions of the government, a local money of account, the '£ currency', was introduced by private individuals as an alternative to English pounds sterling. Merchants issued and redeemed small notes payable in £ currency. This created the basis of a new local currency system by setting £ currency prices for merchandise, commodities, wages and even British Treasury bills; see Decker (2010, 86–87, 121–136; 2011).}
55 {Thus the price of the land at the time of the note issue is set at 100 A-dollars.}

56 {From here to end of sentence added by editor.}
57 {From here to end of paragraph added by editor.}
58 {This setting of a money price is reflected in the fact that there is, contrary to common belief, no 'natural price' of gold (Stadermann 2002, 40; 2006, 56). For example, in the nineteenth century the Bank of England and other central banks such as the German Reichsbank set the price of gold in their currency units through the purchase of gold and commercial bills (Stadermann 2002, 24–30). The reasons for the relative success of the gold standard 'was neither a natural quality nor any constancy of the inherent labor value within metal ... it was a secure asset because of the stabilizing activities of the money-issuing banks' (Stadermann 2008, 236). Similarly, the first bank of New South Wales in 1817 was able to stabilize its note issues at par with British Treasury bills and create a uniform monetary standard based on its discount operations, despite the remoteness of its location (Decker 2010, 150–151; Decker 2011). In the above cases, the banks fixed the price of gold and the price of private debt in their note issue (when discounting bills or purchasing credit contracts, one unit of private bill-based debt is set to one unit of central bank money). The purchase of private debt as the second asset (see Stadermann 2008, 237) next to gold allowed the banks to control their note supply and in this way to stabilize the fixed prices of gold and private bill-based debt relative to other prices.

Today's central banks no longer stabilize the price of any asset and primarily pursue an inflation target (among other targets). However, 'no clear functional relationship exists between the change in the money supply and the index numbers used in statistics to express the price level'. As a result, 'central banks follow the concept of *just muddling through*' (Stadermann 2008, 232, 234; emphasis in original). Thus central banks can set asset prices but not the price level.

On this basis, Stadermann (2002, 126–128) has suggested as an alternative monetary policy to directly fix the price of a selected number of fixed-income securities by outright central bank sales and purchases. Short-term refinance operations, analogous to the purchases of bill-based credit, with the selected securities as collateral, would control the central bank money supply and stabilize the prices of securities that are fixed in this way relative to other prices. Hence, a standard based on fixed-income securities as the currency foundation could be created analogous to the former gold standard.}
59 {As evidenced in New South Wales, where the early colonial government lost control over its money of account; see Decker (2010, 160).}
60 In the two most important central bank systems in the world, the US Fed and the Eurosystem, the term is one week.
61 {In fact, nineteenth-century bank notes in the form of promissory notes payable on demand were easier to enforce than normal debt contracts; see, for example, Rogers (2004 [1995], 180–181) and the discussion of bank notes in Decker (2010, 26–31).}
62 {This is typically ensured by covenants written into the bond contract. For example, this may restrict or prohibit the issue of new debt or the sale of assets; see Copeland and Weston (1992, 512).}
63 This was nevertheless attempted in the early period of the Eurosystem, an association of the European Central Bank and the 12 national central banks of the European Monetary Union. The Banca d'Italia attempted to provide a state credit (to Lebanon) not out of the state's funds but directly out of the Banca d'Italia. The ECB could only just prevent it (Pwe./Tp. 2005, 10).
64 The Old View assumes currencies based on precious metal in which bank notes are redeemable in gold. Here, as evident from Federal Reserve notes prior to 1935, gold is seen as actual or 'lawful money'. However, gold is not the produced commodity 'money' but is property, like, for example, the produced commodity 'machine'. What is redeemable against bank notes is in fact not money as such but merely a particular type of property, whose price can be stabilized by the note-issuing bank

more easily than bills, mortgage securities, etc. For example, during the era of the gold standard, the Bank of England promised everyone presenting its sterling notes for redemption 7.32 g of gold per £ (Stadermann 1994b, 174).

65 {The debt of the private sector owed to the bank; Pesek and Saving (1967, 142).}
66 {In Pesek and Saving's (1967, 142–143) economic accounts, the bank produces a net asset (debt to the private sector) without a matching liability when it prints [sic] money. This is seen to be analogous to a manufacturer producing a machine (creating a net capital asset), which is then leased to the private sector, which creates a debt to the private sector in its economic account reflecting the leased asset.}
67 Alvano Cencini (2001, 84) points out in a recent paper that money as such does not represent net wealth. Money is not produced like a good but issued. However, he then regresses into a production view: '[n]et wealth ... [is] formed through the association of money and current output'. Cencini argues that only after the issued money has resulted in new production and incomes can it form net wealth for the income recipients, for example in the form of bank deposits. Again it is overlooked that money can only be issued by the burdening of property assets, which as net wealth is available the moment additional property is burdened, and not only when more output has been produced.
68 Stuart Enghofer and Manuel Knospe brought this statement to our attention; see Enghofer and Knospe (2005).
69 {Example added by editor.}
70 This was already sensed by Geoffrey Crowther (1940, 47): 'The bank does not "create" money out of thin air; it transmutes other forms of wealth into money'.
71 {Original: Geldvermögen.}
72 {Original: 'die zur Geldemission fähigen Forderungen ... nur nebenbei' behandelt werden.}
73 {Original: 'Die herrschende Theorie' hat 'die Summe der Forderungen und die Summe der Verbindlichkeiten zu Null addiert und ... ein per saldo nicht bestehendes Geldvermögen' angenommen.}
74 {Original: Dieser Schachzug ist genauso lustig, als würde man – da die gekaufte Menge auf dem Güter- und Resourcenmarkt mit der verkauften Menge identisch ist – behaupten, der Resourcen- und Güterreichtum der Gesellschaft sei ebenfalls Null.}
75 {Stadermann (1992, 185–186) defines wealth as the subset of financial assets that are eligible for central bank refinancing operations, or as central bank collateral (e.g., commercial bills, government securities). Eligible central bank assets are in turn claims against the tangible assets of the issuer and represent a liability to the issuer. The netting of those liabilities (i.e., eligible assets) that underpin the current stock of money against the total value of tangible assets underpinning all eligible assets results in the value of eligible assets that can still be used for additional money creation (Stadermann 1992, 189; see also Stadermann 2006, 91–92).}
76 {Original: Als Vermögen bleiben die auf Geld lautenden Forderungen der Vermögenseigentümer auf die wirtschaftlichen Werte in den Haushalten und Unternehmen übrig, die einer weiteren Ausweitung der Geldemission dienen können.}
77 {For example, asset-backed securities.}
78 {See also Stadermann (2006, 91–92), who notes that the adding up of financial assets and liabilities to zero 'obstructs the view precisely on those elements that provide the insights of how a monetary economy functions' (original: 'versperrt gerade die Einsicht in das Funktionieren einer Geldwirtschaft') because it is no longer apparent 'which part of the estimated tangible assets is already burdened and which is free from burden and still usable for refinancing operations' (original: 'welcher Teil des geschätzten Realvermögens bereits belastet und welcher von Belastungen frei und zur Refinanzierung noch einsetzbar ist'). As a result, 'the distribution of property in a society is obscured' (original: 'Die Verteilung des Vermögens wird verschleiert, wo Forderungen und Verbindlichkeiten auf Nominalvermögen zu Null saldiert werden').}

79 Spahn (1998, 389) – see also Spahn (1999, 28–30 and 74; and 2001, 60–62) {original: Jedermann-Geld.}. Spahn attempts to question the explanation of money given by ownership economics. In his view it is not clear why the burdening of creditor property is money and that of the debtor only loan security. This question suggests that Spahn does not understand the difference between money and credit. *Creditor property backs a money note*, i.e., not credit; however, *debtor property backs a credit contract*, i.e., not money.

Moreover, in Spahn's view, ownership economics has not identified that deposit liabilities of modern commercial banks are claims to money and not property. However, he does not recognize that such claims are always claims against the property of the bank. The modern commercial bank is characterized by the fact that it cannot create money. Therefore, money notes, which are only created by the central bank, represent an asset, i.e., property, in the books of the commercial bank. This is different from the central bank, where money notes appear as liabilities. If claims from deposit holders cannot be fulfilled out of this property type, the commercial bank will need to turn other property titles (assets) into money and, in case of emergency, subject its own capital to a debt recovery action.

Steuart knew that as long as the note issuer 'anyone' represents '[a]n honest man, intelligent and capable to undertake a bank ... without one shilling of stock' (Steuart 1767, vol. II, 152), who only issues notes against good loan security and retains the interest proceeds as capital, he can be as well regarded as the Bank of England. Surely such an honest 'anyone' would have to start with a debtor's money; however, he could quickly turn this into a creditor's money by the transformation of profits into own capital.

80 Original: 'Le prêt dans sa norme juridique, les sûretés, les taux de l'intérêt ne semblent pas avoir été pratiqués pour la première fois dans les temples. Les contrats privés sont plus anciens que les contrats sacrés. Nous croyons que ce sont des particuliers, marchands ou propriétaires, qui ont été les inventeurs du contrat de prêt ... les sanctuaires ... ont imité les capitalistes privés'.

81 {Last two sentences of this paragraph added by editor; see Decker (2010, 77–81; 2011).}

82 {See Heinsohn and Steiger (1996, 260–261).}

83 Steuart (1767, vol. II, 149), interestingly in a footnote that was added later, uses the metaphor of the melting down of solid property ('solid property may be melted down') to describe the use of landed property in money credit. Moreover, he recognizes the commonalities between land and other personal property ('personal estates'). While he does not recognize these commonalities as the ownership aspect of the different property variants, he acknowledges that they are functioning as property when he points out the commonality of physically different property positions in their ability to secure credit. This commonality is indeed provided by the abstract notion of ownership alone.

84 {This did not change the fiduciary nature of the money note/coin. Greek coins were counted, not weighed; see Seaford (2004, 126, 136). It should be noted at this point that explanations for the invention of coinage are controversial to this day, with reasons 'canvassed almost to the point of exhaustion' (Harris 2008a, 3).}

85 {Cohen (2008, 78–79) suggests that the money supply in Athens was made elastic and was substantially increased by bank deposits. For Rome, Harris (2008b, 192–193) makes a similar case showing that transferable instruments (*nomina*) were heavily relied on in payments.}

86 {In this case the state-issued coins no longer represent 'money notes' issued in credit contracts but a state-issued settlement asset, the key purpose of which was to settle loan contracts in an acknowledged way (Decker 2010, 2012). Tyre has argued that state rulers applied a 'making charge' (Tyre 2011), with coins simply lighter than bullion of equivalent price (see also Seaford 2004, 140).}

87 {Original: Die Münze schufen wohl Privatleute für wirtschaftliche Zwecke, doch lassen Bilder wie der lyd.[ische] Löwe, die Biene von Ephesus u. a. erkennen, daß die Ausgabe bald in staatliche Regie gelangte.}
88 {The Bank set and stabilized the price of precious metal expressed in its own bank money by selling and repurchasing bank money (Wee 1977, 341). The actual agio between bank guilder and current guilder depended on the actions of the bank and was not identical with the intrinsic agio derived from the difference in weight between bank guilder and current guilder; see Steuart (1767, vol. II, Book IV, Chapter XXXIX), who had already identified the critical role of the brokers; and the discussion in Stadermann (1994a, 48–49). This is therefore another example of how bank operations set asset prices.}
89 The term 'Emporium' refers to trading cities whose merchants controlled the intermediate trade; i.e., foreigners could not deal with other foreigners directly.
90 {Money in the form of bank notes; gold coinage is a variant of property.}
91 {Last two sentences of paragraph added by editor.}
92 See Bagehot (1873, 88). In Bagehot's view, the note issue by banks preceded deposit taking because it was much easier to establish.
93 'A note issue is mainly begun by loans' (Bagehot 1873, 89).
94 {End of paragraph is editor's clarification.}
95 {Original: Zettelbanken.}
96 In the US banking crisis of 1907, clearing houses issued loan certificates to the amount of 500 million dollars, representing 4.5 percent of the money supply M1 (demand deposits and cash) or 50 percent of cash (Gorton 1997, col. 99b).
97 {The Bank of England was incorporated with limited liability; extremely rare at the time. Partnerships had unlimited liability.}
98 {For example, bank bills from non-related third-party banks and government securities.}
99 However, in the Eurosystem a commercial bank is able to submit debt titles of private enterprises or government departments to their national central bank. These are only accepted with a haircut, which can be up to 25 percent. The German Bundesbank only accepts debt titles of private enterprises (European Central Bank 2005, 47–54).
100 This principle has been watered down in the Eurosystem. Here 'tradable debt titles with limited and 'impaired liquidity' are accepted along with 'non-tradable debt titles' that are 'hardly liquid' (European Central Bank 2005, 53) {original: 'marktfähige Schuldtitel mit begrenzter' und 'eingeschränkter Liquidität' akzeptiert sowie sogar 'nicht marktfähige Schuldtitel', die 'kaum liquid sind'}. The European Central Bank understands completely that a lack of liquidity can result in losses to the Eurosystem, a circumstance that it tries to address with haircuts and other measures to control risk.
101 This principle has been watered down in the Eurosystem, because it does not include close relationships between commercial banks and public departments (European Central Bank 2005, 44, fn. 15 and 47, fn. 22). This implies a privilege for state-owned banks, which are closely related to government departments, and therefore provides an opportunity to by-pass the prohibition of monetizing state debt; see also Heinsohn and Steiger (2011); Spethmann and Steiger (2005, 59); and Steiger (2006f [2004]).
102 {Arms-length market transaction involving an unrelated third party avoid the moral hazards associated with related party transactions and their uncertain asset valuations.}
103 The lack of distinction between the debt and asset aspects of the same title has induced Riese, as shown in Section 2.3.3, to identify money that is created by a central bank in a credit contract as a central bank asset. According to Riese, the central bank can keep this asset or provide it to debtors against interest.

104 {Original: Zettelbank.}
105 {Or equivalently by entering into repurchase agreements.}
106 {Strictly speaking, the commercial bank debtor typically receives a bank deposit. However, additional central bank money is needed for the corresponding increase in bank reserves.}
107 {From here to end of paragraph added by editor; see Heinsohn and Decker (2010).}
108 {Last sentence of paragraph added by editor.}
109 The uniform character of central bank money (with bank notes equal to deposits), in contrast to the old German Bundesbank and the Fed {before October 2008}, is no longer maintained in the Eurosystem. The deposits of commercial banks with their national central banks earn interest (European Central Bank 2005, 26 and 63) like demand deposits of a commercial bank. Accordingly, deposits of Eurosystem national central banks have to be defined as claims to central bank money and no longer as central bank money per se.
110 {This paragraph added by editor.}
111 {This paragraph added by editor.}
112 {Here and in the following paragraphs of the original text, the German term 'weiterverleihen' (on-lending) is used to summarize the operations of a commercial bank. The text has been modified to better reflect the fact that commercial banks lend by deposit creation and on-lend central bank money only in the sense that this money underpins new deposits as a reserve.}
113 {Last sentence of paragraph added by editor.}
114 {In fact, central bank money cannot be held by the central bank but only by its counterparties and non-banks. If notes are returned to the central bank they must be booked out or destroyed. In a note-creation process the notes only materialize as valid instruments when they are actually received by the debtor.}
115 {And not as a bank.}
116 {This paragraph added by editor.}
117 {This paragraph added by editor.}
118 {See the Federal Reserve announcement on 3 November 2010 of the purchase of $600 billion in longer-term US government debt from the private sector.}
119 {The security must be repurchased by the commercial bank at the initial sale price plus interest.}
120 {However, this transfer of price risk enhances susceptibility to asset price inflations, as assets can be securitized into debt titles at inflated prices and then refinanced (Stadermann 2008, 239).}
121 {Original: Niederstwertprinzip.}
122 {Original: Eigenkapital.}
123 {This paragraph added by editor; see Heinsohn, Decker and Heinsohn (2009) and Heinsohn and Decker (2010).}
124 {See Schulz (2009) for a similar situation in Poland.}
125 {Prior to embarking on unconventional measures in response to the global financial crisis of 2008; see Heinsohn and Decker 2010.}
126 It does not follow from this that successful central banks *must* prefer state debt for their operations. For example, since the mid-1980s the Bank of England has replaced the previously used Treasury bills by commercial bills (Axilrod and Wallich 1992, col. 77a). This is most likely a response to the fact that the British Chancellor of the Exchequer, as shown above, does not sell his titles directly on the open market but through the Bank of England, with the associated dangers of monetizing state debt. {Similarly, the Reserve Bank of Australia widened the range of securities that it was prepared to accept in its repurchase agreements in 2004 in response to a decline in the volume of Australian Commonwealth Government Securities experienced since the mid-1990s. Eligible securities now included bills and certificates of deposit issued by commercial banks (Reserve Bank of Australia, media release, 4 March 2004).}

127 This is not recognized by Paul C. Martin (2008) when he argues, contrary to ownership economic theory, that money presupposed powerful governments.
128 {Original: Zentralstelle.}
129 {Original: privatrechtlich geregelter Teil der Wirtschaft.}
130 {Original: Daher leiste dieses Amt 'mit der Ausgabe von Banknoten kein Austauschversprechen. Der Inhaber einer Banknote kann … die Zentralstelle nicht im Wesentlichen der Zwangsvollstreckung zur Erfüllung einer Forderung zwingen'.}
131 {Original: Leistungsversprechen.}
132 {Original: in der Abwicklung des Zahlungsverkehrs und der Geldwertsicherung.}
133 For an insightful consolidation of the balance sheets of both Bank of England departments, whose separated balance sheets still exist (however without the note reserve), showing the consequent cancellation of the note reserve, see Andréadès (1904, 296), Stadermann and Steiger (2001b, 85) and Stadermann (2002, 54).
134 Goodhart (1999, 228) has shown that the frequently encountered opinion in the literature that Bagehot demanded a 'policy of *expensive* money' (Riese 1993, 457) {original: 'Politik des *teuren* Geldes'} or even a 'penalty rate' (Humphrey and Keleher 1984, 94) cannot be supported based on *Lombard Street*. The high interest rate merely means that it should be above the market rate 'early in the panic', but not during the panic. Here the interest rate should be determined by market conditions, which suggests a high rate of interest anyway. This in turn implies that the central bank must grant credit neither against a preferential interest rate nor bad loan security (see Bagehot 1873, 197).
135 {The link between state debt and the 'core' of the economy was demonstrated during the Eurozone sovereign debt crisis. Greek state titles were downgraded to 'junk' status in April 2010. This in turn strongly affected the performance of the stock market amid fears that government-imposed austerity programs would significantly depress future earnings.}
136 {This sentence added by editor.}
137 {This paragraph added by editor.}
138 {This paragraph added by editor.}
139 {This paragraph added by editor.}
140 {Of course, the matching loan asset is also booked out.}

4 The market as the result of the ownership-based economy

1 {The oldest consumer credit information agency in Germany.}
2 Mercantilism cannot be judged in this general way. Steuart (1767, vol. I, 178), who concluded this school, knew very well that the type of trade that was of interest to him did not originate from the barter of basic consumer goods. He looks from the start at enterprises that are controlled by money and whose products are only produced for the sole purpose of sale: 'People, I shall suppose, who formally knew but one sort of clothing for all seasons, willingly part with a little money to procure themselves different sorts of apparel properly adapted to summer and winter, which the ingenuity of manufacturers in their desire of getting money may have suggested to their invention'.
3 {Original: Die Folgen der Befreiung [von den feudalen Fesseln] waren für die Bauern nicht nur positive … Die 1. Generation kannte … die marktwirtschaftlichen Bedingungen nicht.}
4 {Original: 'kapitalloser' Unternehmer, Banken und Zentralbanken.}
5 {Original: Haushalten.}
6 {Original: sein Geld.}
7 {Original: Eine wie auch immer geartete Bindung der Geldschöpfung an Eigentum ware dysfunktional.}

Notes   163

8   The authors' analysis runs quickly into a contradiction to its assumption of the irrelevance of property when their mere *description* of monetary policy operations cannot avoid conceding, with grinding teeth, that 'the banks have to deposit financial instruments as *security* for the period of their central bank loans' (Heine and Herr 1999, 337; emphasis added) {original: die Banken für die Dauer des Kredits Wertpapiere als *Pfand* bei der Zentralbank hinterlegen müssen}.
9   {Original: Vikar.}
10 {Original: Eigenkapital.}
11 {This refers to German accounting rules.}
12 {Original: die meisten Unternehmen auch Eigenkapital aufweisen.}
13 {Original: Denn das Eigenkapital eines Unternehmens kann durchaus als Direktkredit des Eigentümerhaushalts an das eigene Unternehmen aufgefasst werden. Implizit ist somit unterstellt, daß Eigenkapital eine Verbindlichkeit des Unternehmens gegenüber dem Eigentümerhaushalt darstellt und im Gleichgewicht die Verwertung von Fremd- und Eigenkapital gleich ist.}
14 {Original: Passiva.}
15 {For example, bank capital in its role as a safeguard against unexpected loan losses.}
16 {Original: Passivseite.}
17 {Original: Sachkapital.}
18 {See the discussion of Heine and Herr (1999) above.}
19 {Original: Vermögensmarkt.}
20 {When already existing money is transferred, both ownership premium and liquidity premium are given up.}
21 Spahn (2001, 58 and 61) has tried to salvage the liquidity premium theory of interest by interpreting Steuart's insight that a debtor is prepared to pay interest because the bank notes obtained in a credit contract circulate. Spahn has therefore argued that the ability to circulate and the liquidity premium are identical. Equating the ability to circulate with the liquidity premium is by all means correct. However, it neglects the fact that the liquidity premium can only enter the world stage because the note-issuing bank has previously burdened its property (capital) and thereby lost ownership premium.
22 {Original: Eigentumsvorbehalt.}
23 {Original: Die 'Nutzengrade' erklären also nicht die Preise, sondern dienen nur noch als gelehrte Floskel, um die einmal gegebenen Preisrelationen als 'richtig' zu behaupten./Zu seiner Bestimmung des maximalen Tauschnutzens war Walras nur gelangt, indem er ... die Preise als *gegeben* ansah. Dies vergißt er im weiteren, um nun umgekehrt von dem nur mit Hilfe seiner Preis-Annahme gewonnenen Theorem die Preise selbst abzuleiten.}
24 {The standard commodity is Walras's *numéraire*, for example, silver of a certain fineness. The unit quantity of the chosen *numéraire* is defined by Walras as the standard ('étalon'); for example, a certain quantity in grams. The unit of account then becomes a set quantity of the chosen *numéraire*; see Walras (1954 [1926], 185–186) and Stadermann and Steiger (2001b, 246).}
25 {From here to end of paragraph added by editor.}
26 {'[D]ifferences between the amounts demanded and the amounts initially held of the various goods' (Patinkin 1965, 6).}
27 {'We denote the real value of the initial money holdings [fiat outside money] – that is, the purchasing power over commodities which these holdings represent – by the term "real balances"' (Patinkin 1965, 17).}
28 {That is, relative to an initial collection of goods and fiat/outside money.}
29 {Example added by editor.}
30 {Original: Nominal- und Sachvermögen.}
31 {Example added by editor; see *The Economist*, 12 February 2011, 69. The flipside is the sale of well-established, commodity-like products. In the absence of cost-reducing

innovation in the production process, the challenge here is to sell an unchanged product at a periodically increased nominal price, which is necessary in order to be able to repay the loan principal with interest at constant factor inputs; see also Stadermann (2006, 141).}
32 {Original: Die relativen 'Tauschverhältnisse' sind nicht Ursache der gerade in Unkenntnis aller Tauschverhältnisse gesetzten absoluten Preise. Vielmehr führen erst die gleichgewichtigen Preissetzungen der Anbieter im Ergebnis auf ein System relativer Preise und auf die Allokation der Güter im Wirtschaftsraum, ohne allerdings mehr als eine Augenblickskonstellation schaffen zu können, da neue Preissetzungen die Statik des Systems immer wieder überwinden.}
33 {The original text refers to the 'Fielmann-Revolution' after the Fielmann optometrist chain.}
34 {Original: daß die Profitrate über knappgehaltene Produktionsprozesse zu einer Form des Zinssatzes wird.}
35 {Original: der Preis für den temporären Verzicht über Geld.}
36 {Sauer (2010, 56) has argued that Heinsohn and Steiger's interest explanation was doubtful because a bank creditor typically has to reserve a lot less property assets than the debtor. For example, the capital of a central bank or private note-issuing bank is always much smaller than its loan assets. Hence the equality of ownership premium and interest in equilibrium implies that the ratio of ownership premium and bank capital is much higher than the ratio of interest and debtor collateral. However, the ownership premium must always be related to the total nominal amount of the money advance, as the bank creditor cannot avoid the associated liability to the full amount of the issued notes. Therefore, the price of the property assets used as collateral or bank capital does not have to be identical to the amount of the advanced notes. Even the price of debtor collateral typically exceeds the amount of the loan.}
37 {In modern property rights systems, human beings are no longer within the scope of chattel property and cannot be sold, mortgaged or owned by a third party.}
38 Evidently, the entrepreneur's value surplus to the amount of the interest payment does not generate a *net profit*. A net profit is only generated when the profit is above the interest obligation. Accumulation is only advanced when the profit is retained for new investments.
39 In Germany, the opportunity of wages laborers to become entrepreneurs by hypothecating their property was significantly reduced by the introduction of the so-called Hartz IV legislation from 2005. While previously the recipient of unemployment benefits only needed to access his property when the benefits provided were insufficient, under Hartz IV, after receiving 12 months of benefits the recipient has to use up his own resources before unemployment benefits are continued. Instead of supporting the access to and the creation of property for a maximum number of economic actors, the legislation has supported the tendency to move from the wage laborer towards the property-deprived proletarian *à la* Marx.
40 {From here to end of (2) added by editor.}
41 One of the absurdities of Germany economic policy is the adding of social contributions, corresponding to a proportional tax of 42 percent, to wage money. This significant increase in labor costs is without parallel world-wide and forces entrepreneurs to take on significantly more debt to begin with. This extreme tax, beginning with the first wage euro, drives investments into labor-saving technological progress or results in the relocation of production abroad. In this way the generation of income from labor is inhibited – the major reason for the German unemployment rate of over 10 percent (2005).

In contrast, Scandinavian countries with similar social benefits have unemployment rates at 50 percent lower than Germany. Here entrepreneurs do not have to take on extra debt for social contributions because these are not part of wages. Instead, production and income is based on relatively low wages, out of which social contributions are financed (in their majority) through taxes on income and consumption.

The paradox that Scandinavian wage laborers find more employment at the same net income is explained by the fact that the individual firms can engage in economic activity with a lesser amount of property hypothecated.

42 {Slaves can be mortgaged, so the pressure to economize on money is reduced.}
43 That 'overinvestment' is not caused by the collective greed of all investors is also recognized by Benoit Mandelbrot and Richard Hudson (2004; German 2005) in their critique of modern financial theory. This assumes that the striving for wealth results in an efficient market which should actually excludes crises. The authors highlight the enormous risk positions in markets and the unavoidability of financial collapses, however, without identifying the need to defend property as the cause for the lack of alternative options.
44 {Original: Diese unterscheiden sich in Nichts von spekulativen Erwartungen, außer darin, daß sie das Ergebnis von Erwartungen in der Vergangenheit sind, während die 'spekulativen' Werte sich aus Erwartungen in der Gegenwart bilden. Die Erscheinungen in der ökonomischen Welt lassen sich nicht nach *Istwerten* und *Erwartungswerten* unterscheiden, sondern nach in Verträgen auf der Grundlage von Erwartungswerten aus der Vergangenheit geronnenen Bewertungen und ebensolchen Bewertungen aus der Gegenwart. Es ist lächerlich, die ersten als real und die letzteren im Gegensatz dazu als *spekulativ* zu bezeichnen, nur weil sich die Erwartungen von gestern *bisher* nicht als ungleichgewichtig erwiesen haben.}
45 {For example, in the aftermath of the global financial crisis, the borrowing of Spanish banks from the ECB at low interest rates and the reinvestment of these proceeds in higher yielding government bonds were reported in June 2010 to have accounted for 40 percent of profits of smaller banks and 20 percent of profits of bigger ones; *The Economist*, 5 June 2010, p78.}
46 {Original: im Blick auf ihre riesigen notleidenden Forderungen überhaupt nicht zur Vergabe von Krediten bereit. Eine derart hartnäckige Zurückhaltung im Kreditgeschäft ist in Japan nie zuvor zu beobachten gewesen.}
47 {A noteworthy exception to this rule occurred in the severe 1843 New South Wales depression. Here the missing collateral was created by legal enactment providing more effective security rights over stock and wool. This helped to resolve the crisis; see Decker (2008).}
48 {Original: 'Statt die Ursache des fehlenden Wechselmaterials zu beseitigen, haben sich die Reichsregierung und die Reichsbank entschlossen, das den Geschäftsbanken fehlende Refinanzierungsmaterial im Zusammenwirken mit den Geschäftsbanken selbst bereitzustellen ... , ohne zu erkennen, daß die Wirtschaft dadurch mit einem sie zerrüttenden Willkürgeld' gepflastert worden ist.}
49 As this historical example shows, creditor's money and debtor's money differ in their very *essence*. The former is based on property and steers the ownership-based economy, whereas the latter destroys the property basis of money and leads to the disintegration of the economy. Köllmann (1999c, 125 and 127) has not understood this *theoretical* difference when he accuses ownership economics of having an 'essentialistic money concept' {original: 'essentialistischen Geldbegriff'} to which the '*history of money* as a descriptive discipline does not provide any clue ... ' {original: 'Geldgeschichte als descriptive Disziplin [keine] Auskunft ... geben könne'}.
50 {This paragraph added by editor.}
51 {European Central Bank, Monetary Policy, Open Market Operations, Ad-hoc communications, 12 September 2011, www.ecb.int; accessed on 13 September 2011.}
52 {See *The Economist*, 17 March 2012, and 'EZB entzieht sich der Umschuldung', *Frankfurter Allgemeine Zeitung*, 16 February 2012.}
53 Anyone who accepts that an ownership-based economy needs actors who can take on debt must also accept the fact that this capacity can be under threat and that solutions must be found to overcome such a situation. For example, anyone who wants to prevent the abolition of property rights may suddenly find himself in a position where

he has to accept a redistribution of property as a compromise. Whoever misunderstands such a preservation strategy as the overturn of the ownership-based society, as does, for example, Gerald Baumberger, a critic of ownership economics (Braunberger 1996), should think about alternative ways to create money; because money creation is the subject in question. If it is not the state that takes on debt in place of its citizens, who either are no longer willing to burden or hypothecate property or no longer have available property left, not many options will be left. In reality, states typically make attempts to aid a recovery by taking on debt on behalf of their citizens. Evidently, the state can also redeem bad loans out of the funds of its citizens through its power to raise taxes. This approach would inevitably be a variant of a Japanese-style redistribution of property.
54 Figures refer to gross debt. Net debt as gross debt minus state assets increased in the same period from 5 to 80 percent (Shiraishi 2003, 5).
55 {December 2005}.
56 The saving of state consumption expenditure is known to be limited due to existing legal requirements, in particular for social security payments. In Japan the rate of state consumption increased from 14 percent in 1991 to 17 percent in 2000 (Shirashi 2003, 6).
57 {It should be noted that Heinsohn and Steiger's positive assessment of the stabilizing effects of fiscal stimulus programs articulated in this chapter at the end of 2005 preempted the newly formed consensus in favor of such interventions in the aftermath of the 2008 global financial crisis. See, for example, Spilimbergo *et al.* (2010, 587–594) for a discussion of such programs.}

5 Issues associated with ownership in developing and transformation countries

1 For more detail see Steiger 2006a and 2012.
2 The current population explosion is an important contributing factor for this, which evidently cannot, in contrast to Europe between 1500 and 1900 (Heinsohn, Knieper and Steiger 1979, 73 and in more detail Heinsohn 2003), be resolved through the conquering of new territories and the establishment of colonies, as demonstrated by the bloody repulsion following the assault of the Spanish African enclaves of Melilla and Ceuta in the autumn of 2005.
3 {In October 2006, the Nobel Committee awarded the Nobel Peace Prize jointly to Grameen Bank and its founder Muhammad Yunus.}
4 {For example, provided in Germany by the Kreditanstalt für Wiederaufbau (KfW), a government-owned development bank.}
5 For a similar development of an ownership-based economy in Australia based on the Lien on Wool and Stock Mortgage Act 1843, see Decker (2005a and 2005b) {see also Decker 2008}.
6 {Original: Grund-Eigenthum.}
7 {Original: Staatliches Geldzeichen.}
8 {Original: Verrechnungszeichen.}
9 The same prohibition holds in Brazil and explains the problem of exorbitantly high interest rates, which obstruct broader development. Commercial bank rates are up to 37 percent higher than the central bank refinancing rate. These are not the result of an 'usury cartel' as has been suggested by the IMF (Goerdeler 2004) but a reflection of the high risk of unrecoverable claims facing banks.
10 {See Schulz (2009, 200–210) for a similar situation in Poland.}
11 {For example, by selling foreign currency assets.}
12 The fact that the success of the developed countries is based on several hundred million enforceable credit contracts, mentioned above, is not even suspected by the authors.
13 {Tenants could purchase their houses or apartments at favorable conditions and were supported through the provision of long-term loans; see Aldenborg (2005, 49–50).}

References

This list includes editor's references.

Adler, B.E. (1998), 'Secured Credit Contracts', in: Newman, P., ed., *The New Palgrave Dictionary of Economics and the Law*, London: Macmillan, vol. 3, col. 405a–410a.

Alchian, A.A. (1992), 'Property Rights', in: Newman, P., Milgate, M. and Eatwell, J., eds., *The New Palgrave Dictionary of Money and Finance*, London: Macmillan, vol. 3, col. 223a–226a.

Aldenborg, U. (2005), *Entwicklung und Transformation in der Logik der Eigentumsökonomik: Theorie und Praxis von Eigentum und genuiner Geldschaffung am Beispiel des Transformationsprozesses in Slowenien*, dissertation, University of Bremen, August.

Andréadès, A.M. (1904), *History of the Bank of England 1640–1903*, translated by C. Meredith, London: P.S. King & Son, 1909.

Andrewes, A. (1967), *Greek Society*, Harmondsworth: Penguin Books, 1971.

Axilrod, S.H. and Wallich, H.C. (1992), 'Open-Market Operations', in: Newman, P., Milgate, M. and Eatwell, J., eds., *The New Palgrave Dictionary of Money and Finance*, London: Macmillan, vol. 3, col. 74b–77a.

Backhaus, J. (2000), '"Property, Interest, and Money: Unresolved Puzzles in Economics". By Gunnar Heinsohn and Otto Steiger', *History of Political Economy*, vol. 32, no. 1, spring, p. 159.

Bagehot, W. (1873), *Lombard Street: A Description of the Money Market*, reprint, New York: J. Wiley & Sons, 1999.

Bailey, M.J. (1998), 'Property in Aboriginal Societies', in: Newman, P., ed., *The New Palgrave Dictionary of Economics and the Law*, London: Macmillan, vol. 3, col. 155b–157b.

Ballin, C. (2005), *Marktrevolution in Schlummernden Märkten*, Berlin: Duncker & Humblot.

Barley, R. (2011), 'Euro Zone Risks Becoming Spanish Prisoner with Bond Buys', *The Wall Street Journal*, 3 September.

Beaufort, J. (2001), 'Abschied vom Tausch? Die Theorie der Eigentumsgesellschaft von Gunnar Heinsohn und Otto Steiger', *IKSF Discussion Papers* (University of Bremen), no. 28, August.

Bethell, T. (1998), *The Noblest Triumph: Property and Prosperity through the Ages*, New York: St. Martin's Press.

Bethell, T. (2008), 'Why Isn't the Whole World Developed? On Property in the Third World', in: Steiger, O., ed., *Property Economics: Property Rights, Creditor's Money and the Foundations of the Economy*, Marburg: Metropolis.

References

Betz, K. (1993), *Ein monetärkeynesianisches und makroökonomisches Gleichgewicht*, Marburg: Metropolis.

Betz, K. (2001), *Jenseits der Konjunkturpolitik: Überlegungen zur langfristigen Wirtschaftspolitik in einer Geldwirtschaft*, Marburg: Metropolis.

Betz, T. (2005), 'Besprechung von Bernd Striegel, Über das Geld: Geschichte und Zukunft des Wirtschaftens, 2005', *Zeitschrift für Sozialökonomie*, vol. 42, no. 146, September, pp. 42–45.

Betz, T. (2008), 'The Property Theories of Bethell, Pipes and de Soto – Similarities and Differences in Emphasis to the Approach of Heinsohn, Stadermann and Steiger', in: Steiger, O., ed., *Property Economics: Property Rights, Creditor's Money and the Foundations of the Economy*, Marburg: Metropolis.

Bindseil, U., Manzanares, A. and Weller, B. (2004), 'The Role of Central Bank Capital Revisited', *ECB Working Paper Series* (European Central Bank), no. 392, September.

Binswanger, H.C. (2003), as quoted in P. Müller, 'Ein paar Prozent Streit: Er wurde gehasst und geliebt, erlaubt und verboten: Eine kleine Geschichte des Zinses', *Die Zeit*, no. 6, 17 February.

Blackstone, B. (2010), 'World News: ECB Notches $20.4 Billion in Bond Purchases – Some Economists Say Central Bank's Move isn't the 'Aggressive' Step Needed to Restore Confidence in Containing Crisis', *The Wall Street Journal*, 18 May.

Blackstone, W. (1893 [1753]), 'Book the Second: Of the Rights of Things', *Commentaries on the Laws of England in Four Books. Notes selected from the editions of Archibold, Christian, Coleridge, Chitty, Stewart, Kerr, and others, Barron Field's Analysis, and Additional Notes, and a Life of the Author by George Sharswood. In Two Volumes*, Philadelphia: J.B. Lippincott Co. (1893), accessed at http://oll.libertyfund.org/title/2140/198689 on June 9 2012.

Blanchard, O. (2003), *Macroeconomics: Third Edition*, Upper Saddle River, NJ: Prentice Hall.

Blenck, D., Hasko, H., Hilton, S. and Masaki, K. (2002), 'The Main Features of the Monetary Policy Frameworks of the Bank of Japan, the Federal Reserve and the Eurosystem', in: Bank for International Settlements (BIS), ed., *Comparing Monetary Policy Operating Procedures across the United States, Japan and the Euro Area: BIS Paper New Series*, no. 9, May, pp. 23–47.

Bofinger, P. (with J. Reischle and A. Schächter) (2001), *Monetary Policy: Goals, Institutions, Strategies, and Instruments*, Oxford: Oxford University Press.

Bogaert, R. (1966), *Les origines antiques de la banque de dépôt: Une mise au point accompagnée d'une esquisse des opérations de banque en Mésopotamie*, Leiden: A.W. Sijthoff.

Bracho, G. and López, J. (2005), 'The Economic Collapse of Russia', *Banca Nazionale del Lavoro Quarterly Review*, vol. 58, no. 232, March, pp. 53–89.

Braunberger, G. (1996), 'Die Vision der Eigentumsgesellschaft: Zwei Bremer Wissenschaftler schreiben die Wirtschaftstheorie um', *Frankfurter Allgemeine Zeitung*, no. 269, 18 November, p. 16.

Bridge, M. (2002), *Personal Property Law*, third edition, Oxford: Oxford University Press.

Brockmeier, T. (1996), *Handlungsrechte (Property Rights) und Armut: Zur Brauchbarkeit neo-liberaler Politikempfehlungen bei der Armutsbekämpfung*, Marburg: Tectum.

Bundesbank (1995), *Die Geldpolitik der Bundesbank*, Frankfurt am Main: Deutsche Bundesbank.

Bundesgerichtshof (1998), 'Das gesamte Bodenreformurteil des V. Senats des Bundesgerichtshofs', Karlsruhe, December 17, *V ZR 200/97*, unpublished manuscript.
Busch, U. (2003), review of Heinsohn, G./Steiger, O.: *Eigentum, Zins und Geld: Ungelöste Rätsel der Wirtschaftswissenschaft*, second edition, 2002, and of Heinsohn, G. and Steiger, O.: *Eigentumstheorie des Wirtschaftens versus Wirtschaftstheorie ohne Eigentum*, 2002, *Utopie kreativ: Diskussion sozialistischer Alternativen* (Berlin), no. 147, January, pp. 86–88.
Cencini, A. (2001), *Monetary Macroeconomics: A New Approach*, London: Routledge.
Chantraine, H. (1979), 'Münzwesen', in: *Der Kleine Pauly*, Munich: Deutscher Taschenbuch Verlag, vol. 3, col. 1447–1452.
Childs, F.H. (1914), *Principles of the Law of Personal Property, Chattels and Choses*, Chicago: Callaghan & Company.
Cohen, E.E. (2008), 'The Elasticity of the Money-Supply at Athens', in: W.V. Harris, ed., *The Monetary Systems of the Greeks and Romans*, Oxford: Oxford University Press, pp. 66–83.
Copeland, T.E. and Weston, J.F. (1992), *Financial Theory and Corporate Policy*, Third Edition, Addison-Wesley: New York.
Cronon, W. (1983), *Changes in the Land*, New York: Hill and Wang.
Crowther, G. (1940), *An Outline of Money*, London: T. Nelson & Sons.
C.W. (2005), 'Ein Finanzmarkt als "Leiter" für die Armen: Mikrokredit-Systeme in der Entwicklungszusammenarbeit', *Neue Zürcher Zeitung* (Internationale Ausgabe), no. 199, 27–28 August, p. 8.
Da. (2005), '"Mezzanine ist keine Modewelle": Finanzprodukte aus dem angelsächsischen Raum für Wachstumsunternehmen attraktiv – Hohe Kosten', *Frankfurter Allgemeine Zeitung*, no. 190, August 17, p. 20.
Dalton, G.B. (1982), 'Barter', *Journal of Economic Issues*, vol. 16, pp. 181–190.
Davidson, P. (1994), *Post Keynesian Macroeconomic Theory: A Foundation for Successful Economic Policies for the Twenty-First Century*, Cheltenham, UK and Brookfield, VT: Edward Elgar.
Davidson, P. (2005), 'The Post Keynesian School', in: Snowdon, B. and Vane, H.A., *Modern Macroeconomics: Its Origins, Development and Current State*, Cheltenham, UK and Northampton, MA: Edward Elgar, pp. 451–473.
Debreu, G. (1959), *Theory of Value: An Axiomatic Analysis of Economic Equilibrium*, New Haven and London: Yale University Press.
Decker, F. (2005a), 'Colonial Currency and Pastoral Expansion: Australia's Early Economic Development from a Property Economic Perspective', *IKSF Discussion Papers* (University of Bremen), no. 34, July.
Decker, F. (2005b), 'The Lien on Wool and Stock Mortgage Legislation from a Property Economics Perspective', *Macquarie University Research Paper* (Macquarie University Sydney), November.
Decker, F. (2008), 'The Legal and Economic History of the Lien on Wool and Stock Mortgage Act 1843 (NSW)', *Legal History*, vol. 12, no. 2, pp. 151–175.
Decker, F. (2010), *The Emergence of Money in Convict New South Wales*, Marburg: Metropolis.
Decker, F. (2011), 'Bills, Notes and Money in Early New South Wales, 1788–1822', *Financial History Review*, vol. 18, no.1, pp. 71–90.
Decker, F. (2012), 'Settlement Assets: The Missing Economic Category in the Theory of Money', in: *SSRN Working Paper*, http://papers.ssrn.com/abstract=2007637.

References

Decker, F. (2013), 'Property Rights', in: J. Wright, ed., *International Encyclopedia of the Social and Behavioral Sciences*, second edition (forthcoming).

Deininger, K. (2003), *Land Policy for Growth and Poverty Reduction: A World Bank Policy Research Report*, Washington, DC: The World Bank and Oxford: Oxford University Press.

Demsetz, H. (1998), 'Property Rights', in: Newman, P., ed., *The New Palgrave Dictionary of Economics and the Law*, London: Macmillan, vol. 3, col. 144a–155a.

Dowd, K. (2000), 'The Invisible Hand and the Evolution of the Monetary System', in: J. Smithin, ed., *What Is Money?*, London: Routledge, pp. 137–156.

Dreher, A. (2005), '"Mehr ist weniger, und weniger wäre mehr": Die Entwicklungsdebatte aus wissenschaftlicher Sicht', *Neue Zürcher Zeitung* (international edition), no. 212, September 10–11, p. 19.

Enghofer, S. and Knospe, M. (2005), *Schulden, Geld und Zins*, University of Bayreuth: Fachbereich Wirtschaftswissenschaften, February 2005, unpublished manuscript.

Epstein, R.A. (1998), 'Possession', in: Newman, P., ed., *The New Palgrave Dictionary of Economics and the Law*, London: Macmillan, vol. 3, col. 62b–68b.

European Central Bank (2005), *Durchführung der Geldpolitik im Euro-Währungsgebiet: Allgemeine Regelungen für die geldpolitischen Instrumente und Verfahren des Eurosystems*, Frankfurt am Main: European Central Bank, February.

European Central Bank (2011a), *The Monetary Policy of the ECB 2011*, Frankfurt am Main: European Central Bank.

European Central Bank (2011b), *Annual Report 2011*, Frankfurt am Main: European Central Bank.

Finley, M.I. (1951), *Studies in Land and Credit in Ancient Athens 500–200 B.C.*, New Brunswick: Rutgers University Press.

Fisher, I. (1906), *The Nature of Capital and Income*, New York: Macmillan.

Fisher, I. (1930), *The Theory of Interest as Determined by Impatience to Spend Income and Opportunity to Invest It*, New York: Macmillan.

Folkerts-Landau, D. and Garber, P.M. (1992), 'The ECB: A Bank or a Monetary Policy Rule?', in: Canzonieri, M.B., Grilli, V. and Masson, M., eds., *Establishing a Central Bank: Issues in Europe and Lessons from the US*, Cambridge: Cambridge University Press, pp. 86–110.

Friedman, M. (1992), 'Quantity Theory of Money', in: Newman, P., Milgate, M. and Eatwell, J., eds., *The New Palgrave Dictionary of Money and Finance*, London: Macmillan, vol. 3, col. 247b–264b.

Friedman, M. and Schwartz, A.J. (1986), 'Has Government Any Role in Money?', *Journal of Monetary Economics*, vol. 17, no. 1, pp. 37–62.

Frisch, R. (1970), 'From Utopian Theory to Practical Applications: The Case of Econometrics – Lecture to the Memory of Alfred Nobel, June 17, 1970', in: http://nobelprize.org/economics/laureates/1969/frisch–lecture.html (last visit: October 4 2005).

Fry, M. (1997), 'The Fiscal Abuse of Central Banks', in: Blejer, M.I./Ter-Minasian, T., eds., *Macroeconomic Dimensions of Central Banks: Essays in Honour of Vito Tanzi*, London: Routledge, pp. 337–359.

German Federal Ministry of Justice (2010), *German Civil Code*, translation provided by Langenscheidt Translation Service, Saarbrücken: Juris GmbH.

Gibbons, J.S. (1870 [1858]), *The Banks of New York, Their Dealers, The Clearing House, and the Panic of 1857*, New York: D. Appleton & Co.

Goerdeler, C.D. (2004), 'Das Wucherkartell der brasilianischen Banken: Kreditnehmer können wegen der hohen Zinsen schnell ins Elend schlittern – Internationaler

Währunsgfonds rügt mangelnden Wettbewerb', *Kurier am Sonntag* (Bremen), no. 25 (143), June 20, p. 4.
Goode, R. (2004), *Commercial Law*, third edition, London: Penguin Books.
Goodhart, C.A.E. (1999), 'Myths about the Lender of Last Resort', in: Goodhart, C.A.E. and Illing, G., eds., *Financial Crises, Contagion, and the Lender of Last Resort*, Oxford: Oxford University Press, 2002, pp. 227–245.
Gorton, G. (1997), 'Clearinghouses', in: D. Glasner, ed., *Business Cycles and Depressions: An Encyclopaedia*, New York: Garland, col. 99a–b.
Graziani, A. (1997), review of Heinsohn, G./Steiger, O.: *Eigentum, Zins und Geld: Ungelöste Rätsel der Wirtschaftswissenschaft*, The European Journal of the History of Economic Thought, vol. 4, no. 1, spring, pp. 158–160.
Graziani, A. (2008), 'Some Observations on Heinsohn and Steiger's "Property Theory of Interest and Money"', in: Steiger, O., ed., *Property Economics: Property Rights, Creditor's Money and the Foundations of the Economy*, Marburg: Metropolis.
Grün, B. (1998), 'Die Geltung des Erbrechts beim Neubauerneigentum in der SBZ/DDR – Verkannte Rechtslage mit schweren Folgen', *Zeitschrift für Vermögens- und Immobilienrecht*, vol. 18, no. 10, October, pp. 537–547.
Grünewald, R. (2001), 'Fibel für Einsteiger in die Eigentumstheorie der Wirtschaft', *IKSF Discussion Papers* (University of Bremen), no. 26, May.
Gurley, J.G. and Shaw, E.S. (1960), *Money in a Theory of Finance*, Washington, DC: Brookings Institution.
Hahn, F.H. (1982), *Money and Inflation*, Oxford: Blackwell.
Harris, W.V. (2008a), 'Introduction', in: Harris, W.V., ed., *The Monetary Systems of the Greeks and Romans*, Oxford: Oxford University Press, pp. 1–11.
Harris, W.V. (2008b), 'The Nature of Roman Money', in: Harris, W.V., ed., *The Monetary Systems of the Greeks and Romans*, Oxford: Oxford University Press, pp. 174–207.
Hausknecht, A. (1995), 'Monetäre Aspekte des vietnamesischen Transformationsprozesses', in: Betz, K. And Riese, H., ed., *Wirtschaftspolitik in einer Geldwirtschaft*, Marburg: Metropolis.
Hausknecht, A. (2001), *Monetäre Aspekte des Transformationsprozesses: Eine Fallstudie Vietnams*, Marburg: Metropolis.
Hawtrey, R.G. (1919), *Currency and Credit*, London: Longmans, second edition (1923); German edition, *Währung und Kredit*, Jena: G. Fischer.
Hawtrey, R.G. (1930), 'Credit', in: *Encyclopaedia of the Social Sciences*, New York: Macmillan, vol. 3, pp. 545–550.
Hawtrey, R.G. (1932), *The Art of Central Banking*, reprint (1970), London: Frank Cass & Co.
Heering, W. (1999a), 'Privateigentum, Vertrauen und Geld: Überlegungen zur Genese von Zahlungsmitteln in Marktökonomien oder: Wie man in Berlin, Bremen und anderswo über Geld denkt', in: Betz, K. and Roy, T., eds., *Privateigentum und Geld: Kontroversen um den Ansatz von Heinsohn und Steiger*, Marburg: Metropolis, pp. 99–143.
Heering, W. (1999b), 'Replik auf die Replik von Gunnar Heinsohn und Otto Steiger', in: Betz, K. and Roy, T., eds., *Privateigentum und Geld: Kontroversen um den Ansatz von Heinsohn und Steiger*, Marburg: Metropolis, pp. 331–339.
Heichelheim, F.M. (1938), *Wirtschaftsgeschichte des Altertums vom Paläolithikum bis zur Völkerwanderung der Germanen, Slaven und Araber*, Leiden: A.W. Sijthoff, vol. I.
Heidelmeyer, W., ed. (1997), *Die Menschenrechte: Erklärungen, Verfassungsartikel, Internationale Abkommen*, Paderborn: F. Schöningh, fourth edition.

References

Heine, M. and Herr, H. (1999), *Volkswirtschaftslehre: Paradigmenorientierte Einführung in die Mikro- und Makrotheorie*, Munich: R. Oldenbourg.

Heinsohn, G. (1976), 'Ursprung und Zerfall des Patriarchats?', *Päd. Extra*, no. 16, pp. 13–17.

Heinsohn, G. (1978), *Theorie für die Entstehung der Hochpatriarchate, der deduktiven Logik und der Notwendigkeit des Geldes – Zwanzig Thesen*, manuscript.

Heinsohn, G. (1984), *Privateigentum, Patriarchat, Geldwirtschaft: Eine sozialtheoretische Rekonstruktion zur Antike* (1982), Frankfurt am Main: Suhrkamp.

Heinsohn, G. (1995), 'Muss die Abendländische Zivilisation auf immer unerklärbar bleiben? Patriarchat und Geldwirtschaft', in: Schelkle, W. and Nitsch, M., eds., *Rätsel Geld*, Marburg: Metropolis, pp. 209–270.

Heinsohn, G. (1998), 'GULag und Auschwitz: Ein Wort zur Klärung der Differenz', *Schriftenreihe des Raphael-Lemkin-Instituts für Xenophobie- und Genozidforschung an der Universität Bremen*, no. 6, April.

Heinsohn, G. (2003), *Söhne und Weltmacht: Terror im Aufstieg und Fall der Nationen*, Zürich: Orell Füssli.

Heinsohn, G. (2005), 'Warum gibt es Märkte?', in Krieg, W./Galler, K./Stadelmann, P., eds., *Richtiges und gutes Management: vom System zur Praxis – Festschrift für Fredmund Malik*, Bern: Haupt, pp. 137–152.

Heinsohn, G. (2008a), 'Where Does the Market Come From? Why the Controversy Between the "Substantivist" Polanyi School and "Formalist" Neoclassical Protoganists of an Eternal and Universal Market Was Never Solved', in: Steiger, O., ed., *Property Economics: Property Rights, Creditor's Money and the Foundations of the Economy*, Marburg: Metropolis.

Heinsohn, G. (2008b), 'Die Verführung zur globalen Zockerei – Essay', *Frankfurter Allgemeine Zeitung – Die Ordnung der Wirtschaft*, 26 April 2008, no. 98, p. 15.

Heinsohn, G. (2008c), 'Fünf Trugschlüsse der Finanzkrise', *Cicero*, November.

Heinsohn, G. (2010), 'Defence of Property as the Cause of Crises', lecture, Erasmus Universiteit Rotterdam, Erasmus Institute for Philosophy and Economics, 10 May 2010.

Heinsohn, G. (2011), 'ROMA QUADRATA: Rätselakkumulation als Impuls auf dem Weg zur Eigentumsökonomik', lecture, Hochschule für Technik, Wirtschaft und Kultur Leipzig, May 11 2011.

Heinsohn, G. and Decker, F. (2010), 'A Property Economics Explanation of the Global Financial Crisis', in: Kolb, R.W., ed., *Lessons from the Financial Crisis: Causes, Consequences, and Our Economic Future*, Hoboken, NJ: John Wiley & Sons, Inc.

Heinsohn, G. (with Decker, F. and Heinsohn, U.) (2009), 'A Property Economics Explanation of the 2008 Global Financial Crisis', in: *SSRN Working Paper*, http://papers.ssrn.com/abstract=1331712.

Heinsohn, G., Knieper, R. and Steiger, O. (1979), *Menschenproduktion: Allgemeine Bevölkerungstheorie der Neuzeit*, Frankfurt am Main: Suhrkamp, second edition (1986).

Heinsohn, G. and Steiger, O. (1977), 'The Significance of "The Wealth of Nations" for an Economic Theory of the Production of Population', *European Demographic Information Bulletin*, vol. 8, no. 4, pp. 138–149.

Heinsohn, G. and Steiger, O. (1981a), 'Geld, Produktivität und Unsicherheit in Kapitalismus und Sozialismus. Oder: Von den Lollarden Wat Tylers zur Solidarität Lech Walesas', *Leviathan*, vol. 9, no. 2, pp. 164–194.

Heinsohn, G. and Steiger, O. (1981b), 'Money, Productivity and Uncertainty in Capitalism and Socialism', *Metroeconomica*, vol. 33, February–October, pp. 41–77.

Heinsohn, G. and Steiger, O. (1983), 'Private Property, Debts and Interest or: The Origin of Money and the Rise and Fall of Monetary Economies', *Studi Economici*, vol. 38, no. 21, pp. 3–56.

Heinsohn, G. and Steiger, O. (1988), 'Warum Zins? Keynes und die Grundlagen einer monetären Werttheorie', in: Hagemann, H. and Steiger, O., eds., *Keynes' Theorie nach fünfzig Jahren*, Berlin: Dunker & Humblot, pp. 315–353.

Heinsohn, G. and Steiger, O. (1989), 'The Veil of Barter', in: Kregel, J.A., ed., *Inflation and Income Distribution in Capitalist Crisis: Essays in Memory of Sidney Weintraub*, London: Macmillan, pp. 175–201.

Heinsohn, G. and Steiger, O. (1996), *Eigentum, Zins und Geld: Ungelöste Rätsel der Wirtschaftswissenschaft*, Reinbek: Rowohlt; third edition: Marburg, Metropolis (2004).

Heinsohn, G. and Steiger, O. (1997), 'Liquidity Premium', in Glasner, D., ed., *Business Cycles and Depressions: An Encyclopaedia*, New York & London: Garland, Garland Reference Library of Social Science, vol. 505, pp. 397–399.

Heinsohn, G. and Steiger, O. (1999a) 'Theorie der Eigentumsrechte und die real bills fallacy: Antworten auf unsere Kritiker', in: Betz, K. and Roy, T., ed., *Privateigentum und Geld: Kontroversen um den Ansatz von Heinsohn und Steiger*, Marburg: Metropolis, pp. 311–339.

Heinsohn, G. and Steiger, O. (1999b), 'Theorie der Eigentumsrechte und die real bills fallacy: Schlußbemerkung', in: Betz, K. and Roy, T., ed., *Privateigentum und Geld: Kontroversen um den Ansatz von Heinsohn und Steiger*, Marburg: Metropolis, pp. 353–358.

Heinsohn, G. and Steiger, O. (2000a), 'The Property Theory of Interest and Money', in: Smithin, J., ed., *What Is Money?*, London: Routledge, pp. 67–100; revised and extended reprint in: Hodgson, G.M., ed., *Recent Developments in Institutional Economics*, Cheltenham, UK and Northampton, MA: Edward Elgar, 2003, pp. 484–517.

Heinsohn, G. and Steiger, O. (2000b), 'Warum eine Zentralbank nicht über ihr Geld verfügen kann', *Ethik und Sozialwissenschaften*, vol. 11, no. 4, December, col. 516a–519a.

Heinsohn, G. and Steiger, O. (2000c), 'Aktien – das Geld der Unternehmen? Oder: Warum man mit "Aktiengeld' so billig bezahlen kann', in: Vielhaber, R., ed., *Die besten Anlagen 2001! Das Fuchs-Jahrbuch für Kapitalanleger*, Berlin: Verlag Fuchsbriefe, pp. 135–142.

Heinsohn, G. and Steiger, O. (2000d), 'Geldnote, Anleihe und Aktie: Gemeinsamkeiten und Unterschiede dreier Wertpapiere', *IKSF Discussion Papers* (University of Bremen), no. 22, September.

Heinsohn, G. and Steiger, O. (2001), 'Property Titles as the Clue to a Successful Transformation', in: Stadermann, H.-J. and Steiger, O., eds., *Eigentum, Freiheit und Haftung in der Geldwirtschaft*, Marburg: Metropolis, pp. 203–220.

Heinsohn, G. and Steiger, O. (2002a), *Eigentumstheorie des Wirtschaftens versus Wirtschaftstheorie ohne Eigentum: Ergänzungsband zur Neuauflage von 'Eigentum, Zins und Geld'*, Marburg: Metropolis.

Heinsohn, G. and Steiger, O. (2002b), 'The Eurosystem and the Art of Central Banking', *Studi economici* (University of Naples), no. 76 (2002/1), pp. 5–30.

Heinsohn, G. and Steiger, O. (2003), 'Crash und Deflation: Zum Verständnis der aktuellen Wirtschaftslage in Deutschland und der Welt', *Frühjahrstagung des Malik Management Zentrum St. Gallen (MZSG)*, March, unpublished manuscript.

Heinsohn, G. and Steiger, O. (2005), 'Alternative Theories of the Rate of Interest: A Reconsideration', in: Fontana, G. and Realfonzo, R., eds., *The Monetary Theory of Production: Tradition and Perspectives (Essays Dedicated to and in Honour of Augusto Graziani)*, London and New York: Palgrave Macmillan, pp. 67–81.

Heinsohn, G. and Steiger, O. (2006a), 'Interest and Money: the Property Explanation', in: Arestis, P. and Sawyer, M.C., eds., *Handbook of Alternative Monetary Theory*, Cheltenham, UK and Northampton, MA: Edward Elgar.

Heinsohn, G. and Steiger, O (2006b), *Eigentumsökonomik*, Marburg: Metropolis.

Heinsohn, G. and Steiger, O. (2008), 'Collateral and Own Capital – the Missing Links in the Theory of the Rate of Interest and Money', in: Steiger, O., ed., *Property Economics: Property Rights, Creditor's Money and the Foundations of the Economy*, Marburg: Metropolis.

Heinsohn, G. and Steiger, O. (2011), 'The European Central Bank and the Eurosystem: An Analysis of the Missing Central Monetary Institution in European Monetary Union', in: Ehrig, D., Staroske, U. and Steiger, O., eds., *The Euro, the Eurosystem and European Economic and Monetary Union*, Münster and Hamburg: LIT-Verlag.

Heinsohn, U. (2001), 'Eigentum und Entwicklung: Zum Zusammenhang zwischen Entwicklung und traditioneller sowie neuer Eigentumslosigkeit', in: Stadermann, H.-J. and Steiger, O., eds., *Eigentum, Freiheit und Haftung in der Geldwirtschaft*, Marburg: Metropolis, pp. 295–335.

Heinsohn, U. (2008), 'Property, Development and de Soto's Approach', in: Steiger, O., ed., *Property Economics: Property Rights, Creditor's Money and the Foundations of the Economy*, Marburg: Metropolis.

Hepburn, S. (2001), *Principles of Property Law*, second edition, Sydney and London: Cavendish Publishing.

Herr, H. (1999), 'Die Rolle des Eigentums im Transformationsprozeß von der Plan- zur Geldwirtschaft', in: Betz, K. and Roy, T., eds., *Privateigentum und Geld: Kontroversen um den Ansatz von Heinsohn und Steiger*, Marburg: Metropolis, pp. 177–199.

Herz D. and Weinberger, V. eds. (2006), *Lexikon ökonomischer Werke: 650 wegweisende Schriften von der Antike bis ins 20. Jahrhundert*, in cooperation with Andreas Blätte.

Hicks, J. (1965), *Capital and Growth*, Oxford: Clarendon Press.

Hicks, J. (1980–1981), 'IS-LM: An Explanation', *Journal of Post Keynesian Economics*, vol. 3, pp. 139–154.

Hicks, J. (1989), *A Market Theory of Money*, Oxford: Clarendon Press.

Hofmann, W. (1964), *Sozialökonomische Studientexte – Band 1: Wert- und Preislehre*, Berlin: Duncker & Humblot.

Horwich, G. (1997), 'Loanable-Funds Doctrine', in: Glass, D., ed., *Business Cycles and Depressions: An Encyclopaedia*, New York: Garland, pp. 400–404.

Humphrey, T.M. and Keleher, R.E. (1984), 'The Lender of Last Resort: A Historical Perspective', in: Goodhart, C.A.E. and Illing, G., ed., *Financial Crises, Contagion, and the Lender of Last Resort*, Oxford: Oxford University Press, 2002, pp. 73–108.

Hutzler, C. and Lawrence, S. (2003), 'Migrants in China Get New Rights: Rural Residents May Seek City Jobs as Directive Ends Past Employment Barriers', *The Wall Street Journal Europe*, January 20, p. A2.

Illig, H. (1996), 'Besitz und Eigentum: Eine Heinsohn-Steiger-Rezension', *Zeitensprünge*, vol. 7, no. 3, September, p. 548.

Immobilia (2004), 'Residential: Enjoying the View, Permits Aside', *Lokale Immobilia* (*Warsaw Business Journal*'s biweekly supplement on real estate, construction and development), May 10, p. L1.

Instituto Democracia y Libertad (2003), *From Dead Capital to Live Capital: The Difference between the ILD and Other Organizations Who Say They Know How to Do the Same Thing*, Lima: Instituto Democracia y Libertad (ILD), April, unpublished manuscript.

International Labour Office (2001), *Collateral, Collateral Law and Collateral Substitutes*, created by Balkenhol, B. and Schütte, H., Geneva: International Labour Office (ILO), Employment Sector: Social Finance Program, Working Paper no. 26.

International Monetary Fund (2005), 'IMF Executive Board Concludes 2005 Article IV Consultation with Argentina', Public Information Notice (PIN) (International Monetary Fund [IMF]), no. 05/83, 30 June.

Israel, J.I. (1989), *Dutch Primacy in World Trade 1585–1740*, Oxford: Clarendon Press.

Jaffee, D. and Stiglitz, J. (1992), 'Credit Rationing', in: Friedman, B.M. and Hahn, F.H., eds., *Handbook of Monetary Economics*, Amsterdam: North-Holland, vol. II, pp. 837–888.

Jao, Y.C., 'Hongkong: Monetary and Financial System', in: Newman, P., Milgate, M. and Eatwell, J., eds., *The New Palgrave Dictionary of Money and Finance*, 1992, vol. 2, col. 314a–316b.

Jevons, W.S. (1957), *The Theory of Political Economy*; fifth edition (1965), New York: Augustus M. Kelley Bookseller.

Jonas, J. (2002), 'Argentina: The Anatomy of a Crisis', *ZEI Working Paper* (Universität Bonn), no. B 12/2002.

Kanatas, G. (1992), 'Collateral', in: Newman, P., Milgate, M. and Eatwell, J., eds., *The New Palgrave Dictionary of Money and Finance*, London: Macmillan, vol. 1, col. 381a–383a.

Kaps, C. (2005), 'Länderbericht: Slowenien – Im Euro-Fieber', *Frankfurter Allgemeine Zeitung*, no. 230, October 4, p. 18.

Kaser, M. (1981), *Römisches Privatrecht*, Juristische Kurz-Lehrbücher, Munich: C.H. Beck.

Keynes, J.M. (1919), 'Inflation', in: *The Collected Writings of John Maynard Keynes, vol. IX: Essays in Persuasion* (1931), London: Macmillan, 1972, pp. 57–58.

Keynes, J.M. (1930), *A Treatise on Money. vol. 1: The Pure Theory of Money*, in: *The Collected Writings of John Maynard Keynes, vol. V*, London: Macmillan, 1971.

Keynes, J.M. (1933), 'A Monetary Theory of Production', in: G. Clausing, ed., *Der Stand und die nächste Zukunft der Konjunkturforschung: Festschrift für Arthur Spiethoff zum 60. Geburtstag*, Munich: Duncker & Humblot, pp. 123–125.

Keynes, J.M. (1934), 'The Propensity to Invest', in: *The Collected Writings of John Maynard Keynes, vol. XIII: The General Theory and After. Part I: Preparation*, London: Macmillan, 1973, pp. 450–456.

Keynes, J.M. (1936), *The General Theory of Employment, Interest and Money*, in: *The Collected Writings of John Maynard Keynes, vol. VII*, London: Macmillan, 1973.

Knapp, G.F. (1905), *Staatliche Theorie des Geldes*, Munich and Leipzig: Duncker & Humblot.

Knapp, G.F. (1924), *The State Theory of Money*, abridged translation from the fourth German edition of 1923, London: Macmillan.

Kolb, R.W., ed. (2010), *Lessons from the Financial Crisis: Causes, Consequences, and Our Economic Future*, Hoboken, NJ: John Wiley & Sons, Inc.

Köllmann, C. (1999a), 'Die Theorie der Eigentumswirtschaft: Methodologische Anmerkungen zu Heinsohns und Steigers "Theorierevolution"', in: Betz, K. and Roy, T., ed., *Privateigentum und Geld: Kontroversen um den Ansatz von Heinsohn und Steiger*, Marburg: Metropolis, pp. 251–181.

Köllmann, C. (1999b), 'Anmerkungen zu den Kritiken von Elke Muchlinski bzw. von Gunnar Heinsohn und Otto Steiger', in: Betz, K. and Roy, T., ed., *Privateigentum und Geld: Kontroversen um den Ansatz von Heinsohn und Steiger*, Marburg: Metropolis, pp. 341–352.

References

Köllmann, C. (1999c), 'Definitionen des Geldes: Eine Kritik des Essentialismus in der Geldtheorie', in: Stadermann, H.-J. and Steiger, O., eds., *Herausforderung der Geldwirtschaft: Theorie und Praxis währungspolitischer Ereignisse*, Marburg: Metropolis, pp. 107–129.

Krüger, M. (1996), 'Unwissende Ökonomen? Der Versuch einer neuen Volkswirtschaftslehre', *Handelsblatt/Der Tagesspiegel*, Literaturbeilage zur Frankfurter Buchmesse 1996, 2–3 October, p. 13.

Krugman, P.R. (1998), 'Japan's Trap', in: *web.mit.edu/krugman/www*, May (last visit: August 22 2005).

Krugman, P.R. and Obstfeld, M. (2003), *International Economics: Theory and Policy – Sixth Edition*, Boston: Addison Wesley.

Lankow, A. (2003), 'Farmers One and All', *The Korea Times*, June 26 (http://times.hankooki.com).

Läufer, N.K.A. (1998), *The Heinsohn-Steiger Confusion on Interest, Money and Property*, University of Konstanz: Fachbereich Wirtschaftswissenschaften, 26 June, unpublished manuscript.

Laum, B. (1924), *Heiliges Geld*, Tübingen: J.C.B. Mohr.

Laum, B. (1965), *Viehleihe und Viehkapital in den asiatisch-afrikanischen Hirtenkulturen*, Tübingen: J.C.B. Mohr.

Leahy, J. (2000): 'Indonesia to Recapitalise Central Bank after Audit Raises "Bankruptcy" Fears', *Financial Times*, January 1, p. 26.

Lehmbecker, P. (2005), 'On the Effect of the Quality of Eligible Collateral on Price Stability: An Empirical Analysis', *IKSF Discussion Papers* (University of Bremen), no. 33, July.

Lerrick, A. (2001), 'A Way Out for Japan: A Solution to the Problems Facing the World's Second Largest Economy that will not Break its Central Bank', *Financial Times*, May 1, p. 13.

Libecap, G.D. (1998), 'Common Property', in: Newman, P., ed., *The New Palgrave Dictionary of Economics and the Law*, London: Macmillan, vol. 1, col. 317b–324a.

Locke, J. (1690a), 'An Essay Concerning the True Original, Extent, and End of Civil Government' [The Second Treatise of Government], in: J. Locke, *Two Treatises of Government*, ed. P. Laslett, Cambridge: Cambridge University Press, 1967, pp. 283–446.

Locke, J. (1690b), *Über die Regierung*, Reinbek bei Hamburg: Rowohlt, 1966.

Loong, L.H. (2005), speech, online as 'Transcript of Prime Minister Lee Hsien Loong's Speech at National Day Rally 2005 on August 21 2005 at NUS University Cultural Centre', http://app.sprinter.gov.sg/data/pr/2005082102.htm.

Lueck, D. (2003), 'First Possession as the Basis of Property', in: Anderson, T.L. and McChesney, F.S., eds., *Property Rights, Cooperation, Conflict, and Law*, Princeton: Princeton University Press, pp. 200–226.

Malinowski, B. (1921), 'The Primitive Economics of the Trobriand Islanders', *The Economic Journal*, vol. 31, March, pp. 1–16.

Malinowski, B. (1922), *Argonauts of the Western Pacific: An Account of Native Enterprise and Adventure in the Archipelagos of Melanesian New Guinea*, Long Grove, IL: Waveland Press, 1984; German edition (1979), *Argonauten des westlichen Pazifik: Ein Bericht über Unternehmungen und Abenteuer der Eingeborenen in den Inselwelten von Melanesisch-Neuguinea*, Frankfurt am Main: Syndikat.

Malinowski, B. (1935), *Coral Gardens and Their Magic – vol. I: Soil-Tilling and Agriculture Rights in the Trobriand Islands*, London: Allen & Unwin, 1966; German

edition (1981), *Korallengärten und ihre Magie: Bodenbestellung und ihre bäuerlichen Riten auf den Trobriander-Inseln*, Frankfurt am Main: Syndikat.
Mandelbrot, B.B. and Hudson, R.L. (2004), *The (Mis)Behaviour of Markets: A Fractal View of Risk, Ruin and Reward*, London: Profile Books.
Martin, P.C. (2008), 'Power, the State and the Institution of Property', in: Steiger, O., ed., *Property Economics: Property Rights, Creditor's Money and the Foundations of the Economy*, Marburg: Metropolis.
Marx, K. (1867), *Das Kapital: Kritik der politischen Ökonomie. Erster Band. Buch I: Der Produktionsprozeß des Kapitals* (1890), in: *Karl Marx-Friedrich Engels-Werke*, vol. 25, Berlin: Dietz (1969).
Matten, C. (2000), *Managing Bank Capital*, second edition, Chichester: John Wiley & Sons Ltd.
McCracken, S. and Everett, A. (2004), *Everett and McCracken's Banking and Financial Institutions Law*, sixth edition, Sydney: Law Book Company.
McGregor, R. (2002), 'Shanghai's Property Boom: "The Housing Market Is the Most Powerful Means to Transform Society and Politics in China"', *Financial Times*, November 13, p. 13.
McIntosh, C. and Wydick, B. (2005), 'Competition and Microfinance', *Journal of Development Economics*, vol. 78, no. 2, December, pp. 271–298.
Ménard, C. and Shirley, M.M. (2005), 'Introduction', in: C. Ménard and M.M. Shirley, eds., *Handbook of New Institutional Economics*, Dordrecht: Springer, pp. 1–18.
Merrill Lynch, Cap Gemini and Ernst & Young (2002), *World Wealth Report*.
Mill, J.S. (1848), *Principles of Political Economy with Some of Their Applications to Social Philosophy*, after the seventh edition (1871), Ashley, W., ed., London: Longmans, Green & Co. (1909); reprint (1976), Fairfield, NJ: A.M. Kelley.
Minsky, H.P. (1975), *John Maynard Keynes*, New York: Columbia University Press.
Mishkin, F.S. (2000), *The Economics of Money, Banking, and Financial Markets: Sixth Edition*, Boston: Addison Wesley.
Moore, B.J. (1988), *Horizontalists and Verticalists: The Macroeconomics of Credit Money*, Cambridge: Cambridge University Press.
Morgenstern, C. (1910), 'Die unmögliche Tatsache' ('The Impossible Fact'), available www.christian-morgenstern.de, last accessed July 22 2012.
Nicholas, B. (1975), *An Introduction to Roman Law*, Oxford: Clarendon Press; revised edition, ed. Metzger, E. (2008).
Niemitz, H.-U. (2000), 'Das Konzept "Eigentum" und seine Rolle in der Diskussion um Chronologie, Evolutionismus, Ethik, Recht und Gesellschaftsvertrag', *Zeitensprünge*, vol. 12, no. 2, June, pp. 318–338.
Niemitz, H.-U. (2008), 'Understanding the Difference Between Moral Standards and Ethics', in: Steiger, O., ed., *Property Economics: Property Rights, Creditor's Money and the Foundations of the Economy*, Marburg: Metropolis.
North, D.C. and Thomas, R.P. (1973), *The Rise of the Western World: A New Economic History*, Cambridge: Cambridge University Press.
Odrich, B. (2001), 'Wo auch der Nullzins nicht mehr hilft: Japans Wachstumsschwäche', *Frankfurter Allgemeine Zeitung*, no. 47, February 24, p. 13.
Österreich-Lexikon (2005), 'Bauernbefreiung', in *aeiou: www.aeiou.at/aeiou.encyclop.b/b165254.htm* (last visit: 21 September 2005).
Parguez, A. and Seccareccia, M. (2000), 'The Credit Theory of Money: The Monetary Circuit Approach', in: J. Smithin, ed., *What Is Money?*, London: Routledge, pp. 101–123.

Patinkin, D. (1965), *Money, Interest, and Prices* (1956), second edition, New York: Harper & Row.

Payandeh, M. (2004), *Konstitution und Erosion der sowjetischen Planungsökonomie und weitere Perspektiven des postsowjetischen Raums aus Sicht der Theorie der Eigentumswirtschaft*, dissertation, University of Bremen.

Pesek, B.P. and Saving, T.R. (1967), *Money, Wealth, and Economic Theory*, New York and London: Macmillan.

Pipes, R. (1999), *Property and Freedom*, New York: Alfred A. Knopf and London: The Harvill Press.

Pipes, R. (2008), 'Russian Patrimonimalism and Its Political Consequences', in: Steiger, O., ed., *Property Economics: Property Rights, Creditor's Money and the Foundations of the Economy*, Marburg: Metropolis.

Pistor, K. (1998), 'Transfer of Property Rights in Eastern Europe', in: Newman, P., ed., *The New Palgrave Dictionary of Economics and the Law*, London: Macmillan, vol. 3, col. 697a–612b.

Polanyi, K. (1944a), *The Great Transformation*, Boston: Beacon Press (1957).

Polanyi, K. (1944b), *The Great Transformation: Politische und Ökonomische Ursprünge von Gesellschaften und Wirtschaftssystemen*, Frankfurt am Main: Suhrkamp (1978).

Polanyi, K. (1957), 'The Economy as Instituted Process', in: Polanyi, K., Arensberg, C. and Pearson, H., eds., *Trade and Markets in the Early Empires: Economies in History and Theory*, Glencoe, IL: Free Press, pp. 243–269.

Polanyi, K. (1977), *The Livelihood of Man*, Pearson, H.W., ed., New York: Academic Press.

Pollock, F. (1888), *An Essay on Possession in the Common Law, Parts I & II*, Oxford: Clarendon Press.

Pollock, F. and Maitland, F.W. (1898), 'Ownership and Possession', *The History of English Law before the Time of Edward I*; reprint (2010) of second edition, with bibliography and notes by Milsom, S.F., Indianapolis: Liberty Fund, vol. 2; accessed at http://oll.libertyfund.org/title/2314/219571 on June 10 2012.

Pryor, F.L. (1977), *The Origins of the Economy: A Comparative Study of Distribution in Primitive and Peasant Economies*, New York and London: Academic Press.

Pwe. and Tp. (2005), 'ECB verhindert unerlaubten Kredit der Banca d'Italia: Italien plante eine verbotene Finanzierung des Staates durch die Notenbank', *Frankfurter Allgemeine Zeitung*, no. 185, August 11, p. 10.

Radelet, S., Clemens, M. and Bhavnani, R. (2005), 'Aid and Growth', *Finance and Development*, vol. 42, no. 3, September (www.imf.org/external/pubs/ft/fandd/2005/09/radelet.htm).

Ricardo, D. (1817), *On the Principles of Political Economy and Taxation* (1821), in: P. Sraffa, ed., *The Works and Correspondence of David Ricardo*, Cambridge: Cambridge University Press, 1951, vol. I.

Richter, R. (1987), *Geldtheorie: Vorlesung auf der Grundlage der allgemeinen Gleichgewichtstheorie und der Institutionenökonomik*, second extended edition (2000), Berlin and Heidelberg: Springer.

Riese, H. (1983), 'Gunnar Heinsohn und die ökonomische Thoerie', *Leviathan*, vol. 13, no. 1, pp. 70–87.

Riese, H. (1993), 'Bagehot versus Goodhart: Warum eine Zentralbank Geschäftsbanken braucht', in: H. Riese, *Grundlegungen eines monetären Keynesianismus: Ausgewählte Schriften 1964–1999 – Band 1: Das Projekt eines monetären Keynesianismus*, Marburg: Metropolis, 2001, pp. 401–468.

Riese, H. (1999), 'Eigentum, Zins und Geld: Die Apokryphen des Gunnar Heinsohn und Otto Steiger', in: Betz, K. and Roy, T., ed., *Privateigentum und Geld: Kontroversen um den Ansatz von Heinsohn und Steiger*, Marburg: Metropolis, pp. 145–155.
Riese, H. (2000a), 'Geld – die unverstandene Kategorie der Nationalökonomie', *Ethik und Sozialwissenschaften*, vol. 11, no. 4, December, col. 487a–498a.
Riese, H. (2000b), 'Replik: Anmerkungen und Antworten', *Ethik und Sozialwissenschaften*, vol. 11, no. 4, December, col. 544a–554b.
Riese, H. (2001), 'Answer to Otto Steiger on the Monetary Explanation of the Rate of Interest', Conference on Monetary Policy in a World with Endogenous Money and Global Capital, Freie Universität Berlin, March 23–25.
Riese, H. (2006 [2001]), 'Money and Wealth in a Monetary Economy: Theoretical Foundation and Macro Policy Implication', presentation at the Conference on Monetary Policy in a World with Endogenous Money and Global Capital, Freie Universität Berlin, March 23–25 2001, unpublished manuscript.
Robertson, D.H. (1940), 'Mr Keynes and the Rate of Interest', in: Robertson, D.H., *Essays in Monetary Theory*, London: P.S. King, pp. 1–39.
Rogers, J.S. (2004 [1995]), *The Early History of the Law of Bills and Notes*, first paperback edition, Cambridge: Cambridge University Press.
Rojas, M. (2002), *The Sorrows of Carmencita: Argentina's Crisis in a Historical Perspective*, Timbro, Sweden: Timbro Förlag.
Roy, T. (1999), 'Eigentum, Besitz und die *regulation by panic* in der Theorie von Heinsohn und Steiger', in: Betz, K. and Roy, T., ed., *Privateigentum und Geld: Kontroversen um den Ansatz von Heinsohn und Steiger*, Marburg: Metropolis, pp. 157–175.
Sachs, J. (1993), *Poland's Jump to the Market Economy*, Cambridge, MA: MIT Press.
Sachs, J. (2005a), *The End of Poverty: Economic Possibilities for Our Time*, New York: The Earth Institute at Columbia University.
Sachs, J. (2005b), *Das Ende der Armut: Ein ökonomisches Programm für eine gerechtere Welt*, Munich: Siedler.
Sahlins, M. (1974), *Stone Age Economics*, London: Tavistock Publications; reprint (2004), London: Routledge.
Sauer, I. (2010), *Die Rolle von Eigentumsrechten und Kreditsicherheiten im zweistufigen Bankensystem und deren Implikationen für die Zentralbankpolitik*, masters thesis in economics, University of Frankfurt am Main.
Schoenmaker D. (2000), 'What Kind of Financial Stability for Europe?', in: C.A.E. Goodhart, ed., *Which Lender of Last Resort for Europe?*, London: Central Banking Publications, pp. 213–223.
Schulz, J. (2009), *Eigentum und Geld als Faktoren ökonomischer Entwicklung*, Marburg: Metropolis Verlag.
Schumpeter, J. (1926), *Theorie der wirtschaftlichen Entwicklung: Eine Untersuchung über Unternehmergewinn, Kapital, Kredit, Zins und den Konjunkturzyklus* (1911); Munich and Leipzig: Duncker & Humblot, second extended edition.
Schwartz, A.J. (2002), 'Earmarks of a Lender of Last Resort', in: Goodhart, C.A.E. and Illing, G., eds., *Financial Crises, Contagion, and the Lender of Last Resort*, Oxford: Oxford University Press, 2002, pp. 449–460.
Seaford, R. (2004), *Money and the Early Greek Mind*, Cambridge: Cambridge University Press.
Shiraishi, K. (2003), *Budget Deficit and Fiscal Discipline: Budget Reform in US and Japan*, Tokyo: Mitsubishi Research Institute: Research Center for Policy and Economy, February 19.

Siddiqi, B. (2005), 'Aiding Development: Tracking the Flows', *Finance and Development*, vol. 42, no. 3, September (www.imf.org/external/pubs/ft/fandd/2005/09/picture. htm).
Silver, M. (1992), *Taking Ancient Mythology Economically*, Leiden: Brill.
Silver, M (1995), *Economic Structures of Antiquity*, Westport, CT: Greenwood Press.
Skaist, A. (1994), *The Old Babylonian Loan Contract: Its History and Geography*, Ramat Gan: Bar-Ilan University Press.
Smith, A. (1776), *An Inquiry into the Nature and Causes of the Wealth of Nations* (1790), ed. by E. Cannan (1904), New York: Modern Library (1937).
Soto, H. de (2000), *The Mystery of Capital: Why Capitalism Triumphs in the West and Fails Everywhere Else*, London: Bantam Press.
Soto, H. de (2008), 'Dead Capital, Fluid Capital and Money', in: Steiger, O., ed., *Property Economics: Property Rights, Creditor's Money and the Foundations of the Economy*, Marburg: Metropolis.
Spahn, H.-P. (1998), 'Besprechung von Heinsohn, G., Steiger, O., Eigentum, Zins und Geld – Ungelöste Rätsel der Wirtschaftswissenschaft', *Jahrbücher für Nationalökonomie und Statistik*, vol. 217, no. 2, pp. 387–390.
Spahn, H.-P. (1999), 'Geldwirtschaft: Eine wirtschafts- und theoriegeschichtliche Annäherung', *Diskussionsbeiträge aus dem Institut für Volkswirtschaftslehre der Universität Hohenheim*, no. 181, September.
Spahn, H.-P. (2001), *From Gold to Euro: On Monetary Theory and the History of Currency Systems*, Berlin and Heidelberg: Springer.
Spethmann, D./Steiger, O. (2005), 'The Four Achilles Heels of the Eurosystem: Missing Central Monetary Institutions, Different Real Rates of Interest, Nonmarketable Securities, and Missing Lender of Last Resort', *International Journal of Political Economy*, vol. 34, no. 2, summer 2004 (printed summer 2005), pp. 46–68.
Spilimbergo, A., Symansky, S., Blanchard, O. and Cottarelli, C. (2010), 'Fiscal Policy for the Crisis', in Kolb, R.W., ed., *Lessons from the Financial Crisis: Causes, Consequences, and Our Economic Future*, Hoboken, NJ: John Wiley & Sons, Inc.
Stadermann, H.-J. (1992), *Wirtschaftspolitik: Grundlagen nationalökonomischen Handelns in einer monetärgesteuerten Weltwirtschaft*, Tübingen: J.C.B. Mohr (P. Siebeck).
Stadermann, H.-J. (1994a), *Die Fesselung des Midas: Eine Untersuchung über den Aufstieg und Verfall der Zentralbankkunst*, Tübingen: J.C.B. Mohr (P. Siebeck).
Stadermann, H.-J. (1994b), *Geldwirtschaft und Geldpolitik: Einführung in die Grundlagen*, Wiesbaden: Gabler.
Stadermann, H.-J. (1999), 'Wesentliche Eigenschaften der Währung und des Geldes: Eine Differenzierung der Währungsemissionen von Staatsbanken und Zentralbanken', in: Betz, K. and Roy, T., eds., *Privateigentum und Geld: Kontroversen um den Ansatz von Heinsohn und Steiger*, Marburg: Metropolis, pp. 73–98.
Stadermann, H.-J. (2000), 'Aus Nichts wird nichts', *Ethik und Sozialwissenschaften*, vol. 11, no. 4, December, col. 534b–537b.
Stadermann, H.-J. (2002), *Das Geld der Ökonomen: Ein Versuch über die Behandlung des Geldes in der Geldtheorie – Mit zwei Schriften David Ricardos im Anhang*, Tübingen: Mohr Siebeck.
Stadermann, H.-J. (2006), 'Nominalökonomik', in: Stadermann H.-J. and Steiger O., eds., *Allgemeine Theorie der Wirtschaft*, vol. 2, Tübingen: Mohr Siebeck.
Stadermann, H.-J. (2008), 'Property Base: A Central Bank's Guide to Adequate Monetary Policy', in: Steiger O., ed., *Property Economics, Property Rights, Creditor's Money and the Foundations of the Economy*, Marburg: Metropolis.

Stadermann, H.-J. and Steiger, O. (1992), 'Maria Theresa Dollar', in: Newman, P., Milgate, M. and Eatwell, J., eds., *The New Palgrave Dictionary of Money and Finance*, London: Macmillan and New York: Stockton, vol. 2, col. 648b – 651a.

Stadermann, H.-J./Steiger, O. (1999), 'James Steuart und die Theorie der Geldwirtschaft', in: Stadermann, H.-J. and Steiger, O., eds., *Herausforderung Geldwirtschaft*, Marburg: Metropolis, pp. 19–49.

Stadermann, H.-J./Steiger, O. (2001a), 'Nominalökonomie. Entwurf einer Theorie gegenseitiger Verpflichtungen', in Stadermann, H.-J./Steiger, O., eds., *Verpflichtungsökonomie*, Marburg: Metropolis, pp. 81–104.

Stadermann, H.-J. and Steiger, O. (2001b), *Allgemeine Theorie der Wirtschaft*, vol. 1: *Schulökonomik*, Tübingen: Mohr Siebeck.

Stadermann, H.-J. and Steiger, O. (2006), 'James Steuart and the Theory of the Monetary Economy', in. J. Backhaus, ed., *The Founders of Modern Economics: The Maastricht Lectures in Political Economy*, Cheltenham, UK and Northampton, MA: Edward Elgar.

Stadermann, H.-J. and Steiger, O. (2010), 'John Maynard Keynes and the Theory of the Monetary Economy', in: J. Backhaus, ed., *The Founders of Modern Economics: The Maastricht Lectures in Political Economy*, Cheltenham, UK and Northampton, MA: Edward Elgar, forthcoming.

Stange, H.O.H. (1960), 'Die altamerikanischen Kulturen', in: *Ploetz-Auszug aus der Geschichte*, Würzburg: Ploetz, 26th edition, pp. 706–710.

Starr, C.G. (1977), *The Economic and Social Growth of Early Greece: 800–500 B.C.*, New York: Oxford University Press.

Starr, C.G. (1982), 'Economic and Social Conditions in the Greek World', in: *The Cambridge Ancient History. Second Edition. Volume III. Part 3: The Expansion of the Greek World, Eight to Sixth Centuries B.C.*, Cambridge: Cambridge University Press, pp. 417–441.

Steiger, O. (1978), 'Prelude to the Theory of a Monetary Economy: Origins and Significance of Ohlin's 1933 Approach', *History of Political Economy*, vol. 10, no.3, pp. 421–446.

Steiger, O. (1979), 'Geld und Ökonomie 14 Thesen', in: Wassmann, B., ed., *L'invitation au voyage zu Alfred Sohn-Rethel*, Bremen.

Steiger, O. (2001), 'Question to Hajo Riese on the Monetary Explanation of the Rate of Interest', Conference on Monetary Policy in a World with Endogenous Money and Global Capital, Freie Universität Berlin, March 23–25.

Steiger, O. (2002), 'Der Staat als "Lender of Last Resort" – oder: Die Achillesferse des Eurosystems', in: Barens, I./Pickardt, M., eds., *Die Rolle des Staates in der Ökonomie – Finanzwissenschaftliche Perspektiven: Festschrift für Otto Roloff zum 65. Geburtstag*, Marburg: Metropolis, pp. 51–84.

Steiger, O. (2005a), 'Eigentum und Recht und Freiheit: Eine Triade und 66 Thesen', in: W. Krieg, K. Galler and P. Stadelmann, eds., *Richtiges und gutes Management: vom System zur Praxis – Festschrift für Fredmund Malik*, Bern: Haupt, pp. 153–178.

Steiger, O. (2005b), 'Schuldnergeld: Der wunde Punkt in der keynesianische Staatstheorie des Geldes', in: Huber, G., Krämer, H. and Kurz, H.D., ed., *Einkommensverteilung, technischer Fortschritt und struktureller Wandel: Festschrift für Peter Kalmbach*, Marburg: Metropolis, pp. 169–188.

Steiger, O. (2006a), 'Property Economics *versus* New Institutional Economics: Alternative Foundations of How to Trigger Economic Development', *Journal of Economic Issues*, vol. 39, no. 1, March.

Steiger, O. (2006b), 'The Endogeneity of Money and the Eurosystem: A Contribution to the Theory of Central Banking', in: M. Setterfield, ed., *Complexity, Endogenous Money and Macoeconomic Theory: Essays in Honor of Basil Moore*, Cheltenham, UK and Northampton, MA: Edward Elgar.

Steiger, O. (2006c), 'Hernando de Soto, "El otro sendero" (1986)', in: Herz, D. and Weinberger, V., eds., *Lexikon ökonomischer Werke: 650 wegweisende Schriften von der Antike bis ins 20. Jahrhundert*, Düsseldorf: Verlag Wirtschaft und Finanzen.

Steiger, O. (2006d), 'Tom Bethell, "The Noblest Triumph: Property and Prosperity through the Ages" (1998)', in: Herz, D. and Weinberger, V., eds., *Lexikon ökonomischer Werke: 650 wegweisende Schriften von der Antike bis ins 20. Jahrhundert*, Düsseldorf: Verlag Wirtschaft und Finanzen.

Steiger, O. (2006e), 'Richard Pipes, "Property and Freedom" (1999)', in: Herz, D. and Weinberger, V., eds., *Lexikon ökonomischer Werke: 650 wegweisende Schriften von der Antike bis ins 20. Jahrhundert*, Düsseldorf: Verlag Wirtschaft und Finanzen.

Steiger, O. (2006f [2004]), 'Which Lender of Last Resort for the Eurosystem?', presentation at the Conference on Monetary Policy in a World with Endogenous Money and Global Capital, Freie Universität Berlin, March 23–25 2001; also as *ZEI Working Paper* [Universität Bonn], no. B04–23, September 2004.

Steiger, O. (2006g), 'Hernando de Soto, "The Myth of Capital: Why Capitalism Triumphs in the West and Fails Everywhere Else" (2000)', in: Herz, D. and Weinberger, V., eds., *Lexikon ökonomischer Werke: 650 wegweisende Schriften von der Antike bis ins 20. Jahrhundert*, Düsseldorf: Verlag Wirtschaft und Finanzen.

Steiger, O. (2008), 'The Fundamental Flaw in New Institutional Economics: The Missing Distinction between Possession and Property', in: Steiger, O., ed., *Property Economics: Property Rights, Creditor's Money and the Foundations of the Economy*, Marburg: Metropolis.

Steiger, O. (2012), *Property Rights and Economic Development: Two Views*, Marburg: Metropolis, forthcoming.

Steiger, O., ed. (2008), *Property Economics: Property Rights, Creditor's Money and the Foundations of the Economy*, Marburg: Metropolis.

Stella, P. (1997), 'Do Central Banks Need Capital?', *IMF Working Paper* (International Monetary Fund), no. 83.

Steppacher, R. (1999), 'Institutionelle Rahmenbedingungen: Eigentumsordnung und Märkte', in: Bieri, H., Moser, P. and Steppacher, R., *Die Landwirtschaft als Chance einer zukunftsfähigen Schweiz oder Dauer-problem auf dem Weg zur vollständigen Ernährung?*, Zürich: Schweizer Vereinigung Industrie und Landwirtschaft (SIL), paper no. 135, pp. 21–34.

Steppacher, R. (2008), 'Property, Mineral Resources and Sustainable Development', in: Steiger, O., ed., *Property Economics: Property Rights, Creditor's Money and the Foundations of the Economy*, Marburg: Metropolis.

Steuart, J. (1761), *A Dissertation upon the Doctrine and Principles of Money, Applied to the German Coin*, in: *The Works, Political, Metaphysical, and Chronological, of the Late Sir James Steuart*, London: D.T. Cadell & W. Davies, 1805; reprint (1967), New York: A.M. Kelley, vol. 5, pp. 171–265.

Steuart, J. (1767), *An Inquiry into the Principles of Political Oeconomy: Being an Essay on the Science of Domestic Policy in Free Nations*, London: A Millar & T. Cadell; reprint (1993), Düsseldorf: Verlag Wirtschaft und Finanzen, Books I and II.

Stevenson, R.W. (1993), 'Poles Forge Private Bank System: Experience Is Scant, Save for Bad Loans', *The New York Times*, February 23 1993, p. 17.

Stiglitz, J.E. and Greenwald, B. (2003), *Towards a New Paradigm in Monetary Economics*, Cambridge: Cambridge University Press.
Stiglitz, J.E. and Weiss, A. (1981), 'Credit Rationing in Markets with Imperfect Information', *The American Economic Review*, vol. 73, pp. 393–410.
Striegel, B. (2005a), *Über das Geld: Geschichte und Zukunft des Wirtschaftens* (2004), second edition, Lütjenburg: Verlag für Sozialökonomie.
Striegel, B. (2005b), 'Was ist Geld und woher kommt der Zins? – Eine Eigentumstheorie des Geldes', *Zeitschrift für Sozialökonomie*, vol. 42, no. 146, September, pp. 24–33.
Svejnar, J. (2002), 'Transition Economies: Performance and Challenges', *Journal of Economic Perspectives*, vol. 16, no. 1, pp. 3–28.
Taylor, J.B. (1993), 'Discretion Versus Policy Rules in Practice', in: *Carnegie-Rochester Conference Series on Public Policy*, 39, pp. 195–214.
Taylor, J.B. (2010), 'Getting Back on Track: Macroeconomic Policy Lessons from the Financial Crisis', *Federal Reserve Bank of St. Louis Review*, May/June, 92(3), pp. 165–76.
Tett, G. (2001), 'Japan Banks Refuse Funds from Bank of Japan: More Aggressive Methods may Now be Needed to Maintain Loose Monetary Policy and Limit Deflation', *Financial Times*, May 10, p. 4.
Theil, W. (2000), 'Bürgerliches Recht, Geld und zinsinduzierte Geldknappheit: Ein Beitrag zur Heinsohn and Steiger-Riese-Kontroverse', *IKSF Discussion Papers* (University of Bremen), no. 21, March.
Theil, W. (2001), 'Eigentum und Verpflichtung: Einige juristische Aspekte', in: Stadermann, H.-J. and Steiger, O., eds., *Verpflichtungsökonomik: Eigentum, Freiheit und Haftung in der Geldwirtschaft*, Marburg: Metropolis, pp. 175–200.
Thornton, H. (1802), *An Enquiry into the Nature and Effects of the Paper Credit of Great Britain*; edited by F.A. Hayek (1939), London: G. Allen & Unwin; reprint (1978), New York: A.M. Kelley.
Thurnwald, R. (1932), *Economics in Primitive Communities*, London: Oxford University Press & International African Institute.
Timberlake Jr., R.H. (1984), 'The Central Banking Role of Clearing House Associations', in: Goodhart, C. and Illing, G., ed., *Financial Crises, Contagion, and the Lender of Last Resort: A Reader*, Oxford: Oxford University Press, 2002, pp. 127–141.
Tinbergen, J. (1969), 'The Use of Models: Experience and Prospects – Lecture to the Memory of Alfred Nobel, December 12, 1969', in: http://nobelprize.org/economics/laureates/1969/tinbergen–lecture.html (last visit: October 4 2005).
Tobin, J. (1963), 'Commercial Banks as Creators of "Money"', in: Carson, D., ed., *Banking and Monetary Studies*, Homewood, IL: Richard D. Irwin, pp. 408–419.
Tyre, R. (2011), Herodotus 4:166, Message #13749, ANE-2 Ancient Near East 2, http://groups.yahoo.com/group/ANE-2/message/13749, last accessed June 10 2012.
UN Millennium Project (2005), *Investing in Development: A Practical Plan to Achieve the Millennium Development Goals*, London and Sterling, VA: Earthscan.
Varmaz, A. (2005), 'Effizienzanalyse deutscher Banken unter Einsatz der Data Envelopment Analysis', lecture, International Scientific Annual Conference Operations Research 2005, University of Bremen, September 7–9.
Walras, L. (1954 [1926]), *Elements of Pure Economics or the Theory of Social Wealth*, translated by W. Jaffé, London: Allen and Unwin.
Weaver, P.M. and Kingsley, C.D. (2001), *Banking and Lending Practice*, published in association with, and approved and recommended by, the Australasian Institute of Banking and Finance, Fourth Edition, Sydney: Lawbook Co.

Wee, H. Van der (1977), 'Monetary, Credit and Banking Systems', in: Rich, E.E and Wilson, C.H., eds., *The Cambridge Economic History of Europe, vol. 5, The Economic Organisation of Early Modern Europe*, Cambridge: Cambridge University Press, pp. 291–392.

Willers, H. (1909), *Geschichte der Römischen Kupferprägung: Vom Bundesgenossenkrieg bis auf Kaiser Claudius – nebst einleitendem Überblick über die Entwicklung des antiken Münzwesens*, Leipzig: Teubner.

Wolff, M (1923), 'Das Sachenrecht', in: Enneccerus, L., Kipp, T. and Wolff, M., eds., *Lehrbuch des Bürgerlichen Rechts*, vol. 2, fifth edition, Marburg: Elwert'sche Verlagsbuchhandlung.

Woodford, M. (2003), *Interest and Prices: Foundations of a Theory of Monetary Policy*, Princeton: Princeton University Press.

World Bank (1975), *Land Reform: Sector Policy Paper*, Washington, DC: The World Bank.

World Bank (2005), *Doing Business in 2005: Removing Obstacles to Growth*, Washington, DC: The World Bank and Oxford: Oxford University Press.

Wray, L.R. (1998), *Understanding Modern Money: The Key to Full Employment and Price Stability*, Cheltenham, UK and Northampton, MA: Edward Elgar.

Wray, L.R. (2000), 'Modern Money', in: J. Smithin, ed., *What Is Money?*, London: Routledge, pp. 42–66.

Zehnder, A.J. (2005), 'Immobilienbrief: Falsche Signale', *Frankfurter Allgemeine Zeitung*, no. 239, October 14, p. 49.

Index

Page numbers in *italics* denote tables.

absolute prices 109, 110–11, 112
accumulation 4, 5, 113–25
Adelman, I. 128
Adler, B.E. 35
aid, development 127, 128
Alchian, A.A. 25
Aldenborg, U. 137
Algeria 133
Alvarez, L.W. 127
Andrewes, A. 7
antichresis 62
Apple 112
appropriation, power of 17
Argentina 124; Austral Plan 91; budget deficits 91–2; convertibility plan 92; currency board 92; hyperinflation 91
Arrow-Debreu model 22
asset prices 97, 120
asset values 66, 67
assets 1, 3, 11, 12, 105; burdening of 2; capital 73; central bank 46–7; commercial banks 47–8, 73; entrepreneurs 103; money as 111; nominal 73
assignats 30, 31
asymmetric information 25, 34, 39, 60, 130, 132
Austria, property rights 101, 128
Axilrod, S.H. 22, 91, 96

Backhaus, J. 148n9
Bagehot, W. 41, 77, 79, 82–3, 94–5, 96
Bailey, M.J. 27
Ballin, C. 113
Bangladesh, microfinance 130–1
Bank of Amsterdam 77
bank deposits 9–10, 70, 79

Bank of England 41, 75, 82, 91, 95, 96, 161n126
Bank Indonesia 88–9
Bank of Japan 93, 123, 125
bank money 18, 20, 31
bank notes 9–10, 20; and credit contracts 79; legal tender status 75, 78; as liabilities 72; redeemability of 43, 44, 93–4, 154n31; *see also* central banks, notes
banks: capital 29, 39, 41–2, 44–5; country 43, 75, 82; credit 79; deposit 79; loan security 153n28; overexposure of 118; state 9–10; transformation countries 135; *see also* central banks; commercial banks; private banks
barley 57–8, 75–6
Barley, R. 124
barter 6, 18, 22, 67, 69, 101, 107, 110
barter paradigm 3, 4, 30, 51, 53, 111
Berlin school 39–52
Bernanke, B. 87
Bethell, T. 29
Betz, K. 44
bills of exchange 19–20
Bindseil, U. 88
Binswanger 144n3
Blackstone, W. 124
Blanchard, O. 89
Blenck, D. 103
Bofinger, P. 89
Bogaert, R. 75
bonds 23, 24; covered 84; government 21, 124; prices 24
booms 120
borrowed base 96
Bracho, G. 137

186 Index

Braunberger, G. 166n53
Brockmeier, T. 130
budget deficits 91–2, 125
Bundesbank 70, 88, 99
burdening of property 1–2, 3, 4, 11, *14*, 52, 55–7, 60, 61, 69, 74, 115; in monetary Keynesianism 52; in neoclassical economics 22; in new institutional economics 25–6, 27, 28
business cycles 113–25

capital 19, 23, 103, 105; bank 29, 39, 41–2, 44–5; central banks 41, 42, 46–7, 80, 84, 85, 89, 94; commercial banks 80, 84, 95; entrepreneurs 103–4; physical 104, 105, 117, 121; scarcity 114; yield 114
capital assets 32, 73
capital flight 98
capital goods 23
capital markets 92, 122
capitalism 16, 17, 18
capitalists 18; entrepreneur 2; money 2
Cencini, A. 109, 158n67
central banks 21–2, 37, 42, 66, 83; assets 46–7; capital 41, 42, 46–7, 80, 84, 85, 89, 94; deposit balances 21; exchange rate stabilization 97; foreign currency assets 88; gold assets 88; inflation control 97–8; insolvency 88–9, 90; interest rate 49–50, 85, 86, 87, 97, 123; as lender of last resort (LOLR) 40, 41, 83, 89–90, 94, 95; liabilities 31, 44, 45, 46, 66, 73, 90; liquidity 45–6; money 31, 36, 38, 40, 46, 114; money creation 83–99; money credit 41, 48, 49; notes 21, 80, 83, 84, 85, 98–9 (redeemability of 93–4); reserves 95–6
Chantraine, H. 77
Chiang Khai-Shek 133, 137
Childs 144n15
China 135, 137–8
classical economics 1, 2, 16, 17–20, 52–3, 101, 106, 111, 114
clearing houses 81, 82; loan certificates 82
coercive orders 4, 12, 28
coins 18, 75, 78, 99; clipping and adulteration 77; making charge 159n86; private 76; state 76–7
collateral: and business cycles 120, 121; land as 131–2; substitutes 130; theft of 77; *see also* loan security
colonial economies 75, 126–7
command systems 4, 5, 8, *14*, 27, 54, 126

commercial banks 40, 42, 44, 49, 72, 80; assets 47–8, 73; capital 80, 84, 95; as central bank counterparties 94; coinage needs 99; as debtors of central banks 83–4, 85, 86, 92–3; defaulting 84; insolvency 90; interest rates 86–7, 122; liabilities 45, 73, 84; liquidity 90, 94, 95; loan security 83–4, 95, 96; ownership premium 85, 87; resource credit 40–1, 48
commercial bills 69, 96
commodities 1, 3, 11, 12, 107; burdening of 2; production of 104, 105
commodity markets 34, 105
commodity money 30, 72, 78–9, 108–9
common property 17, 18, 19, 25, 27
competition: centralization of 130, 131; monopolistic 110; oligopolistic 110; polypolistic or perfect 109–10
consumers: preferences 112, 113; utility maximization 108
consumption 1, 2, 4, 5
contracts: employment 115, 116; enforcement of 2, 4, 55–7, 133; nominal 107; sales 54, 59, 60, 105, 106, 111, 116, 121, 152n4; supplier 116; *see also* credit contracts
Costa Rica 88
costs 107; minimization of 108, 109
country banks 43, 75, 82
covered bonds 84
credit 7, 9, 19, 118; in kind 57–8; money 41, 48, 49, 58; open (unsecured) 63; resource 40–1, 48; supply and demand 24
credit banks 79
credit contracts 52, 54–5, 56–7, 70, 71, 72, 75, 79, 83, 100, 111, 116; bank notes and 79; barley in early 57–8; entrepreneurs 29, 104, 105; in Keynes/Keynesian economics 29, 34–5; loan security in 60, 63, 100; money notes and 59, 61–2; in neoclassical economics 24; ownership premium and 54, 59–62, 63–4; pure (money-creating) 59–60, 61, 62, 70;
risk 29–30, 34–5 (equalization of 64)
credit markets 24–5, 34, 68, 69; equilibrium in 34, 35
credit money 70
credit rationing 24–5, 33, 34–5, 35, 39, 132
credit risk 29, 38–9, 64
creditors 55, 56, 59; credit risk 64; money 31, 36, 37, 72, 104; risk premium 64

Cronon, W. 146n18
Crowther 158n70
currency 76; devaluation 97; foreign currency assets 88; inconvertible 98; transformation countries 136–7
currency boards, Argentina 92
Currency foundation 150n41
current prices 108, 109, 110
customary rules 4, 28
Czech Republic 8, 135, 136

Dalton, G.B. 6
Davidson, P. 36
de facto possession 1, 3, 4, 5–10, 11, 12, *13–14*, 28, 54, 129
de jure possession 2, 3, 54, 129; in an ownership-based society 10–12, *13*, 15
Debreu, G. 21
debt enforcement actions 1
debt markets 124, 125
debt titles 31, 32, 33, 37, 84, 92–3
debtors 55, 56, 59; liquidity premium 64; money 31, 36, 37, 64–5, 72, 104, 105; risk premium 64
Decker, F. 97, 156n54, 157n58
deficit spending 125
deflation 22, 121
Deininger, K. 131–2
demand 113; excess 109, 110
demand deposits 70–1, 79
Demsetz, H. 16, 25, 26, 148n10
Denmark 133
deposit banks 79
devaluation, currency 97
developing countries 127–33; infrastructure projects 128–9; land rights 131–3; loan security 130, 131, 132; microfinance 130–1; property rights 128, 129–33
development aid 127, 128
discount loans 96
distribution 4, 5
dollar notes 78
domination, theory of 18
Dowd, K. 79

economic activity 3–5, 11–12, *13–14*, 15, 28–9, 52–3, 55
economic development 127–8
economic ethnology 5–6
economization 55
efficiency 28
employment contracts 115, 116

endogenous money 36, 40
enforcement of contracts and rights 2, 4, 55–7, 133
Enghofer, S. 99
England: country banks 43; land ownership 132; property-owner-based production 78
entrepreneur capitalits 2
entrepreneurs: and credit contracts 29, 104, 105; as economic agents 100–7
Epstein, R.A. 26, 27
equilibrium prices 112
European Central Bank (ECB) 70, 124, 160n100
European Economic Community (EEC) 125
European Monetary Union 70, 93
Eurosystem 88, 93, 160n99, 100 and 101, 161n109
excess demand 109, 110
excess supply 109, 110
exchange rates 97
exchange ratios 112
exchange value 21
exogenous money 40
expectations, speculative 118–19
exploitation 18

factor prices 107, 109, 112
Federal Reserve 87, 88, 92; interest rates 87; quantitative easing 87
Federal Reserve Bank of New York 85
feudal systems 4, 5, 7–8, 11, 27, 28, 54, 56, 57, 126
fiat money 21, 22, 38
Finance and Development 127
financial crises 122–5; (2008) 85, 90, 97; sovereign debt crisis (2010–) 124
financial markets 40, 68, 104, 121
first possession 27
Fisher, I. 20, 66–7, 110, 112
Folkerts-Landau, D. 89
foreign currency assets, central banks 88
foreign investment, in transformation countries 136
France 125
freedom 12
Friedman, M. 22, 48, 71, 78, 89, 94
Frisch, R. 127
Fry, M. 88

Garber, P.M. 89
Geldzins 146n12
general equilibrium 22, 108, 109, 110

188 Index

Germany 92, 124, 125; accommodation bills (Finanzwechsel) 124; Bundesbank 70, 88, 99; Democratic Republic (GDR) 8 (land reform fund 8–9); insolvency law 56; Mefo-Wechsel 124; Nazi 93, 124; private note-issuing banks 83; SCHUFA 100; state treasury warrants (Darlehenskassenscheine) 124
gold 7–8, 22, 43, 78, 79, 88, 157n58, 159n64
gold standard 157n58
Goodhart, C.A.E. 89, 90
goods markets 69, 111
goods prices 107, 109
Gorton, G. 82
government bonds 21, 124
Grameen Bank 130
Great Depression 122
Greece 93, 124; Ancient 77
Greenwald, B. 34, 35, 106, 107, 122
growth 28
Grün, B. 9
Gurley, J.G. 72
Güterzins 146n11

Hahn, F.H. 35
Hardenberg, K.A. von 132
Hausknecht, A. 44, 103
Hawtrey, R.G. 41, 60, 67, 81, 95
Hayek, F. von 118
Heering, W. 153n26
Heichelheim, F.M. 57
Heine, M. 44, 45, 101–2, 103
Heinsohn, G. 21, 24, 40, 49, 51, 52, 57, 63, 68, 88, 97, 101, 104, 119, 132, 136
heredium 152n18
Herr, H. 44, 45, 101–2, 103
Hicks, J. 33–4, 122
hoarding 23, 24, 32, 52, 98
Hofmann, W. 107
Holland 77–8
homo economicus 3, 5, 18
Horwich, G. 23
Huber, E. 129
Hudson, R.I. 165n43
Hutzler, C. 138
hyperinflation, Argentina 91
hypothecation of property 1, 2, 4, 9, *14*, 52, 55–7, 59, 60, 61, 64, 69, 70, 74, 85, 104, 106, 111, 118, 129; in new institutional economics 25–6, 27, 28; and state socialism 9; in transformation countries 137

Inca Empire 8
India, colonial administration 126–7
Indonesia 88–9
inflation 22, 91, 97–8, 121, 123
informal property 129
infrastructure projects, developing countries 128–9
innovation 112, 113, 117–18, 119–20
inside money 96
insolvency 56, 88–9, 90
Instituto Libertad y Democracia (ILD) 129
interest 1, 4, 6, 9, 54–5, 57–65, 75, 76, 100, 103, 112, 113–14, 154n38; and burdening of property 3; central bank theory of 49–50; in classical economics 1, 19, 53; in command systems 7; Keynes's theory of 32–3, 50, 63, 114; in kind 57, 58; in monetary Keynesianism 51, 53; in neoclassical economics 1, 22–4; in state socialism 10
interest rates 1, 2, 24, 66, 67, 112, 114, 115, 121; central banks 49–50, 85, 86, 87, 97, 123; commercial banks 86–7, 122; equilibrium 34; and financial crises 122; level of 63; pure 63
International Development Association (IDA) 131
International Labour Office (ILO) 130
International Monetary Fund (IMF) 91, 92
investment 23, 24, 33, 122; in capital assets 32; foreign, in transformation countries 136; Keynes's theory of 29–30, 52; over- 118, 119, 120, 165n43; risk 29–30
Ireland 124
IS curve 33, 122
IS/LM model 33, 122
Israel, J.I. 78
Italy 124

Jaffee, D. 34
Jao, Y.C. 83
Japan 125, 133; budget deficits 91; debt titles 93; stagnation 123
Jevons, W.S. 107
Jiang Zemin 137–8
Jonas, J. 92

Kanatas, G. 35, 36
Kapitalzins 148n7
Kaps, C. 137
Keynes, J.M. 2, 23, 38, 64, 86, 105, 111, 114; on credit contract risk 29; on hoarding 24, 98; on liquidity premium

49; on loan security 29; theory of interest 32–3, 50, 63, 114; theory of investment 29–30, 52; theory of money 31–2, 67, 71
Keynes 144n3, 145n2, 149n17
Keynesian economics 1, 2, 16, 29–52, 53, 86, 101–2
Knapp, G.F. 30
Knospe, M. 99
Köllmann, C. 152n9
Krugman, P.R. 89, 123

labor: division of 18; free wage 115–16, 117
labor theory of value 18
land 19, 26; as collateral 131–2; economic activation of 11; ownership 26, 132, 133
land reform fund 8–9
land rights: Austria 101; developing countries 131–3
Lankow, A. 133
Laos 133
Läufer, N.K.A. 156n50
Laum, B. 6, 57
lawful money 78, 79
Lawrence, S. 138
Leahy, J. 89
lease agreements 2, 56
leasehold 132
legal systems, transformation countries 137
legal tender status 75, 78, 79
Lehmbecker, P. 98
lender of last resort (LOLR) 40, 41, 82, 83, 89–90, 94, 95
Lenin, V.I. 134
Lerrick, A. 123
liabilities 42, 74, 81, 84, 103; bank notes as 72; central bank 31, 44, 45, 46, 66, 73, 90; clearing house 82; commercial banks 45, 73, 84; entrepreneurs 103
Libecap, G.D. 27
liquid resources 23
liquidity 105; central banks 45–6; commercial banks 90, 94, 95
liquidity crisis 41–2, 95, 96
liquidity preference 33
liquidity premium 2, 32, 33, 49, 61, 63, 64, 69, 86, 104, 105, 114, 115, 122, 163n21
LM curve 33, 122
loan certificates, clearing house 82
loan principal 67
loan security 6, 7, 55, 58, 75, 121, 123, 153–4n28; in classical economics 18–19; commercial banks 83–4, 95, 96; in credit contracts 60, 63, 100; developing countries 130, 131, 132; in Keynes/Keynesian economics 29, 33–6, 38, 39, 41–2, 43–4; in neoclassical economics 24
loanable funds 23
Loong, L.H. 136
López, J. 137
Lucretius 8
Lueck, D. 27

Malinowski, B. 5, 6, 7
Mandelbrot, B.B. 165n43
marginal cost 110
marginal product ratios 108
marginal productivity 107
marginal products 108, 109
marginal rate of substitution 108
marginal revenue 110
marginal utility 21, 107, 108, 109
market economy 21
market prices 109, 110
markets 6, 7, 10, 21, 100–25; capital 92, 122; classical notion of 101; commodity 34, 105; financial 40, 68, 104; goods 69, 111; hierarchies 102; money 111, 122; neoclassical idea of 101; *see also* credit markets
Marx, K. 18, 116, 134
material reproduction 4; in de facto possession-based systems 5–10, *13–14*; in ownership-based society with economic activity *13*
McGregor, R. 137
McIntosh, C. 130–1
Ménard, C. 25
Menger, C. 107
mercantilism 16–17
Mesopotamia 74–5, 76
microeconomics 108, 109
microfinance 130–1
Mill, J.S. 126, 127
Minsky, H.P. 36, 38–9
Mishkin, F.S. 89
monetarism 22, 89
monetary economy 39–40
monetary Keynesianism 39–52, 51–2, 53, 69, 86, 101, 102, 103, 105, 106, 114–15
money 1, 4, 6, 7, 36, 53, 72–4, 100; of account 30, 66–71, 70, 104, 105, 108, 111, 112, 114; as an asset 111; bank 18, 30, 31; central bank 31, 36, 38, 40, 46, 114; in classical economics 18–19, 20;

money – *contd.*
commodity 30, 72, 78–9, 108–9; credit 70; creditor's 31, 36, 37, 72, 104; current 31; debtor's 31, 36, 37, 64–5, 72, 104, 105; endogenous 36, 40; entrepreneur 104–5, 105–6; exogenous 40; fiat 21, 22, 38; gold as 7–8; inside 96; Keynes's theory of 31–2, 67, 71; lawful 78, 79; as means of payment 40; as measure of value 19; member bank 31; in neoclassical economics 21–2; net wealth of 72–4, 158n67; neutrality of 22, 110; New View of 72–3; *numéraire* 30, 67, 101, 110, 163n24; Old View of 72, 73; outside 21, 96, 97; paper 18, 19, 30–1; private ownership paradigm of 4; proper 30, 31, 67, 68, 70, 71; quantity of 110, 111; representative 30, 31, 32; state 30, 31, 36–7, 71; in state socialism 9–10; temporary loss of 1; as unit of account 19; velocity of circulation 110
money capitalists 2
money creation 1, 2, 3, 72, 121, 122, 123; central banks 83–99; credit-based 19, 59–60, 61, 62, 70, 73; entrepreneurs 102; in monetary Keynesianism 40, 41, 50, 51–2; in neoclassical economics 22; by the private note-issuing bank 74–83
money credit 41, 48, 49, 58
money markets 111, 122
money notes 70, 71, 72, 159n79; and credit contracts 59, 61–2
money prices 7, 107–13
money supply 33, 36
money wages 115, 117
monied class 19
monopolistic competition 110
monopoly 110
Moore, B.J. 36, 86
moral hazard 28, 132
mortgages 136
Mycenaean-Greek feudalism 7–8

Nazi Germany 93, 124
neoclassical economics 5, 16, 18, 20–9, 53, 58, 101, 106, 113, 114, 122; barter paradigm 3; burdening of property in 22; consumption in 1, 2; credit contracts in 24; *homo economicus* 3, 5; interest in 1, 22–4; markets in 101, 106; money in 21–2; prices in 107, 110–11, 112; property rights in 20, 21, 25–8
net wealth 72–4, 158n67
new institutional economics 16, 25–9

new Keynesianism 35–6, 69
New South Wales 152n8, 156n54, 157n58
Nicaragua 88
Nigeria 133
nominal assets 73
nominal contracts 107
nominal price anchor 67
non-borrowed base 96
North, D.C. 27
Norway 133
numéraire 30, 67, 101, 110

Obstfeld, M. 89
Odrich, B. 123
oligopolistic competition 110
original accumulation 114
Österreich Lexikon 101
outside money 21, 96, 97
overinvestment 118, 119, 120, 165n43
overproduction 118, 119, 120
ownership 25–6, 53, 55; abolition of 134; land 26; and possession distinguished 1; private 4, 12, 27; shared 27; state 12; in state socialism 8–10
ownership-based societies 4–5, 10–12, *13–14*, 15, 16, 52, 56, 57
ownership premium 1, 3, 54, 59–62, 63–4, 67, 86, 100, 114, 122, 123; commercial banks 85, 87; entrepreneurs 102, 105, 106
ownership rights 26
ownership titles 10, 54, 55

paper money 18, 19, 30–1, 123–4; *see also* bank notes; money notes
Paraguay 88
Parguez, A. 146n20
partial equilibrium analysis 108
Patinkin, D. 110–11
Payandeh, M. 135
perfect competition 109–10
Pesek, B.P. 73
phantom property 123–4
physical capital 104, 105, 117, 121
Pistor, K. 27
Poland 135, 136
Polanyi, K. 6, 101
polypolistic competition 109–10
Portugal 124
possession 18, 20, 21, 25, 26, 53; de facto 1, 3, 4, 5–10, 11, 12, *13*, 28, 54, 129; de jure 2, 3, 10–12, *13*, 15, 54, 129; first 27; and ownership distinguished 1; rights of 2, 26; sale of 1, 2; transfer of 2, 60, 61
possession-based systems 4, 5

post-Keynesianism 36–9, 111
poverty 126, 127–33
power relations 18
preferences, consumer 112, 113
price level 110, 111
prices 10; absolute 109, 110–11, 112; for accounting purposes 108; asset 97, 120; bond 24; current 108, 109, 110; equilibrium 112; factor 107, 109, 112; goods 107, 109; market 109, 110; money 7, 107–13; nominal anchor for 67; relative 18, 21, 67, 107–13; share 120
price setting 66, 156n47, 157n58
primitive accumulation 114
private banks, note-issuing 74–83, 99, 145n4
private ownership 4, 12, 27
private property 17–18, 25, 27
privatization, transformation countries 134
production 4, 11; over- 118, 119, 120
productivity 24; marginal 107
profit 1, 2, 18, 19, 32, 105, 114, 120; rate of 114, 120
promissory notes 32, 64–5
property: common 17, 18, 19, 25, 27; informal 129; phantom 123–4; private 17–18, 25, 27; sale of 1, 2; *see also* burdening of property; hypothecation of property
property law 1
property rights 5, 10, 11, 16, 25, 53, 54, 100; developing countries 128, 129–33; enactment of 12; in neoclassical economics 20, 21, 25–8; in new institutional economics 25–8; ownership aspect of 1–2, 55; possessory aspect of 1, 2; in transformation countries 135–6, 137–8
property titles 47, 55, 67–8, 69
Prussia 132–3
Pryor, F.L. 7
public debt 124, 125

quantitative easing, Federal Reserve 87

Radelet, S. 127
real balances 110
real-bills doctrine 19, 69
real bills fallacy 20
recession, innovation and 119–20
reciprocity 4, 5, *14*, 54, 57
relative prices 18, 21, 67, 107–13
rental/lease agreements 2, 56
rents 18, 19
representative money 30, 31, 32

reproduction *see* material reproduction
repurchase (repo) agreements 44, 70, 88, 92, 154n37
Reserve Bank of Australia 161n126
reserves, central banks 95–6
resource credit 40–1, 48, 102
Rhee, S. 133
Ricardo, D. 18, 19
Richter, R. 71, 79, 93, 94
Riese, H. 39, 40–2, 45–6, 47, 48–50, 51, 73, 81, 88, 102, 104, 114
risk: asymmetric distribution of 35; credit contracts 29–30, 34–5; creditor 29, 38–9; debtor 29–30, 38; investment 29–30
risk management 130, 131
risk premium 2, 63, 64
Robertson, D.H. 23, 24, 34
Rojas, M. 124
Roy, T. 154n38, 155n39
rule of law 12, 133
Russia 93, 133; financial crash (1998) 136–7

Sachs, J. 128, 135
Sahlins, M. 5–6, 7
sale of property 1, 2, 27
sales contracts 54, 59, 60, 105, 106, 111, 116, 121, 152n4
Sauer 172n36
saving 23, 32, 33, 105, 114
Saving, T.R. 73
savings 23, 24, 52
scarce resources 5, 28–9, 53
Schoenmaker, D. 89, 90
SCHUFA 100
Schumpeter, J. 20
Schwartz, A.J. 22, 89, 94
Seccareccia, M. 146n20
securities, tradable 84
Securities Markets Programme (SMP) 124
security rights 3
seigniorage 99
Senegal 133
settlement assets 144n9, 154n31
share issues 104
share prices 120
shared ownership 27
Shaw, E.S. 72
Shirley, M.M. 25
Singapore 136
Skaist, A. 75
Slovenia 137
Smith, A. 17, 18, 20

social finance programs 130
social safety nets 4, *14*, 57, 126; loss of 57, 58
socialist systems *see* state socialism
Soto, H. de 129
South Korea 133
sovereign debt crisis 124
Soviet Union 134–5
Spahn, H.-P. 42–4, 154n38, 159n79, 163n21
Spain 124, 125
speculators 118–19
Stability and Growth Pact 125
stabilization programs 128
Stadermann, H.-J. 18, 21, 30, 31, 37, 43, 44, 48, 63, 68, 74, 77, 78, 91, 97, 107, 112–13, 119, 124, 150n41, 156n47, 156n54, 157n58, 158n75, 158n78
stagnation, Japan 123
Stalin, J. 134
Stange, H.O.H. 8
Starr, C.G. 7, 75
state, as lender of last resort 90
state banks 9–10
state debt titles 92–3, 96–7
state-issued coin 76–7
state money 30, 31, 36–7, 71
state-owned companies 9, 10
state ownership 12
state socialism 4, 8–10, 11, 133–5; interest in 10; money in 9–10; ownership in 8–10
Steiger, O. 18, 21, 24, 30, 31, 36, 37, 40, 45, 49, 51, 52, 63, 68, 78, 86, 88, 89, 90, 91, 104, 107, 112–13, 119, 132, 136
Stein, K. 132
Stella, P. 88
Steuart, J. 16–17, 41, 64–5, 79–80, 81, 95, 113, 159n79, 159n83
Stevenson, R.W. 135
Stiglitz, J. 24–5, 34–5, 39, 106, 107, 122–3, 130, 132
Striegel, B. 155–6n45
sub-Saharan Africa 128
supplier contracts 116
supply, excess 109, 110
surplus-value 116
Svejnar, J. 137
Sweden: commercial banks 91; Riksbank 99

Taiwan 133
tax collection 56, 93
Taylor, J.B. 97
technical progress 116–18, 119–20
Tett, G. 123
Thomas, R.P. 27
Thornton, H. 41, 42–3, 75
thrift 24, 114
Thurnwald, R. 5
Timberlake Jr., R.H. 82
time preference, neoclassical theory of 23
Tinbergen, J. 127–8
Tobin, J. 71, 72
total utility 108
tradable securities 84
transaction costs 22
transformation countries 133–8; banks 135; currency 136–7; foreign investment in 136; hypothecatable property 137; legal systems 137; property rights 135–6, 137–8
tribal systems 4, 5–7, 11, 27, 28, 54, 56, 57, 126

UN Millennium Project 128, 135
unburdened property 18
unit of account 30, 67, 108
United States 82; inflation 91; Treasury 87–8 (Term Asset-Backed Securities Loan Facility (TALF) 85); *see also* Federal Reserve
Uruguay 88
use right 55, 56
use value 21
utility 152n9; marginal 21, 107, 108; maximization 3, 108, 109; total 108

value: asset 66, 67; labor theory of 18
Varmaz, A. 39
Varro 152n18
velocity of circulation 110

wage labor 115–16, 117
wages 121; money 115, 117
Wallich, H.C. 22, 91, 96
Walras, L. 22, 78, 107
wealth, net 72–4, 158n67
Wee, H. Van der 79
Weintraub, S. 36
Weiss, A. 24–5, 34, 39
Wicksell, K. 78
Willers, H. 57–8
Woodford, M. 66
World Bank 130, 131
Wray, L.R. 36, 37, 38, 39
Wydick, B. 130–1

zemindars 126–7